PRESS

SAP PRESS is issued by
Bernhard Hochlehnert, SAP AG

SAP PRESS is a joint initiative of SAP and Galileo Press. The know-how offered
by SAP specialists combined with the expertise of the publishing house Galileo
Press offers the reader expert books in the field. SAP PRESS features first-hand
information and expert advice, and provides useful skills for professional
decision-making.

SAP PRESS offers a variety of books on technical and business related topics
for the SAP user. For further information, please visit our website:
www.sap-press.com.

Jörg Thomas Dickersbach, Gerhard Keller, Klaus Weihrauch
Production Planning and Control with SAP
2006, approx. 400 pp.
ISBN 978-1-59229-106-9

Stephen Birchall
Invoice Verification for SAP R/3
2006, 80 pp.
ISBN 978-1-59229-083-3

Jitendra Singh
Implementing and Configuring SAP Global Trade Services
2006, 200 pp.
ISBN 978-1-59229-096-3

Martin Murray
Understanding the SAP Logistics Information System
2007, 328 pp.
ISBN 978-1-59229-108-3

Roland Fischer
Business Planning with SAP SEM
2005, 403 pp.
ISBN 978-1-59229-033-8

D. Rajen Iyer

Effective SAP® SD

Get the Most Out of Your SAP SD Implementation

Galileo Press

Bonn • Boston

ISBN   978-1-59229-101-4

1st edition 2007, 2nd reprint with corrections 2008

Editor Jawahara Saidullah
Copy Editor John Parker, UCG, Inc., Boston, MA
Cover Design Silke Braun
Layout Design Vera Brauner
Production Steffi Ehrentraut
Typesetting SatzPro, Krefeld
Printed and bound in Germany

Contents at a Glance

Contents

6   Financials and Controlling: Key Influence and Interface 193

7   Influence of SM and QM in SD Processes 223

Sales accounts for goods and services sold by a company in a certain period, containing valid sales price and distribution data, help distribute the goods and services to the customer. In a simple supply chain model, a company procures or manufactures goods and services to meet the customer's request. The Sales and Distribution module of SAP helps in selling the goods and services to the customer and making sure they reach the customer.

1 Introduction and Overview

In a classic supply chain model, a sales and distribution system helps a company build the understanding of delivery of services or goods with their customers and makes use of the logistics infrastructure to fulfil agreements. In other words, sales and distribution helps you register contracts, agreements, or order acknowledgements with your customer and fulfil them.

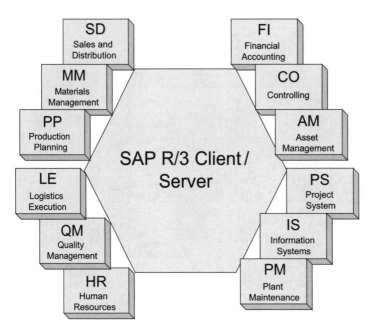

Figure 1.1 Key Modules of an SAP R/3 System

The Sales and Distribution module is a key element of the SAP logistics process, which directly interfaces with the other critical logistics functions, like materials management and logistics execution. As a back end, the fulfilment of the order or delivery of goods and services are supported by the Materials Management or Logistics Execution module. SAP Sales and Distribution closely connects with the mySAP Customer Relationship Management, which comprehends and extends the solution for managing your business relationships with your customers. Figure 1.1, shows a few of the key modules in the SAP R/3 system.

Figure 1.2 highlights some of the new functionality introduced with mySAP ERP. Last but not least, Sales and Distribution interfaces very closely with Finance to track all costs and prices associated with the sales. Keep in mind that though this book was written on SAP ECC 6.0, it will be relevant for all releases higher than R/3 4.5.

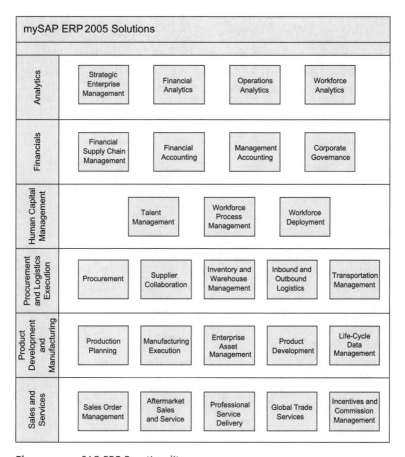

Figure 1.2 mySAP ERP Functionality

Let's now get an idea of how Sales and Distribution fits into SAP's ERP systems.

1.1 Sales and Distribution in the SAP World

Take a simple scenario, in which the sales process begins with the customer ordering goods or services from you and asking for the requested delivery date. This basic information can be used to create a document in Sales and Distribution called a sales order. You then can trigger shipping activities at an appropriate time so that the customer receives the material in time. As soon as the material leaves the company, you post a goods issue order to update stock and values. You then create a billing document and send the customer the invoice. As soon as the customer pays for the materials, the incoming payments are posted in Financial Accounting.

Sales can start with the pre-sales information to plan and evaluate your marketing and sales strategies and provide a basis for establishing long-term business relationship with your customers. Related activities include tracking lost sales, recording presales data to help negotiate large contracts, and selling goods and service to large organizations that require documentation of the entire process.

Sales and Distribution is one of oldest SAP components and is an integral part of the ERP system. It has evolved over time and become stronger with the different releases and versions. The customer-facing processes have moved to the SAP business suites—mySAPCustomer Relationship Management (CRM)—and SAP Sales and Distribution ties very closely with the CRM process. The functions that help in managing the customer relationship are now part of the mySAP CRM; e.g., Marketing, Channel Management, and Field Services. It supports all customer-focused business areas, from marketing to sales and services, as well as customer interaction channels, such as Web and mobile client. Figure 1.3 shows a typical SAP E-Commerce application for mySAP CRM. Sales and Distribution is part of the mySAP ERP Central Component with mySAP ERP.

To emphasize the process, let's take the example of a standard order also called a sales order. A sales order is an electronic document that captures and records your customer's request for goods or services. The sales order contains all pertinent information for processing the customer's request throughout the whole process cycle.

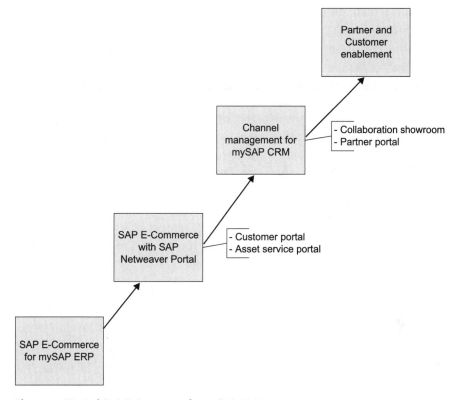

Figure 1.3 Typical SAP E-Commerce for mySAP CRM

1.1.1 Meeting Customer Requirements

A standard order within sales and distribution registers your customer's request for delivery of goods or services at a specified time. A standard order might contain the following:

▶ Customer and material (service) information

▶ Price agreement for all financial statement items

▶ Information about delivery dates and delivery quantities

▶ Information about shipping processing

▶ Information about billing

To process a standard order, the sales component will automatically suggest data from the master records and control tables (or business rules) that has been maintained or put aside ahead of time. Understanding these business rules or processes and how they are configured will help in designing our processes later in the book.

Sales and Distribution needs to closely link to other components or processes for confirming or acknowledging the order to the customer. Before you can confirm the delivery date with the customer, you might want to check the availability of the goods on the requested date and also transfer this requirement to material (service) planning. Sales and Distribution depends on Materials Management to organize and monitor the actual procurement of the material. The material can be procured by producing it in-house or buying it from an external vendor.

Figure 1.4 shows the view of a standard order entry.

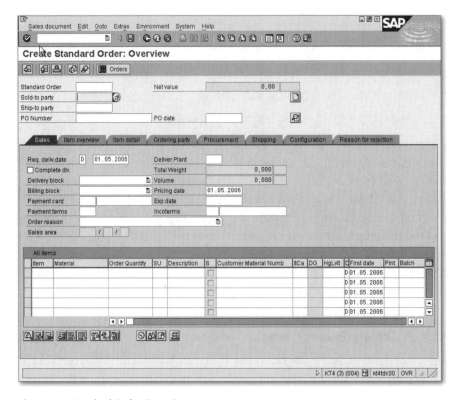

Figure 1.4 Standard Order-Entry Screen

The way in which a material is obtained for a customer can depend on the material itself, as well as on the sales transaction. So your sales order could trigger procurement to be fulfilled in any of the following ways:

▶ Available to stock

▶ Guaranteed replenishment (purchase requisition or purchase order, planned order, or production order)

▸ Triggers make to order production

▸ Triggers outbound delivery via an external supplier (third-party business transaction)

▸ Organize outbound delivery via another warehouse (stock transfer)

1.1.2   Shipping Materials to the Customer

Materials can be shipped to the customer if they are available at the specified time. The shipping process in Sales and Distribution begins when you create the delivery. The delivery controls, supports, and monitors numerous sub-processes for shipping, such as the following:

▸ Picking and confirming the quantity

▸ Packing

▸ Planning and monitoring the transport

▸ Posting the goods after it is issued out of stock

These processes are closely tied to the Logistics Execution functions of the ERP Central Component. Creating a delivery document involves copying information from the sales order, such as materials and quantities, onto the delivery document. If you have warehouse management, the delivery document would be transferred within the warehouse via transfer order to control the movement of the goods within the warehouse. The posting of goods issue can bring about a change based on a quantity basis as well as on a value basis in stock. Changes based on value are made on the relevant balance sheet accounts in financial accounting.

1.1.3   Getting Paid for Services or Goods

Once you have fulfilled the customer order, you would like to get paid for the goods or services. This is accomplished by creating a billing document for goods and services. Creating a billing document involves copying information from the sales order and delivery document into the billing document. As a result, delivery items and order items (services, for example) can be models for the billing document.

This billing document is a sales-and-distribution document that serves several important functions, including the following:

- The sales and distribution document acts as the basis for creating invoices.
- The billing documents serves as a data source for financial accounting to help you monitor and process customer payments.

When you create a billing document, the G/L accounts are normally determined automatically and the relevant data is posted. The system carries out the following:

- A debit posting on the customer's recievables account
- A credit posting on the revenue account

To enable this, billing in Sales and Distribution supports the following:

- Creating invoices for goods and services
- Creating credit memo and debit memo
- Cancelling previously posted billing document
- Automatically transfering billing document data to accounting

When you get a payment from the customer, you post the payment against the invoice and reconcile the differences. When you post an incoming payment, the data on the relevant G/L account is posted automatically. The system carries out the following:

- A debit posting on the cash account
- A credit memo on the customer's recievables account

> **Note**
>
> Payment process is part of the Financial Accounting component of the ERP Central component. Refer to Figure 1.5 displaying the key processes in Sales and Distribution.

Figure 1.5 gives you an overview of Sales and Distribution processes, displaying the link between the sub-processes in customer order management within the system. The structure of the blocks from the top to bottom represents the normal sequence of event in the sales and distribution process.

Sales and Distribution uses the organizational elements and structure within SAP to processes its functions through the supply chain. These organizational elements could represent the company's functional structure.

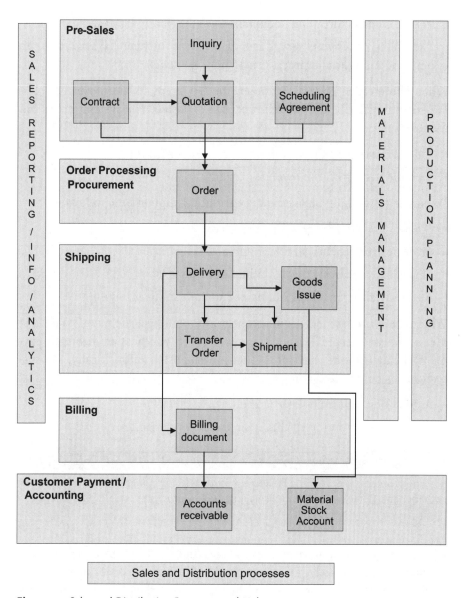

Figure 1.5 Sales and Distribution Processes and Linkages

1.2 Key Influence of the Organizational Structure

Organizational structure is a very important and key step in Sales and Distribution implementation, as it requires a thorough analysis of how your organization wants to run its business. Organizational units in the SAP system

represent the structure of an enterprise organization. In other words, organizational units are legal and/or organizational units within enterprises.

SAP R/3, R/3 Enterprise Sales and Distribution, or mySAP Sales and Services use a range of organizational units designed exclusively for mapping sales and distribution processes, such as sales organization and distribution channel. There are other organizational units, which sales and distribution refers to or links to in order to process a business transaction.

SAP provides you with different accounting, logistics, and human resources organizational units to help portray your company structure. As a first step, you want to analyze the structure and business procedures in your company and match them to the SAP structure.

Different organizational elements are defined as examples in the standard SAP version. You might have to extend the elements to fit your business needs, as the standard delivered ones wouldn't cover all of them. You can always work with the structures delivered as a clarification tool and help the project team interpret the applications of these structures.

> **Tip**
>
> I recommend that that only a limited number of persons be authorized to maintain the organization elements, as these have downstream impacts that will not be easy to change.

1.2.1 Organizational Units

A group can be represented in the system using the terms client and company code. Generally, a client represents a group, while a company code represents a company in the sense of an independent accounting unit. A client is a self-contained technical unit. General data and tables that are used for several organizational structures are stored at this level.

A company code is seen as a completely independent accounting unit that can be represented as the smallest organizational unit of external accounting. This includes the entry of all accounting transactions and the creation of all proofs of a legally required individual account closing, such as the balance sheet and the profit-and-loss statement. Examples of a company code could be a corporate group, or a subsidiary.

A company is an organizational unit in accounting, representing a business organization according to the requirements of commercial law in a particular

country. A company can comprise one or more company codes. The finance and controlling group is involved in defining the company code.

You can use the company code and business area to represent a group from a financial accounting viewpoint. A business area is a separate business unit for which cross-company-code internal reporting can be carried out. Business areas are not limited by company codes. You will use business areas if you want to calculate profit and loss statements independently of the company code. In the case of postings made from Sales and Distribution, the business area can be derived automatically.

Figure 1.6 depicts the basic information needed to define a company code. Apart from the further company key being referenced in other tables as a foreign key, there are a few things you should note because of their influence on the Sales and Distribution process. Some of these are listed below:

▸ The currency mentioned here are used for financial posting and account. Please note your sales currency could be different from this currency.

▸ Documents printed use the address defined here.

▸ The language key entered here determines the display text, entering text and document print.

Figure 1.6 Defining Company Code

You can reach it via the transaction code SPRO. Click on **SAP Reference IMG** (Implementation Guide), to display **IMG** and then follow the rest of this path: **Enterprise Structure • Definition • Financial Accounting**. Then, click on **Define Company**.

Sales Organization

Sales Organization is an organizational unit in Logistics that groups the enterprise according to the requirement of sales and distribution. A sales organization is responsible for distributing goods and services. Therefore, it is also liable for the sold products and responsible for the customers' right of recourse. A typical example would be a regional, national, or international subdivision of the market.

A sales organization is uniquely assigned to a company code. More than one sales organization can be assigned to a company code. To use the Sales and Distribution functions in the SAP system, you need at least one sales organization. In the sales statistics, the sales organization is the highest summation level. All sales and distribution documents—that is, all orders, outbound deliveries, and billing documents—are assigned to a sales organization. Figure 1.7 on the next page displays the screen shot of sales-organization definition. Before you define a sales organization, you should consider the following:

▶ A sales organization can be assigned to one company code legally.

▶ A sales organization could have more than one plant assigned to it.

▶ The address maintained in the sales organization is used for document printing.

▶ The sales organization controls the maintainance of master data and control data. For example the customer master, pricing, and print outputs. Note that a sales organization can't share any master data with other sales organizations, so these need to be created seperately.

▶ Sales document types (order types) can be specific to sales organizations. This also means that when a document is created, all the items within the order belongs to the sales organization.

▶ You can assign employees and sales offices to the sales organization.

▶ As mentioned above, the sales organization is the highest summation level for sales statistics, with its own statistics currency.

Here is the menu path for defining the sales organization within the Display IMG: **IMG • Enterprise Structure • Definition • Sales and Distribution**. Then, do the following:

1. Click on **Define, copy, delete, check sales organization**.

2. In the pop-up window, choose **Define Sales Organization**.

You can define a sales organization with a description and can maintain the statistical currency and various address text names. You can have a sales

organization calendar, if it is different from your factory calendar. You can also make use of the customer inter-company billing, if this sales organization represents an internal customer; i.e., if you are selling to a sister company or another subsidiary. If you want to activate the rebate processing, check **Rebate Processing Active**.

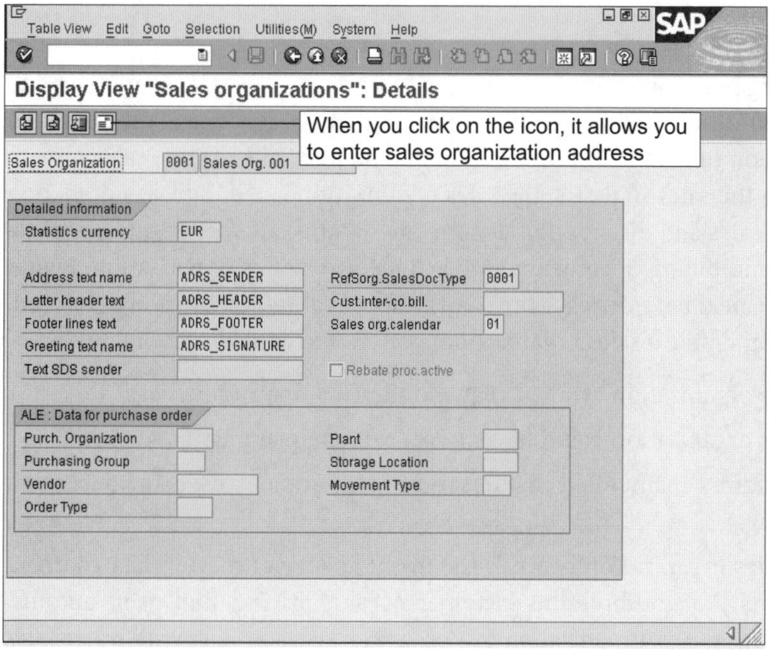

Figure 1.7 Sales Organization Definition

The configuration parameters within the section **ALE: Data for purchase order** as shown in Figure 1.7 is used if you have a distributed business model; that is, if a sales order triggers a purchase order in a different logical system for procuring the part. You can define here the purchase organization, purchasing group, vendor, and purchase order type for the purchase order created based on the sales organization in the sales order. It also allows you to define the plant, storage location, and movement type for material movement from the plant stock.

When you click on the Address icon—the icon representing a postcard, in the definition of sales organization—it allows you to maintain address and search terms. You can maintain the address in different international languages and modes of communication; e.g., fax, email, print, etc. Figure 1.8 displays the address details of the sales-organization configuration definition.

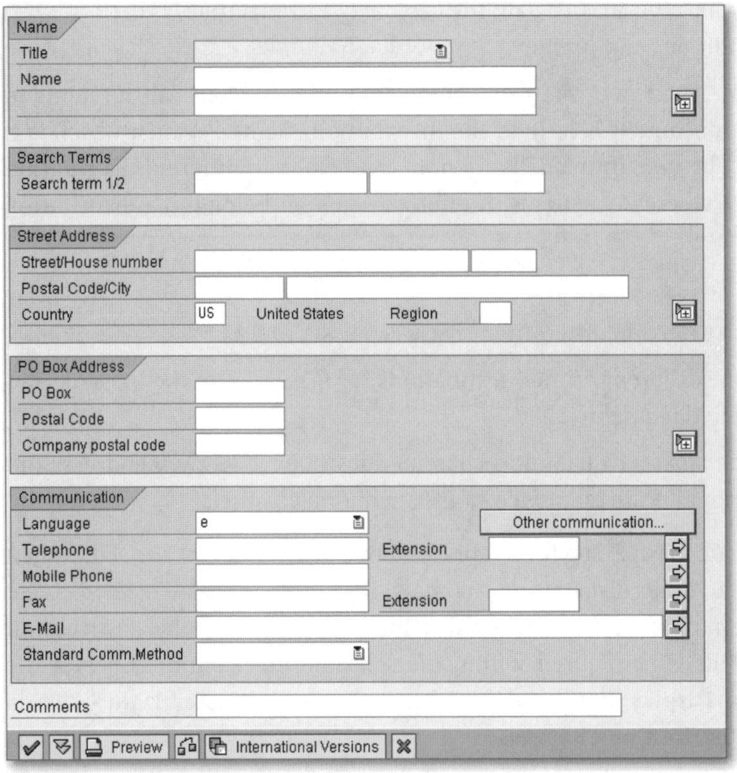

Figure 1.8 Sales Organization Address Information

Distribution Channel

A distribution channel is a means through which sales-related materials reach the customers. In other words, the distribution channel characterizes the way in which goods and services are distributed. This also can represent the company's strategies to distribute goods and/or services to your customers. Several distribution channels can be assigned to a sales organization.

To use the sales and distribution functions in the system, you need at least one distribution channel. Among other things, you can use the distribution channel to do the following:

▶ Define responsibilities

▶ Carry out flexible price structure

▶ Differentiate sales statistics

▶ Allocate a distribution channel to one or more sales organizations

▶ Allocate one or more plant

- Define your own master data for customer and materials as well as your own conditions and pricing

- Determine your own sales document type (order type). All the items in the sales document belong to the distribution channel against which is it created. The item in the delivery note can belong to different distribution channels, whereas the items in billing document belong to a distribution channel.

- Sales office

- Serve as a selection criterion in many reports and lists

- Determine different printer destinations for messages on the basis of sales and billing documents.

- Remember that a distribution channel doesn't have its own address, and you cannot allocate employee to a distribution channel.

You can create master data for a representative distribution channel that then is also used in other distribution channels. To do this, you also have to create the allocation of the representation distribution channel to other distribution channels. This is configured within the sales and distribution area via the menu path: **Display IMG · Sales and Distribution · Master Data · Define Common Distribution Channels**.

Once there, you can define the shared distribution channel that applies for condition and customer and material data. This helps you minimize the cost of creating and maintaining the master data. You can also update statistics for each distribution channel without creating the master data for the different sub-areas of the organization. Figure 1.9 shows you the configuration step where you can define the common distribution-channel mappings.

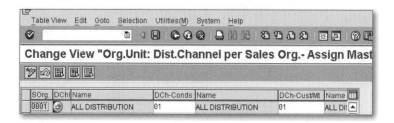

Figure 1.9 Common Distribution Channel Mapping

A Sales Office definition is optional, as you can use sales and distribution function without creating a sales office. A sales office can be a location with address and you can assign to this office. You can also maintain sales groups

in the same manner, but this is optional. You can assign a sales group to one or more sales offices, and you can assign people to particular sales groups.

Division

A division can be used to group materials and services. Several divisions can be assigned to a sales organization. To use the sales and distribution functions in the system, you need at least one division. A division also can represent a certain product group,. Therefore, you can restrict price agreements with a customer to a certain division. In addition, you can conduct statistical analysis by division.

Division is not only a key organization element in sales and distribution, it also represents a business area account assignment for logistics transactions in financial accounting. The business area is determined by the plant and the division in the material master record. The same reasons as those we listed for the distribution channel apply here as well. You can can allocate a division to one or more sales organizations and distribution channels.

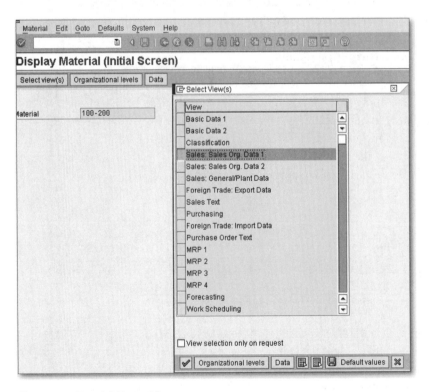

Figure 1.10 Material Master Views

A material is assigned to one division only. You specify the division in the first sales-and-distribution view of the material master maintenance screen. Business area is allocated to a division from plant. Figure 1.10 displays the screen shot of material master maintenance with different views. The typical transaction codes for material master maintenance are MM01 (material master create), MM02 (material master change), and MM03 (material master display).

The menu path to define division is: **Display IMG · Enterprise Structure · Definition · Logistics-General.** Once you are there, you can do the following.

1. Click on **Define, copy, delete, check division**

2. In the pop-up window, select **Define Division**

Figure 1.11 displays the Sales Organizational Data 1 view, seen as **Sales: sales org. 1.**

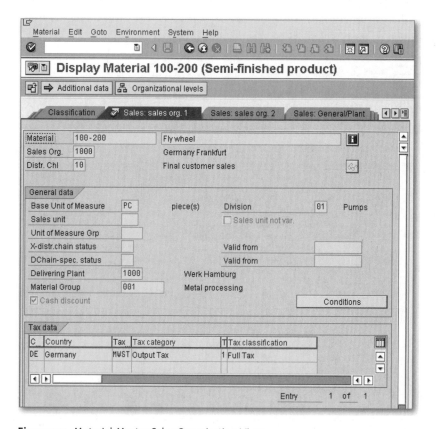

Figure 1.11 Material Master Sales Organization View

> **Note**
>
> In the various chapters of this book, I will be referring to the sales and distribution master data. That includes material master data specific to sales processes, pricing condition, customer master data, etc., as appropriate and needed.

Plant

The plant is a location where the material stock is kept. It could represent a production facility in the system. The plant and storage location are organizational units that can be used by all logistics areas of the SAP system. materials management is primarily concerned with the material flow. From a materials-management point of view, a plant is above all a location where material stock is kept. In production, a plant represents a manufacturing facility. You can see the details behind the plant definition in Figure 1.12.

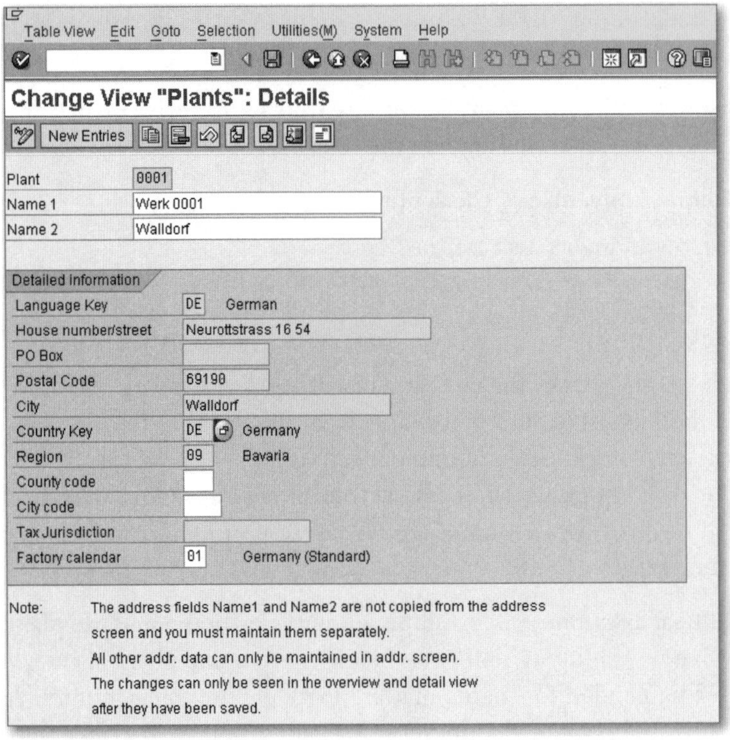

Table View	Edit Goto Selection Utilities(M) System Help

Change View "Plants": Details

New Entries

Plant	0001
Name 1	Werk 0001
Name 2	Walldorf

Detailed information

Language Key	DE	German
House number/street	Neurottstrass 16 54	
PO Box		
Postal Code	69190	
City	Walldorf	
Country Key	DE	Germany
Region	09	Bavaria
County code		
City code		
Tax Jurisdiction		
Factory calendar	01	Germany (Standard)

Note: The address fields Name1 and Name2 are not copied from the address
screen and you must maintain them separately.
All other addr. data can only be maintained in addr. screen.
The changes can only be seen in the overview and detail view
after they have been saved.

Figure 1.12 Plant Definition

In the Sales and Distribution module, a plant represents the location from which materials and service are delivered and corresponds to a distribution

center. In sales and distribution, the plant has a central function with the following characteristics:

▶ To use the sales and distribution functions in the system, you need at least one plant.

▶ Each plant is uniquely assigned to a company code.

▶ The assignment between sales organizations/distribution channel and plant doesn't have to be unique.

▶ The plant is essential for determining the shipping point.

A plant has the following attributes:

▶ Address

▶ Language

▶ Country

▶ Its own material master data with different views for MRP, Purchasing, Sales and Costing, among other aspects

The menu path to define the plant is: **Display IMG · Enterprise Structure · Definition · Logistics-General**. Then, do the following:

1. Click on **Define, copy, delete, check plant**

2. In the pop-up window, select **Define Plant**

Shipping Point

Shipping is an integral part of the sales and distribution processing. The shipping point is the highest-level organizational unit of shipping that controls your shipping activities. Each outbound delivery is processed by exactly one shipping point. The shipping point could be a loading ramp, a mail depot, or a rail depot. It can also be a group of employees responsible for organizing very urgent deliveries.

The organizational assignment of a shipping point is carried out at the plant level. More than one shipping point can be assigned to one plant, although this is only recommended for plants that are located close to each other. A shipping point can be divided into several loading points. A delivery is always initiated from exactly one shipping point. Thus, all items of a delivery belong to one shipping point. Groups of deliveries can also belong to one shipping point. A shipping point has an address. The shipping point is used as a selection criterion for processing deliveries for picking, goods issue and

printing documents. The configuration details behind the shipping point definition are shown in Figure 1.13.

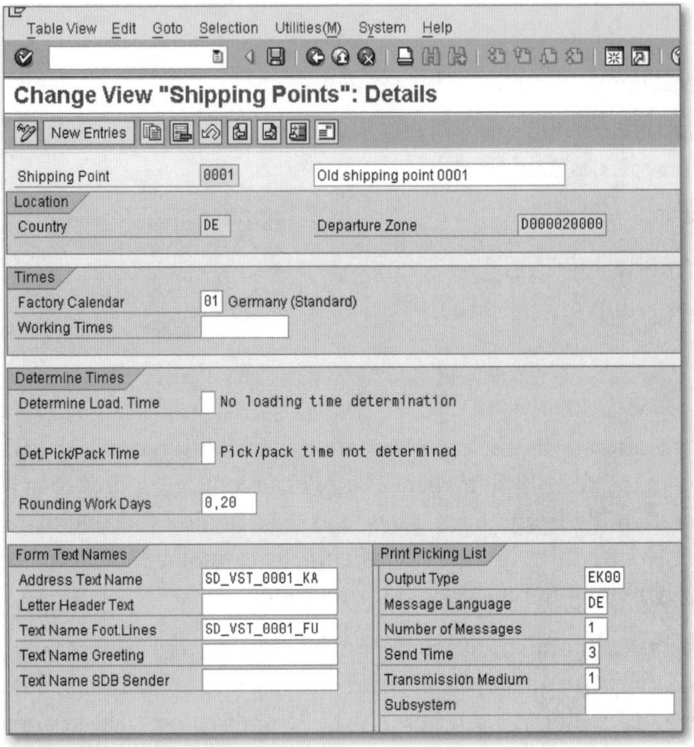

Figure 1.13 Shipping Point Definition

The menu path to define the shipping point is: **Display IMG · Enterprise Structure**. Then, do the following:

1. Click on **Definition**

2. Click on **Logistics Execution**

3. Click on **Define, copy, delete, check shipping point**

4. In the pop-up window, select **Define shipping point**

1.2.2   Linking Organizational Structures

In Section 1.2.1, you inserted your own company structure in the system by allocating the organization units in sales and distribution. We now need to link or assign the organizational elements in Sales and Distribution to each other and to link other functional area organizational elements (Finance,

Logistics) to sales and distribution, which in turns connects the Sales and Distribution to Finance and Logistics processes. The following is a list of the linkages or assignment of the Sales and Distribution organization structures defined in Section 1.2.1:

► Assign sales organization to company code

► Assign distribution channel to sales organization

► Assign division to sales organization

► Set up sales area

  ► Assign sales office to sales area

  ► Assign sales group to sales office

Sales Area

A sales area is a combination of sales organization, distribution channel, and division. It defines the distribution channel a sales organization uses to sell product of a certain division. Each sales and distribution document is assigned to exactly one sales area. This assignment cannot be changed. A sales area can only belong to only one company code.

When processing sales and distribution documents, the system accesses various master data that depend on the sales area. This master data includes, customer master data, material master data, price, and discounts. The system also carries out a number of checks concerning the validity of certain entries according to the sales area.

> **Note**
>
> A simple organizational structure may often be better than a complex one. It simplifies master-data maintenance, for one thing. You should not define complex organizational structure in order to have detailed reporting options. I advise using the fields in the master data screen and documents for this purpose.

Links Between Sales and Distribution and Other Areas

Let us look at some of the linkages between the sales and distribution organization elements and other functional areas:

► **Assign Sales Organization**
  As a pre-requisite, within Sales and Distribution, you should have assigned the Sales Organization to the Company Code. Similarly you

should assign the Plant, which is a logistics organizational element to Company Code. Then you need to assign the Sales Organization to Plant and the Distribution Channel for logistics interfaces.

▶ **Assign Sales Area to Credit Control Area**
The credit control areas are defined in the FI module. The credit limit of a customer is also determined in a control area there. By linking the customer master record to the credit limit, a link is also established between the Financial Accounting (FI) and Sales and Distribution (SD) modules.

▶ **BusinessArea Account Assignment**
Revenue in financial accounting and value posting for goods movement in inventory accounting can be represented separately for each business area. A business area is defined in the FI module, so this needs to be a collaborative effort with the finance department. Here you need to assign business area by sales area and assign plant/division to business area.

> **Note**
>
> For business-area account determination, you will have to define for each sales area the rules that the SAP System will use to find a business area. You will have to use the default settings and cannot change the rules for determining the business area in Customizing.

The menu path for assignments is: **Display IMG · Enterprise Structure · Assignment · Sales and Distribution**. There are other assignment or linkages for the organizational structure that belong to other functional areas, such as, Financial Accounting, Materials Management, which are also important for sales and distribution functions. Figure 1.14 displays the list of assignments in the implementation guide configurations steps, which are also listed below:

▶ Assignment of company code to company, and assignment of company code to credit control area in Financial Accounting

▶ Assignment of plant to company code within Logistics-General

▶ Assignment of business area to plant/valuation area/division within Logistics-General

▶ Assignment of shipping points within Logistics Execution.

You can run a consistency check for enterprise structure in Sales and Distribution. It will provide you with the results of any missing definition, allocations and you can correct them before you proceed further. While you are in the Display IMG, expand or click on **Enterprise Structure**. Then, do the following:

1. Expand or click on **Consistency Check**

2. Click on **Check enterprise structure** for Sales and Distribution

Now that we understand the key organizational elements within SD, let's go over some of the key business processes within the SD functions. These functions are interfaced closely with other modules, like Materials Management, Finance, Production Planning, or Quality Management and might link across these functions for an end-to-end process.

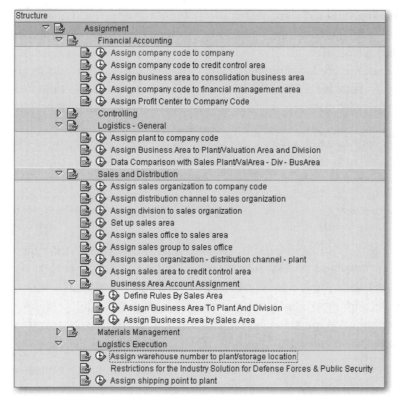

Figure 1.14 Assignments for Organizational Elements

1.3 Key Processes in Sales and Distribution

Every sales activity you undertake in SAP R/3 Enterprise or mySAP ERP is recorded in a sales document. You can represent different business processes such as sales, shipping, and billing with the following specifically designed document types:

- ▶ Sales document types (e.g., inquiries, quotation, or standard orders)
- ▶ Delivery types (e.g., deliveries, or return deliveries)
- ▶ Billing document types (e.g., invoices, credit memo, or debit memos).

Each document is identified by a unique document number as well as being assigned an overall status. The overall status depends on the status of the different steps of the sales activity.

Sales activities could start with a pre-sales event or activity, follow up with order processing and shipping, and end with billing. Pre-sales activity might consist of inquiry, quotation, scheduling agreement, or a contact. These pre-sales activities might lead to a firm commitment in the form of a sales order. This falls under the order-processing cycle. Shipping the goods or service to the customer involves a shipping process, which calls for the creation of delivery note, pick, pack, and issuance of the material. You can now use the billing process to bill the customer for the goods or services delivered.

Along the path from pre-sales to product shipment, the sales and distribution process interfaces closely with materials management for goods and service procurement. Materials management closely interfaces with production planning (provided it is used in your company) for internally manufactured goods. When a goods or material is issued from the stock, this activity is interfaced with the Finance module. Also, when billing documents are created, this activity interfaces with Finance (customer payment and accounting) for accounts receivable.

The entire chain of documents: inquiry, the quotation, the sales order, the delivery, the invoice, and the subsequent delivery free of charge creates a document flow or history. The flow of data from one document into another reduces manual activity and makes problem resolution easier. Figure 1.15 displays a typical document flow within the sales cycle.

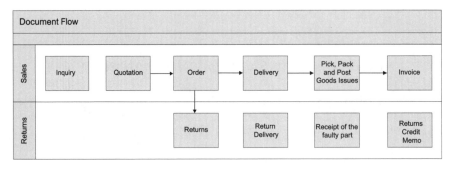

Figure 1.15 Sales Document Flow

1.3.1 Sales Document Structure

The sales document consists of a document header and as many items as required. Each item can, in turn, contain as many schedule lines as needed. The document header contains general data and default values that are valid for the entire document. Depending on the settings in Customizing, some of these default values can be manually changed at the line-item level.

The document items contain data about the goods and services ordered by the customer. This includes material numbers, descriptions, prices, and terms of delivery and payment. Data for shipping and procurement is located in schedule lines. Because the delivery deadline and order quantity are found in schedule line, each item with delivery requirements must contain at least one schedule line.

The general data that is valid for the entire document is recorded in the document header. This might include the identifying numbers of the sold-to party, ship-to party, and payer, the document currency and exchange rate, the pricing procedure, and so on. Whereas data in the document header applies to all the items in the document, data in the item is specific to that item; e.g., material number, quantity, or plant from which the part is being delivered.

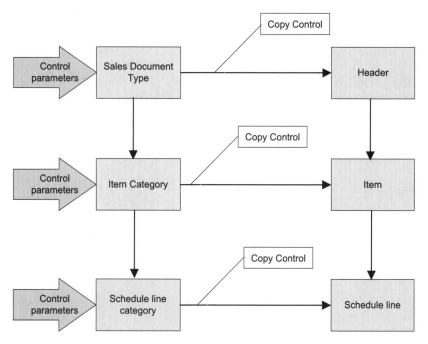

Figure 1.16 Sales Document Structure

An item consists of one or more schedule lines. The schedule line contains all the data that is needed for delivery. Suppose for example that a customer orders 20 units of a particular material, which you enter as one item in the sales order. You can only deliver 10 pieces now, but can deliver the remaining 10 pieces next month, so you need to schedule two deliveries. The data for these deliveries (dates, confirmed quantities, etc.) is stored in two separate schedule lines.

In sales documents where certain delivery data such as contacts is not relevant, the system does not create a schedule line for that data. Data that is recorded in the schedule line includes the schedule line quantity, delivery date, and confirmed quantity. Figure 1.16 displays the typical document structure with sales and distribution documents.

1.3.2 Sources of Document Data

During the data input for sales documents, the system supports you by analyzing various sources of information. The aim is to make the document creation easier by using default values or fixed reference data. Let's look at several ways the information can be maintained and defaulted into the sales document in the creation process; i.e., the different information sources a document looks for during creation:

▶ **Master Data**
The system reads the master data defined for a customer, a material, or pricing condition. For example, the specific terms of payment for a customer can be found. The sales information from a material master can serve as the source of the delivery plant.

▶ **Existing Document Data**
Document data that has already been entered or determined automatically by the system can be used to enter additional document data. For example, the delivery plant is used along with other information to determine the shipping point.

▶ **Customizing**
Default values for creating documents can be defined in Customizing. For example, you can set a default value for the delivery date or configure a delivery or billing block in the sales document type.

▶ **Hard-Coded Controls**
Hard-coded controls can be used to weight the different sources of information. In using a weight factor, the value is multipied by a number to increase or decrease the importance of the information.

▶ **Default Values from Master Data**

From the customer master record of the sold-to party, the system presents sales, shipping, pricing, and billing data. In addition, the system copies customer-specific master data about texts, partners, and contact people at the customer site.

For each material in the in the sales order, the system automatically presents data from the relevant material master records, such as data for pricing, delivery scheduling, availability check, tax determination, and weight and volume determination. It is advisable to store as much data as possible in the master data records, as this will save time and prevent erroneous data.

You can enter different types of master data in SAP SD, such as information on business partners, materials, customer/material, item proposals, bills of material, prices, discounts, taxes, freight, output, and texts. The system will access this data during order processing. Figure 1.17 shows you how a sales document pulls data from different sources.

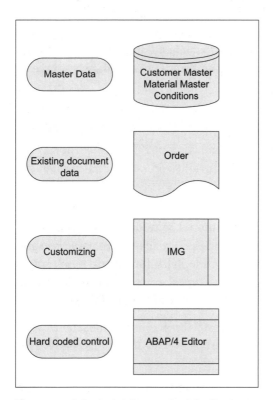

Figure 1.17 Information Sources for Sales Documents

1.3.3   Controlling Business Processes in Sales

Customizing and configuration are used interchangeably in the SAP world and they mean the same thing. The Display IMG structure begins with the SAP Customizing Implementation Guide. The standard delivered business processes through the implementation guide can be referred to as configuration. You can adapt the standard delivered configuration to your company's requirement, which is Customizing. Sales processes are controlled by Customizing for sales documents. SAP provides the customizing tool through the Implementation Guide for different SAP systems, which helps implement the SAP system with a configuration that meets the company's requirements or enhances the system. Customizing can be done at header, item, or schedule-line level, depending on the structure of the document.

Functions outside of the document type—such as pricing, partners, and outputs—that are maintained in basic functions for sales and distribution and linked to the document type. The sales document type is not completely configured until you have processed all the necessary basic functions.

Customizing for the sale document types controls the behavior of sales documents at the header level. You will configure settings that are valid for the whole sales documents. Different sales documents delivered with the system represent different business process. For example, within pre-sales the sales document types are inquiry (IN) and quotation (QT). Examples from Outline Agreements are quantity contract (QC), scheduling agreement (DS), and general value contract (WK1). The sales phase has standard order (OR), rush order (RO), cash sale (CS), consignment fill-up (CF), and delivery free-of-charge (FD). In the complaints phase you will find returns (RE), credit memo request (CR), subsequent free-of-charge (SDF), and debit memo request (DR).

Figure 1.18 shows the configuration setting for sales document type quotation (QT). To reach this configuration step, follow this menu path from the Display IMG: **Sales and Distribution • Sales • Sales Document Header**. You can then click on **Define Sales Document Types**. You can access the Implementation Guide (IMG) or display the IMG, in one of the two following ways:

▸ As you log on and enter the SAP Easy Access, follow the menu path: **Tools • Customizing • IMG • Execute Project • SAP Reference IMG**. This will bring up the Display IMG.

▸ Alternatively, after you log on on and are in the SAP Easy Access within the command bar at the top, type in the transaction code SPRO, and hit enter. Click on **SAP Reference IMG** to bring up the Display IMG.

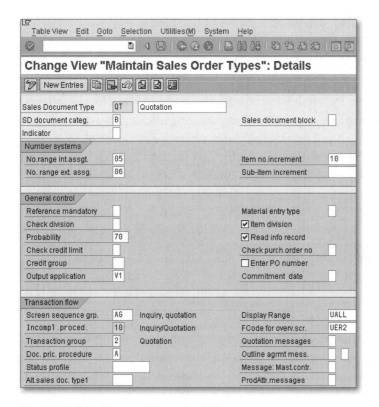

Figure 1.18 Sales Document Type: Quotation

Document Category

Let's go over some of the key definitions for this. SD document category defines the classification for the document type (inquiry, order, scheduling agreement, returns). In the number-systems section, you define number range for internal and external assignment, item number increment, and sub-item number increment.

The general control section allows you to check for any reference document requirement; e.g., you are not able to create a delivery without referencing a sales order. You also can check for credit limits in terms of warnings, error messages, or blocks from further processing, and access credit-management functions. You can define other checks as well. For example, you may want to check for an item division from material master or copy from the header of the document-processing function. You may wish to determine whether the purchase-order number must be validated whether any of customer material information must be read, or whether to use the commitment date for calculation.

The transaction flow allows you to screen sequences encountered when entering a sales document. You can also define the messages displayed, based on the checks and assignment of incompletion procedure. This is done at a different place in the configuration step. We will describe that later in this book.

Let's take an example of another order type, as we move on to other sections. Figure 1.19 displays the standard order type (OR) configuration definitions.

Shipping			
Delivery type	LF	Delivery	Immediate delivery
Delivery block			
Shipping conditions			
ShipCostInfoProfile	STANDARD	Standard freight information	

Billing			
Dlv-rel.billing type	F2	Invoice	CndType line items	EK02
Order-rel.bill.type	F2	Invoice	Billing plan type	
Intercomp.bill.type	IV	Intercompany billing	Paymt guarant. proc.	01
Billing block			Paymt card plan type	03
			Checking group	01

Requested delivery date/pricing date/purchase order date		
Lead time in days		☑ Propose deliv.date
Date type		☐ Propose PO date
Prop.f.pricing date		
Prop.valid-from date		

Contract			
PricProcCondHeadr		Contract data allwd.	
PricProcCondItem		FollUpActivityType	
Contract profile		Subseq.order type	
Billing request	DR	Check partner auth.	A
Group Ref. Procedure		☐ Update low.lev.cont.	

Figure 1.19 Standard Order Type

Within the scheduling agreement you can define the usage of the material being shipped (spare part or a replacement part for example). The shipping section allows you to define delivery type and choose whether you want a delivery block or the shipping condition to be defaulted when the order is created. The billing section allows you to maintain different billing types based on the process (if is it delivery related, order related or inter-company). You can also define billing plan (milestone or periodic) by defining the billing type. The checking group allows you to maintain the check for payment cards.

Within the section for requested date/pricing date/purchase order date, you can control the price date, request a delivery date proposed in the document and what format to use (week, day, month or posting period). The contact section provides the relevant contact information; e.g., the price procedure condition proposed for header, item, any pre-defined contract profile, and what kind of order type and billing type is used for billing.

Within the availability check section you can define the business transaction, which controls the rule-based availability check based on business context. This entry makes it possible to use the availability check settings in the APO planning system for this order type.

Definition and Configuration

The definition and configuration of sales document types can be divided into three parts as seen below:

- **Define Sales Document Types**

  Here we define the control specifications for the documents types we reviewed above. You need to be aware that sales document types are not isolated but are closely linked with delivery types and billing types. You can default a billing block, if the billing department has to review the orders (e.g., returns).

- **Define Additional Sales Functions**

  When you define your own sales document type or make changes to the existing ones to meet your company requirements, make sure some additional functions are taken in account, such as:

  - Number ranges for sales document types

  - Screen sequence

  - Usage indicator

  - Reason for rejection

  - Check against the division for header and item

- **General SD Functions**

  You need to configure a number of general SD functions for sales document types. For example, you can have:

  - A specific pricing function based on sales document type.

  - An output type specific to sales document type

Sales Area Differentiation

Sales can be differentiated into four major areas, which are:

- ▶ Customer inquiries and quotations
- ▶ Sales orders
- ▶ Contracts and agreements
- ▶ Complaints, such as returns, repair, credit memo and debit memos

You can create special orders with sales, for example cash sales where you sell the goods and get cash in return, and rush order, where you deliver the product immediately and bill the customer later.

A customer scheduling agreement is an agreement with the customer specifying the delivery quantity and dates. You fulfill the agreement by creating deliveries. A customer contact is an outline agreement that captures data on when a goods or services will be sold within a given time period.

Apart from these standard business processes, you can also implement more specialized business processes, such as make-to-order item, third party, consignment stock, and configurable products. Now that we understand the basics of Sales and Distribution, I will introduce you to mySAP ERP and highlight the functionality introduced with different releases.

1.4   What is New in mySAP ERP?

As we all know, a new technology platform is important for future systems strategy. Release R/2 was a centralized computing model used for automating business processes. SAP R/3 replaced this with client-server architecture for better efficiency and control. Companies are looking at leveraging the IT investment they have done so far with SAP R/3 and make their businesses adaptable with mySAP ERP. MySAP ERP is the latest technology advancement, with a focus on strategic value and an enterprise service architecture (ESA) model.

With the release of SAP 4.6C, we had the application layer and SAP basis layer. SAP R/3 Enterprises has SAP R/3 Enterprise, SAP Web Application Server, Extension Sets, and Add-on Industry Solutions. With mySAP ERP 2004, the main components (Sales and Distribution, Materials Management, Finance, etc.) are part of the SAP ERP Central Component. augmented by Extension Sets, Industry Solutions, Strategic Enterprise Management, Inter-

net sales, Self Service, and more. Most important, mySAP ERP is packaged with SAP NetWeaver. The application platform consists of J2EE and an ABAP stack above the database and operating system abstraction. With mySAP ERP, you have the option of switching the framework between enterprise extensions and industry extensions.

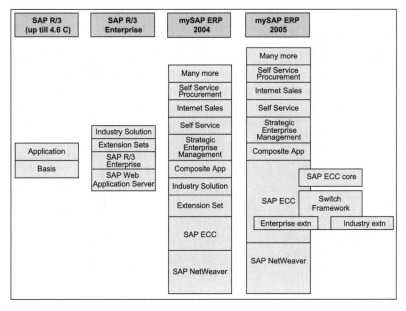

Figure 1.20 mySAP ERP Evolution Pause

Figure 1.20 illustrates the mySAP ERP evolution in terms of how the different layers have emerged with the technology and the application components. In summary, the key differences between SAP R/3 and mySAP ERP is highlighted below in Table 1.1.

SAP R/3	mySAP ERP
Client-server architecture	Enteprise Service Architecture
SAP Web Application Server	Designed for SAP NetWeaver
Transactional user	Business user
Data-centric	Message-centric
Enterprise processes	End-to-end processes
Real-time data processing	Real-time business

Table 1.1 SAP R/3 vs. mySAP ERP

1.4.1 Functionality Enhancements Within SAP R/3 Releases

Now we can look at some high-level enhancements from SAP R/3 4.0 through 4.6 releases:

▶ **Cancel Goods Issue Posting**
With release R/3 4.0A, you can now cancel goods issue posting for deliveries. This helps simplify the delivery management process.

▶ **Deliveries Sent to Internal/External Departments**
Deliveries can be sent to internal and external department in many different ways, starting with release R/3 4.0A. The aim of release 4.0 is to create a common basis for an EDI/ALE messages in this area. This function was developed for both inward and outward messages, and particular attention is paid to improving performance. This enhancement ensures standardization and integration of the delivery process to improve the logistics.

▶ **Define Downpayment**
It is possible to define downpayment as part of the sales order with release 4.0A. In the capital goods, engineering, and construction industries, it is common to agree upon a downpayment with the customer for manufacturing and delivering a contracted object. This enhancement improves sales-order management by allowing the use of downpayments with enough flexibility to automate the process.

▶ **Free Goods**
The use of different types of free goods was introduced with release R/3 4.0A. With an exclusive agreement, the manufacturer will ship free goods in addition to the customer's order quantity. The free item could be the same as the product ordered or another product. For an inclusive agreement, the manufacturer will ship part of the customer's order quantity for free. Both of these are supported by the new free goods functionality.

▶ **Material Information System**
Also known as MAIS, this was introduced in release R/3 4.0A. The MAIS procedure ensures continuity of information between customers and suppliers (e.g., the automotive industry). This enhancement allows reduction of errors and a better data consistency. It also speeds up the delivery process.

▶ **Payment Cards**
These are gradually replacing cash as a means of payment, proving to be indispensable to customers and a valuable tool to businesses as well. As payment cards have gained in popularity, card technology has advanced at an explosive rate. With R/3 4.0A, payment-card processing was intro-

duced, which not only provides flexibility in procurement and sales management but also helps automate the process.

▶ **Shipment Cost Processing**
This was introduced with R/3 4.0A. Shipments are an important and integral part of the logistics chain. Shipment activities need to be organized swiftly and efficiently to achieve high levels of customer satisfaction and at the same time minimize logistic costs. This enhancement offers control and visibility on shipment cost processing.

▶ **Value Contracts**
These were introduced with R/3 4.0A. The value contract describes the outline agreement with the customer. It contains the validity period, the agreed-upon total value, and rules controlling the release of the contract. As a result, it is possible to define the specific customers who can call off against the contract, in addition to the relevant materials. Special pricing agreements can be stored in the value contract and can be defined at different levels. For example, the value contract can contain prices that are relevant for individual materials or discounts that apply to all materials released.

▶ **PRICAT Messages**
PRICAT messages are SAP delivered iDocs templates used for transferring price data and catalogs for goods and services. They are customer-specific. With R/3 4.5 A Sales and Service, we have on the outbound side the R/3 system supporting the creation of PRICAT messages. The system creates an intermediate document (IDoc), which is converted to an EDI file in PRICAT format by an EDI subsystem. The allows use of logical messages to transfer data on price and catalogs for goods and services to a customer.

▶ **Repair Processing**
With R/3 4.5A Sales and Service, Repair Processing was introduced. When a customer wants to repair a faulty piece of equipment, you can document this request with a service notification and enter into the system as a customer repair order. You can also arrange to collect the faulty product from the customer. Once you have recieved the piece of equipment to be repaired and have performed a technical check, you can manage it as individual customer stock for the customer repair order. This enhancement provides a comprehensive set of new functionalities that covers end to end a process specifically designed for service and repairs (e.g., receiving products from the customer, repairing them, returning them, and billing the customer).

▶ **Sales and Service Revenue Recognition**
With R/3 4.5A Sales and Service, revenue recognition was introduced. It works closely with Sales and Distribution, Financial Accounting, and Con-

trolling application components. This functionality increases your choices or when revenue recognition takes place. You can select from several standard industry techniques the revenue-recognition method that best meets your company's needs.

▶ **Linking Distribution Centers and WMS**
With 4.5A, it is possible to link a distribution center as an independent component with the SAP R/3 system or to link the SAP R/3 Warehouse Management System. The creation of a distribution center as an independent component makes it easier to model decentralized systems using ERP and Warehouse Management System (WMS). This enhancement provides more efficiency and flexibility in driving down the cost of the supply chain while increasing productivity and improving customer service.

▶ **Simpler Navigation**
With 4.6A, navigation through many of the processes such as invoice creation, assembly processing, sales activity processing, and telephone sales has become simpler. The enhancement improves productivity and saves time by easier navigation through sales and billing. The improvements have been made to the following functions:

▶ Sales document processing

▶ Billing document creation

▶ Condition maintenance

▶ Sales activity processing

1.4.2 Sales Order Management

Within the scope of sales and services in mySAP ERP 2005, we find Sales Order Management, Aftermarket Sales and Service, Professional-Service Delivery, Global Trade Services, and Incentive and Commission Management.

MySAP ERP focuses on user productivity by providing a role-based central point of access, pushing relevant information actively to the users, providing guided procedures for common tasks, and embedding analytics for better decision making. A user can have his or her logon screen as a single point of entry or represent the actual workload, providing a quick access to transactions and reports. Users can define their personal object work lists (POWLs) in contrast to SAP R/3, where users had to search for information by starting different reports with personal selection variants. Figure 1.21 shows you how easy it is to define the POWL.

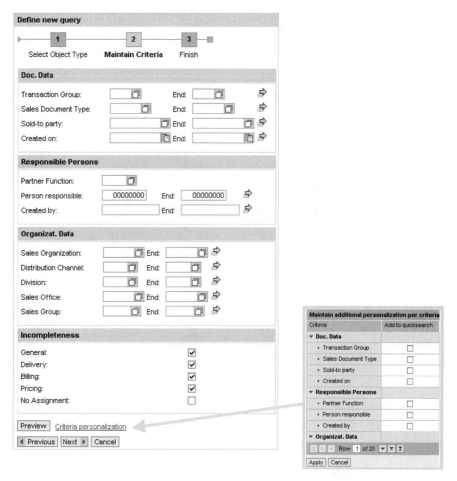

Figure 1.21 Personal Object Work List

High performance is achieved through an intelligent cashing mechanism that provides:

▶ Real-time information upon request

▶ Refresh running asynchronously for high usability

▶ Work lists that remain available until results are refreshed

Sales Order Management has new user interfaces for sales documents: Inquiries, quotations, and sales orders. It allows you to adjust the user interfaces (UI) according to the company's individual sales processes. The approach is to reduce complexity and unnecessary information for occasional users. The technology behind this UI is ABAP Web Dynpro, and it is built on top of the new service, application program interface, which decou-

ples the UI from business logic. This also provides high performance for volume transactions. SAP E-Commerce for mySAP ERP, available within Sales Order Management, has introduced some new features, listed below:

▶ **Design**

 ▶ Frameless Business to Consumer (B2C)

 ▶ New order header

 ▶ Enhanced display of search

▶ **User Management**

 ▶ Super user concept

 ▶ Authorization roles (role-based authorization)

 ▶ Web-based user management

 ▶ Transaction code SU05-SU01 user concept migration in business-to-business (B2B) and business-to-customer (B2C) during log-on

▶ **Catalog**

 ▶ Option for catalog display only (no ordering because of authorization roles)

 ▶ New ABAP-based catalog replication trigger from ERP back end

 ▶ Enhanced search functionality

▶ **Order Management**

 ▶ Multiple order types in shop management

 ▶ Contract release order

 ▶ Bill of material (BOM) explosion

 ▶ Credit card support in B2B

1.4.3 New Features in mySAP ERP 2005

Web auction (selling with eBay) is a new function introduced in mySAP ERP 2005. It is a complete auction-to-cash process allowing business to enable an additional sales channel. Selling via eBay provides ways to create and manage listings on eBay while leveraging existing product data and handling order management, fulfillment, and financial process. It allows optional check-out in a Web store for closer integration with SAP E-Commerce.

With mySAP ERP, you can integrate Web auction management. It allows you to select products and add eBay-specific information, schedule, and publish eBay listings. Buyers can bid and browse on eBay.com. Other functions are

integrating order management and fulfillment, monitoring auctions and sales on eBay.com, and managing the feedback from eBay. With mySAP ERP, the winning bidder can check out directly at the eBay site with the checkout capability integrated with SAP E-Commerce and the B2C scenarios. Within the mySAP ERP Sales and Service, there are four major areas:

▶ **Sales Order Management**
Within Sales Order Management, you have: Accounts Processing, Internet Sales, Managing Auctions, Inquiry Processing, Quotation Processing, Trading Contract Management, Sales Order Processing, Mobile Sales, Inbound Telesales, Contract Processing, Billing, Returnable Packaging Management and Consignment.

▶ **Aftermarket Sales and Service**
Aftermarket Sales and Service includes Phase-in Equipment, Phase-Out Equipment, Asset Scrapping, Product and Warranty Registration, Warranty Claim Processing, Service Contract Processing, Service Plan Processing, Mobile Measurement and Counter Reading, Service Employee Resource Planning, Service Notification Processing, Service Order Processing, Billing, Returns Processing, and In-House Repair Processing.

▶ **Professional-Service Delivery**
Professional-Service Delivery consists of Project Planning and Scoping, Resource and Time Management, Quotation Processing, Sales Order Processing, Project Execution, Time and Attendance, Managing Employee, Time and Attendance, Travel Expense Management, Project Accounting, Resource-Related Billing, and Resource-Related Inter-company Billing.

▶ **Incentive and Commission Management**
Incentive and Commission Management consists of Incentive Business Configuration, Incentive Plan Maintenance, and Incentive Processing.

Let's now move on to gain an overview of Analytics

1.4.4 SAP Analytics

The objective of the SAP analytics has been to empower the business users. The common challenge of analytics systems is that they are typically centralized, and the IT group becomes the bottleneck in delivering the reports, while the business users need insights whenever windows of opportunity open.

SAP Analytics approaches this challenge by providing business users with an insight-actionable, managed self-service environment with ad hoc creations

of key performance indicators (KPIs), hierarchies, queries, and semantic views. The business users are exposed to the logic of analysis and not the technical complexity. SAP Analytics provides a new tool for reporting analytical data, because as a consultant you will have to work with your business users and end users and can use this along with other reporting tools.

Figure 1.22 shows you typical output of SAP analytics. Different pictorial or graphical representation of data gathered on the fly are available, along with user interfaces that are configurable based on user definitions and role.

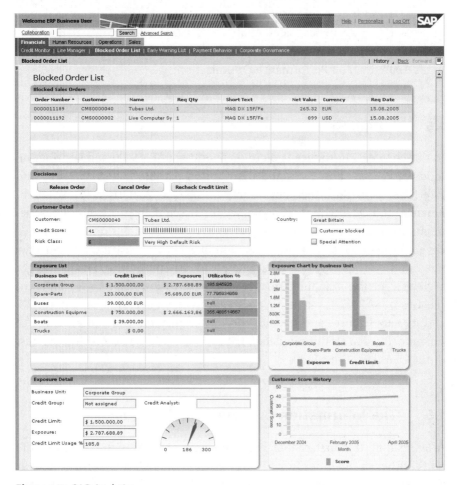

Figure 1.22 SAP Analytics

Analytics within mySAP ERP consist of the following areas:

▶ End-User Service Delivery

▶ Stratetegic Enterprise Management

▶ Financial Analytics

▶ Operations Analytics

▶ Workforce Analytics

Operations Analytics consists of: Sales Planning, Procurement Analytics, Inventory and Warehouse Management Analytics, Manufacturing Analytics, Transportation Analytics, Sales Analytics, Customer Service Analytics, Program and Project Management Analytics, Quality Management Analytics, Asset Analytics, and Performance Optimization.

1.5   Summary

In this chapter, I introduced you to the world of SAP's Sales and Distribution module. We saw how Sales and Distribution fits into the SAP strategy and interfaces with the other key functions such as Materials Management, Finance, and Quality Management. We discussed the key organizational elements for representing your company in an effective business model. We covered the key business processes within Sales and Distribution and how you can use the configuration parameters to customize them. Finally, we got a glimpse of the new functionality and features introduced with different releases of SAP ERP systems. We also gave you an overview of mySAP ERP and its new features and functionality. Later chapters will address some of functionality and features in detail. Let us now take a quick look into the rest of the chapters of this book.

1.6   The Information Contained in This Book

After reading this first chapter, you can now proceed with the rest of the book, either in the order in which the chapters appear or according to your own requirements. Therefore, please take a look at the chapter descriptions and decide for yourself how you would like to use this book.

Chapter 2 will cover the master data and configuration application and settings in detail. Master data is the key source of information to be determined in the sales and distribution transactions and documents. It also explains the

data determination and processing of sales documents. We will touch on important aspects of configuration, in order to control the sales document type, item category, and schedule line category. These configurations allow you to define your sales processes through documents and transactions. SAP uses the document flow to link subsequent and preceding processes. These documents carry the information across the supply chain and act as a process event.

Chapter 3 will explain sales and distribution key techniques, gotchas, and tips. Pricing is one of the most powerful functionalities in Sales and Distribution, and this module uses condition techniques to determine pricing. Condition techniques are a very effective and powerful way of defining the business process for search sequences and determining information based on complex business rules. Understanding this will help you take full advantage of the pricing functionality. You can also apply condition techniques in other areas, such as output determination and text determination. We will learn about the partner determination and see how it can best be applied to your business. Movement of data from one document to another within sales is controlled by copy control and requirement.

The Materials Management (MM) module is one of the key interfaces to Sales and Distribution. The sales and distribution process has many influences on the Materials Management process. *Chapter 4* takes up the most commonly and frequently influence on the materials management processes by sales and distribution functions and processes. A sales order triggers a requirement and checks for availability in Materials Management. We will understand the fundamentals of availability. Cross-company process sales use Materials Management in the physical movement of parts from one location to another, triggered by the sales process. Inter-company and cross-company movements are initiated within Materials Management and use Sales and Distribution functions. Similarly sales processing uses third-party processing and sub-contracting with MM functionality. Another influence of sales process on Material scheduling is seen with the agreements.

Having understood the influence of Materials Management, we will move in *Chapter 5* to the processes that are extensions of SD within the supply chain. Transportation and shipment executions within Logistics Execution are used extensively in the sales and distribution process. Another important aspect of supply chain is warehouse management, embedded very closely with the sales process. The decentralized warehouse management supports business-process outsourcing.

Chapter 6 will touch briefly on the Financial and Controlling interface. The billing document is part of the sales and distribution function, but carries financial information. Integration of the billing document and its configuration is explained in this chapter. Account determination helps recognize the different financial elements within a transaction between you and customer. This chapter explains some financial supply chain management processes and functions that work with logistics systems to create an end-to-end process. Discussion of the interface with Profitability Analysis helps you understand the financial reporting of the sales activities performed in the company.

Chapter 7 outlines the concepts of service management and processing of service orders. Service order is another aspect of sales with functionality to support service-order processing for customers. Complaints and returns are process-derived from the service management functions, and we will see how they are set up in SAP. Quality management is embedded within the sales process, so this chapter will explain the key quality process in application for sales processing. Workflow concepts are also explained, to help you understand the functionality behind workflow.

Having explained the configuration settings for sales and distribution and sales business processes, we will devote *Chapter 8* to report analysis, user productivity, and development tools from a technical point of view. Quick views, queries, lists, and reports are fast ways of extracting the data and presenting it. We will study traditional information reporting via the sales information system for analytical reporting and the business intelligence warehouse. Any implementation involves configuration settings, customization, personalization, or modification and enhancement, if these are not provided by the standard delivery configurations. We will learn the concepts and applications of modifications and enhancements.

We will end this book with the *Chapter 9*, which will review the various techniques and ways with which data is transferred into and out of SAP system. These include data transfer for the purpose of doing conversion from legacy system, use of output types for notifying external partners or printing documents and sending emails. Different SAP systems communicate with each other through application linking, and remote function call helps trigger functions from one system to another. We will look at the specific SD communication to the Global Trade Services system and the interface with Customer Relationship Management.

1.7 How to Read This Book

Features and functionality discussed here apply to SAP R/3 through mySAP ERP from the Sales and Distribution point of view. I have tried to cover the most important aspects of the Sales and Distribution module, and if specific functionality is germane to a specific release, I have tried to address it. This book is intended to provide in-depth knowledge of Sales and Distribution, to serve as a reference for understanding the key concepts, and to give you the details behind the power of this module.

This information can be very helpful for business analysts, technical analysts, super users project leads, progam managers, or consultants who are actively involved in a new SD implementation. It will also be useful for those wanting to upgrade, enhance, and make the best of the SD functionality. Other readers can use it as a refresher for SAP SD, because it provides details of SD functionality, features, and processes not easily understood or documented. This book describes some of the key interfaces with SD and technical concepts behind implementations. I wrote this book to give you a strong foundation and to help you build on your Sales and Distribution expertise. This should help you make use of the untapped functionality within one of oldest and most powerful SAP modules.

Let's now proceed with the rest of this book, starting with Chapter 2 where I will cover master data and configuration application and settings.

This chapter will walk you through the key possible sources of information for master data and its configurations. The system reads the master data defined for a specific customer, which could be a material or a condition. With Customizing, you can define default values for creating documents and the business processes they define.

2 Sales and Distribution Master Data and Configuration: Applications and Processing

Master data for Sales and Distribution (SD) consists of information that helps you process your transaction, in terms of the business partner you are dealing with or the goods or services you might provide to your customer. Master data helps you determine the information needed to process the transaction. Several sources of data can be copied into a sales order or into another SD document. Most of them are default values that you can overwrite in the sales and distribution document, if necessary.

The sources of data include customer master data, material master data, condition master data, and output and control tables. The condition master data is created and maintained in the sales and distribution master data for automatic pricing. Output is information sent to the customer via various media, such as mail, EDI, or fax.

Control tables are created and maintained through Customizing. The default values of several data can be controlled in the sales and distribution documents, depending on the tables' settings.

A previous sales document can serve as a source of data for another sales document. For example, a quotation can serve as a data source for a sales order. Figure 2.1 shows you the different ways in which information can be pulled into sales transactions, for example, from orders or quotations.

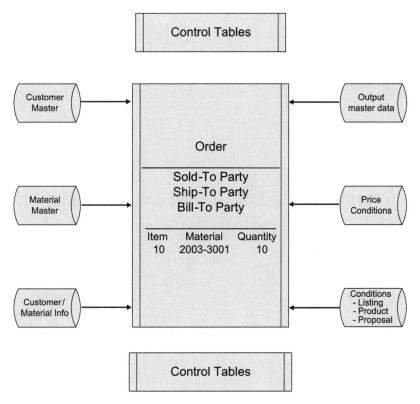

Figure 2.1 Data Origination and Determination in Sales Transactions

2.1 Master Data in Sales and Distribution

As mentioned earlier, data defaults into the sales document from the master record; e.g., from the customer master record of the sold-to party, the system proposes sales, shipping, pricing, and billing data. For each material in the sales order, the system automatically presents data from the relevant material master records, such as data for pricing, delivery scheduling, availability check, tax determination, and weight and volume determination.

You should store as much data as possible in master records in SAP R/3. This will save you time during order entry and help you to avoid incorrect entries. You can enter different types of master data in R/3, such as, information on business partners, materials, customer/material, item proposals, bills of materials (BOMs), prices, discounts and rebates, taxes, freight, output, and text. The system will frequently access this data during order processing.

2.1.1 Customer Master Data

The customer master data can be grouped into three categories, which are discussed below:

▶ **General Data**

The general data is relevant for sales and distribution and for accounting. It is stored centrally (client specific) in order to avoid data redundancy. It is valid for all organizational units within a client.

▶ **Sales Area Data**

The sales area data is relevant for sales and distribution. It is valid for the respective company code. The customer master includes all the data necessary for processing orders, deliveries, invoices, and customer payments. In order to maintain in the customer master the general data that is relevant for sales and distribution and accounting, the data are grouped on several tab pages.

▶ **Company Code Data**

The general data is maintained independently of the organizational units. The general data in the customer master is set up on the following tab pages:

> ▶ Address

> ▶ Control Data

> ▶ Payment transactions

> ▶ Marketing

> ▶ Unloading points

> ▶ Export data

> ▶ Contact persons

Customizing allows you to hide certain fields on a tab page or make them required entry fields. Configuration allows you to define account groups and select field for customers. This can be accessed through the transaction code OVT0. You can also reach it via the Implementation guide (IMG) general transaction code SPRO, and then clicking on **SAP Reference IMG**. This will bring up the tree structure under the SAP Customizing Implementation Guide. Then, do the following:

1. Expand or click on **Logistics – General**

2. Expand or click on **Business Partner**

3. Expand or click on **Customers**

4. Expand or clisk on **Control**

5. Double-click on **Define Account Groups and Fields Selection for Customers**

This transaction code lists all the groups within the SAP system, both SAP standard delivered and any custom ones created by your company.

If you want to create a new Customizing entry, I recommend copying with reference to a standard configuration entry and making necessary modification to the copy based on your company's requirement. You see the details behind the one available in the SAP standard system; select one group, and double-click on the selection. In the change view **Customer Account Groups: Details** screen, you can select one of the field statuses by double-clicking and selecting a group below that selection. This will bring up a screen that is shown in the Figure 2.2.

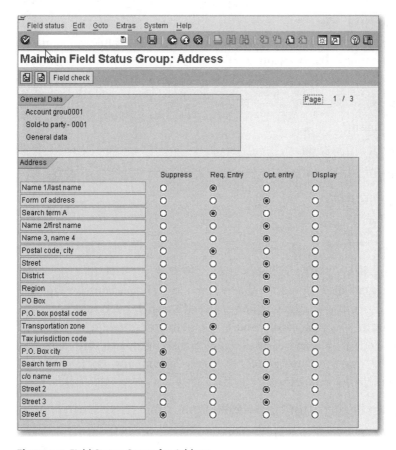

Figure 2.2 Field Status Group for Address

Similarly, you can also define screen layout to be transaction dependent. Number ranges are defined and assigned by account group. Other control configuration related to customer is found under the path: **Customers • Control**.

You can maintain the sales area data in various ways, depending on the sales area (sales organization, distribution channel and division). The sales area data in the customer master is shown on the following tab pages:

- Sales (e.g., Sales office, currency, sales district, price group)
- Shipping (e.g., Shipping condition, deliverying plant, transportation zone)
- Billing document (e.g., Output tax classification, payment condition)
- Partner functions (e.g., ship-to party, bill-to party, payer)

Partner functions are stored for the customer master in the customer master sales area data (tab page: **Partner functions**). During sales-order processing, they are copied as default values into the documents. The business data in a sales document is taken from the master data records for the different business partners. For sales-order processing, you need the mandatory partner functions of sold-to-party, ship-to-party, payer, and bill-to party. In the course of processing a sales order, these can differ from each other or they can be identical. Here are the most commonly used business partner functions in a sales transaction:

- Sold-to party: Places the order
- Ship-to party: Receives goods or services
- Bill-to party: Receives the invoice for goods or service
- Payer: Responsible for paying the invoice

Other partner functions, such as contact person or forwarding agent, are not absolutely necessary for sales-order processing. Because the ship-to party can be in a different place than the sold-to party, the delivery address and tax information are taken from the ship-to party's master record. As the payer is responsible for paying your receivables, the payment conditions in the document come from the payer's master record. The bill-to party data contains the address to which the invoice should be sent. This address could be different from that of the payer. Figure 2.3 shows a view of the **Customer** master record.

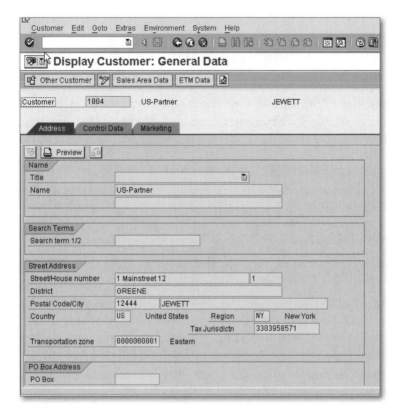

Figure 2.3 Customer Master Views

The customer maintenance for sales and distribution can be reached through the SAP Easy Access menu: **Sales and Distribution • Master Data • Business Partner • Customer • Create • Sales and Distribution**. This also can be reached through the transaction code VD01 (create). You will also find an option, **Complete**, under **Create**. This allows you to create a customer entry with company-code data. This can also be reached through the transaction code XD01 (create with accounting and sales data).

> **Note**
>
> VD02 is a change-customer record, and VD03 is for display. This numbering standard applies to all the transactions; e.g., XD02 is for change customer records with accounting information and XD03 for display.

Table 2.1 lists some other common transaction codes for the customer master.

Transaction Code	Description
VD04/XD04	To display customer account changes—any changes made to the customer master fields
VD05/XD05	To block or unblock customer by sales area specific order, delivery, billing, or sales support.
VD06/XD06	To set a customer for deletion
VD07/XD07	To maintain reference customer for consumer

Table 2.1 Customer Master Maintenance Transaction

To maintain the company code data relevant for accounting in the customer master, the data fields are grouped on several tab pages, which are:

▶ Account management (e.g., reconciliation account)

▶ Payment transactions (e.g., payment methods, payment block)

▶ Correspondence (e.g., dunning procedure, accounting clerk)

▶ Insurance (e.g., amount insured)

Note

When you change a master record after using it to create documents (orders, deliveries, billing documents, and so on), the changes do not affect the documents already created. The address in the customer master, however, is an exception. If necessary, therefore, you would have to change the data (but not the address) in the documents manually.

Configuration related to customer master data is found under the **Display IMG**. Once there, do the following:

1. Expand or click on **Sales and Distribution**

2. Expand or click on **Master Data**

3. Expand or click on **Business Partner**

Within that data, you can perform Customizing related to the customer and contact person. Some examples of Customizing are: defining customer hierarchy, defining customer classification for marketing, defining sales districts for sales, defining shipping priorities for shipping, defining customer calendar for shipping and for billing, and defining billing schedule, terms of payment, and incoterms, etc. These definitions are then maintained in the customer master. For the contact person, there are certain configuration

parameters, such as buying habits and attributes. Table 2.2 lists samples of some master data tables with regard to the customer master.

Table	Description
ADR	Address tables
CDCLS	Cluster structure for change documents
CDHDR	Change document header
KNA1	General data in customer master
KNAS	Customer master (VAT registration numbers general section)
KNAT	Customer master record (tax groupings)
KLPA	Customer/vendor linking
KNB1	Customer master (company code)
KNB4	Customer payment history
KNB5	Customer master (dunning data)
KNBK	Customer master (bank details)
KNEX	Customer master: legal control, sanctioned party list
KNKA	Customer master credit management: central data
KNKK	Customer master credit management: control area data
KNMT	Customer material info record data table
KNVP	Customer master partner functions
KNVS	Customer master shipping data
KNVV	Customer master sales data

Table 2.2 Sample Customer Master Data Tables

2.1.2 Material Master Data

The material master comprises the following areas:

▶ Basic Data

▶ Sales and Distribution Data

▶ Purchasing Data

▶ Accounting

▶ Costing

▶ Warehouse Management

Basic data is relevant for all areas and is valid for all organizational units within a client. The sales organization data is relevant for sales and distribution. It is valid for sales organizations and their respective distribution channels. The sale: plant data is also relevant for sales and distribution; it is valid for the delivery plant.

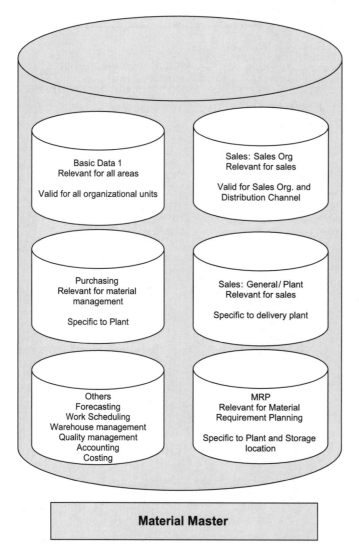

Figure 2.4 Material Master Views

Additional data relevant for different organizational units is available as well. The data for **Sales: Sales Org. 1** and **Sales: Sales Org. 2** as well as the sales text, is valid for the sales organization and the distribution channel. The **Sales:**

General/Plant data and the **Foreign Trade: Export** data is valid for the delivering plant. Figure 2.4 displays the **Material Master** with different views and the relevant data contained.

Customizing allows you to control the following activities with sales document type definition:

▸ Whether multiple materials can be entered with various divisions for an order

▸ Whether the system will respond with or without warning messages

▸ Whether the division on item level is copied from the material master record or whether the division in the document header is also copied into the item.

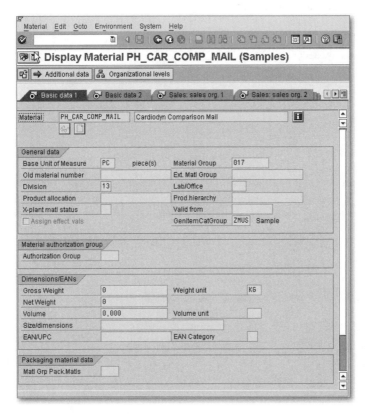

Figure 2.5 Material Master Views Screen

Later in this chapter, we will see how sales document types are configured to reflect the above functionality. Configuration allows you to play with the settings based on the standard defaults based on your business requirement.

Figure 2.5 shows the **Basic data 1**, **Basic data 2**, **Sales: sales org. 1**, **Sales: Sales org. 2** and **Sales: General/Plant Data** (not shown).

As with any relational data, material master information is stored in different tables. Table 2.3 lists some typical material master tables. Keep in mind that this not an exhaustive list.

Table	Description
KNMT Customer	Material info record data table
MAEX	Material master: legal control
MAKT	Material descriptions
MARA	General material data
MARC	Plant data for material
MARD	Storage location data for material
MARM	Units of measure for material
MBEW	Material valuation
MDKP	Header data for MRP document
MDMA	MRP area for material
MDVM	Entry in MRP file
MPOP	Forecast parameters
MKAL	Production versions of material
MVKE	Sales data for material
MPGD_MASS	Planning data
MLAN	Tax classification for material

Table 2.3 Sample Material Master Tables

Some commonly used materials management transactions are listed in Table 2.4.

Transaction code	Description
MM01	Material create
MM02	Material change
MM03	Material display

Table 2.4 Materials Management Transactions

Transaction code	Description
MM04	Display changes made to material master fields after it has been saved
MM06	Flag material for deletion
MM11	Schedule creation of material
MM12	Schedule material change
MM13	Activate a schedule change based on a key date
MM16	Schedule a material for deletion
MM03	Display material
MM19	Display material based on key date
MM14	Display any planned changed to the material master
MM17	Mass maintenance

Table 2.4 Materials Management Transactions (cont.)

Tip
Material master maintenance transactions can be accessed through the SAP Easy Access menu, via this path: **Logistics • Materials Management • Material Master**.

Within the SD configuration, certain settings or parameters control the influence of material or product that has been determined and processed in a sales transaction.

2.1.3 Condition Master Data

Condition master data are similar to the master data, except that they are determined based on business logic or configuration settings, such as pricing conditions retrieved through access sequence. The condition master also uses condition techniques. We will cover the fundamentals of condition techniques in Chapter 3, as applied in the pricing procedure.

Pricing

The condition master data includes prices, surcharges, discounts, freights, and taxes. You can define the master record for condition (condition records) to be dependent on various data. In Customizing, you can control the data on which prices, surcharges, and discounts, freights, or taxes can be dependent. The condition type defines the multiple use of a condition. You can have a

percentage, a quantity-dependent or amount-dependent surcharge period. You can maintain values within a condition record (price, surcharge, and discount) according to scale.

Output

Output is any information that is sent to the customer via communication media such as mail, EDI, or fax. Examples include the printout of a quotation or an order confirmation, order confirmation via EDI, or an invoice or fax. As with pricing, output determination takes place using condition techniques. Output can be sent for various sales and distribution documents (order, delivery, billing document).

In the output master data, you define the transmission medium, the time, and the partner function for an output type. Output can be sent as soon as data is saved or by means of a standard program that is run regularly (RSNAST00).

Configuration

Configuration allows you to control the item proposals. Some of the defaults include technical parameters, such as assignment of a number range and item number. If you want an item to be proposed as the customer frequently buys it, than you might want to specify it as part of customer master record. The related configuration can be found under the menu path: **Sales and Distribution • Master Data • Item Proposal.**

Material Determination

While creating a sales document, material determination allows you to find certain material automatically using a key already stored in the system, rather than have to enter the material number. The key could be a customer-specific material number or the International Article Number (IAN). With this technique, the material that is keyed in is automatically replaced by the material found during the creation. The configurations can be found in the Display IMG if you follow this path: **Sales and Distribution • Basic Functions • Material Determination.**

Material determination uses the condition technique. This involves identifying fields, which helps determine the master record (which becomes part of the condition table), the search strategy (access sequence), and the condition type

or material determination type. This process is also referred to as define the material determination procedure. To become active, these procedures need to be assigned to sales document type. Within the material determination, you can also set up a configuration for material substitution with reasons.

Product Proposal

Within Basic Functions, you can set a configuration for a dynamic product proposal. A product proposal is a list of products for a specific customer that is automatically proposed during sales-document processing. You can define the material that should appear and in what sequence. The product proposal is based on various sources; e.g., order history, listed material, excluded material, item proposal, customer material info records, and customer specific data sources. With Customizing, you should maintain the following for product proposals:

▶ Define customer procedure

▶ Define document procedure

▶ Assign document procedure to order types

▶ Maintain table of origin for product proposal

▶ Define product proposal procedure and determine access sequence

▶ Maintain online and backgrond online procedure determination for product proposal

Listing/Exclusion

Another configuration, which uses condition techniques, is listing and exclusion. Material listing and exclusion allows you to define, which material can be sold to a specific customer. The following steps are involved in this process:

1. Define access sequence and assign a condition table

2. Define type of material listing or exclusion and assign an access sequence

3. Define procedure and assign appropriate types

4. Assign procedures for the listing or the exclusion to sales document types

We have seen the various locations that information that can be stored within the SAP SD function. Now let's see how they are determined for processing.

2.2   Sales and Distribution Processes: Data Determination and Processing

When a customer calls in to request a part or service and you agree to provide the goods and service, you need to acknowledge it with a sales order or agreement. To ease the data-entry process and save time, you would like to default much of the predefined data and process it through the business logic based on your business model and set of rules. Data determination helps you default these data into the sales document and processing guides you through the end of the process.

A wide range of activities are carried out in SD. Different business processes can be identified and controlled by means of the sales document type. The standard system features many different sales document types for sales processes that are carried out on a regular basis. Here are some examples of document types that are delivered standard in the system:

▶ Standard order for invoiced sales on fixed delivery dates

▶ Rush order and cash sales for sales from the plant (with or without invoice)

▶ Free deliveries for sale on fixed deliveries dates (without invoice)

▶ Returns for return goods (credit memo/replacement delivery)

Figure 2.6 shows the different functions performed by the sales document while processing it through. You can implement these processes as they are or use them as a basis for mapping your own processes. The sales document type controls the sales documents. Similarly, the delivery type can be used to control the shipping documents and the billing type can be used to control the billing documents.

Depending on the transaction, certain functions are carried out automatically. These functions can be activated or deactivated directly via sales document type; e.g., for your standard sales process, you want the system to automatically determine the time at which your customer can receive the order goods.

To do so, you need to activate the shipment scheduling and availability check functions. These functions, however, are not required for credit memo requests. Another example is pricing not carried out for free deliveries. Figure 2.7 shows you the standard order type configuration screen.

Figure 2.6 Sales Document Functions

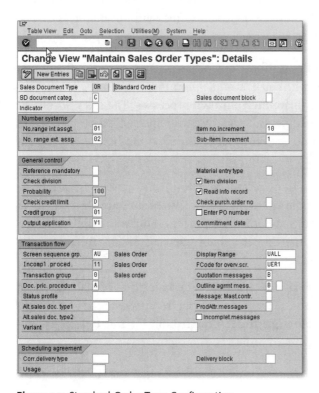

Figure 2.7 Standard Order Type Configuration

Just to walk you through few example of data determination through configuration, let me describe a business scenario involving plant, shipping point and route determination. The content of Plant, Shipping point determination, and Route fields in a sales document can be determined automatically and acts as a basis for delivery scheduling.

2.2.1   Plant

The plant plays a central role in Logistics. In SD, it is the delivering plant. When processing an item, the system automatically attempts to determine the associated delivering plant from the master data. The entry can later be changed manually. The system uses the following search strategy:

▸ Checks if a specification exists in a customer-material info record

▸ Checks if a specification exists in a customer master record

▸ Checks if a specification exists in the material master record

If nothing is found, no delivering plant is set in the sales document type. Without a plant, an item cannot be processed further. For example, attempts to automatically determine the shipping point or tax are unsuccessful, the availability cannot be checked, and an outbound delivery cannot be made.

2.2.2   Shipping Point Determination

The shipping point is the organizational unit in the system that is responsible for processing shipping. To determine a delivery date for a customer order, the system must take into account all the required lead times for the different shipping and transportation sub-process. For the shipping point, you can define the times required for preparing and packing the goods.

Figure 2.8 on the next page shows the different configuration steps involved in shipping point determination and the assignments to the shipping condition, loading group, and plant, which determine the primary shipping and the manual shipping points.

The shipping point is normally determined automatically for each item in the sales document. The automatic default value can be changed manually later if you have planned for a different shipping point.

The system uses three fields as search keys for determining the shipping point automatically. The data is normally defined in the following master records:

- Shipping condition from the sold-to party (view: **Shipping**)

- Loading group in the sales-specific material data (view: **Sales: General/ Plant Data**)

- Delivering plant (view: **Sales: Sales Org.1**)

The shipping conditions can be used to define in the system the delivery type requested by the customer.

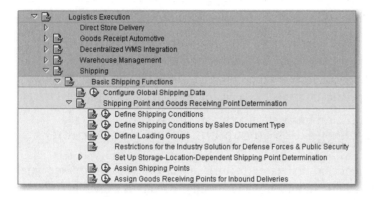

Figure 2.8 Shipping Point Determination

2.2.3 Route Determination

The route is the path a delivery follows from the delivery plant to the ship-to party. It can comprise more than one section. It has a start point and an end point. The route can be used to define the actual transit time (length of the time for which the goods are in transit) and the lead time for transportation planning.

The route is normally determined automatically for each item in the sales document. This default value can be changed manually later if you have planned a different route.

The system tries to determine a route for every item to be delivered. The system uses four fields as search keys for determining the route automatically. This data is normally defined in master records and in Customizing. The following is a list of the key determination data for a route determination:

- The departure zone in the customizing for the shipping point

- Shipping condition from the sold-to party (view: shipping of customer master record)

▶ Transportation group in the sales-specific material data (view: Sales: General/Plant Data)

▶ Transportation zone in the general data for the ship-to party

The configuration related to Shipping can be found within the display IMG. While in Display IMG, follow this path: **Logistics Execution • Shipping Basic • Shipping function • Shipping Point and Goods Receiving Point Determination**. You can also find the Route configurations under the Basic Shipping functions under Routes.

We saw how the determination happens with the configuration setting within the SD processes. Now let's look at the how sales processes are controlled through sales document type.

2.3 Controlling Sales Document with Sales Document Type

The instruments for Customizing, which take place at each level in the sales document, are the sales document type, item category, and schedule line category. The Customizing for a sales document type controls the behavior of a sales document at the header level. Sales processes are controlled by Customizing for sales documents. You need to make settings in Customizing so that the item and schedule line categories are determined in the sales document.

To complete the setup of a business process in your system, you need to configure the system to forward data from the sales document to subsequent documents, according to your needs. You can do this in copy control. A section in another chapter will describe copy control and requirements.

Additional configuration must be done outside of the document type. Much of that Customizing, such as pricing, partners, output, and so on, is maintained in basic functions. The procedure is then linked to the document type (item category or schedule line category). Figure 2.9 on the next page displays the different functions performed during a sales document creation or change.

You need to configure several general sales functions (basic functions) for the sales documents. These include partner determination, pricing, output determination, credit management, incompleteness checks, and delivery scheduling. You can fine-tune these settings at each level within the sales document.

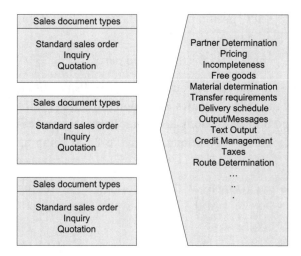

Figure 2.9 Functions Within Sales Document Type Configuration

The sales document is not completely configured until you have processed all of the necessary basic functions. For example, you configure the sales document type and pricing procedure separately; then assign the procedure to the sales document type. You can also create default output types for each sales document type. To do this, assign the relevant output-determination procedure to the sales document type in Customizing for output.

Figure 2.10 lists all the basic function configurations with the SAP SD. Basic functions are the functionality and features within **Sales and Distribution**, configured and defined outside of the sales document type and later assigned to the sales document type for invoking this functionality.

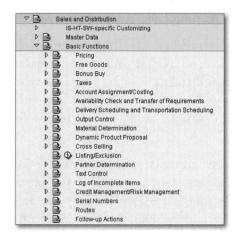

Figure 2.10 SD Basic Functions

2.3.1 Configuring Sales Document Types

Customizing for a sales document type controls the behavior of a sales document at the header level. You will configure settings that are valid for a whole sales document. Some of this data is fixed values, and some appears as default values. Different sales document types are delivered with the system to represent the different business processes. Figure 2.11 illustrates the different sales document applications in different phases of the sales process.

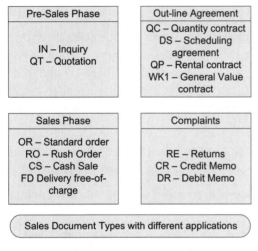

Figure 2.11 Sales Document Types:Application

In Customizing for the sales document type, you configure settings that influence the sales process, such as the sales document category, delivery, and billing blocks, or the document types for subsequent deliveries and billing documents.

The default values that appear when you create a document can be saved or can be overwritten with different values at different levels of the document to match particular procedures. You can set a rule for customer delivery date or certain basic requirements for contracts. In addition, you can activate various checks, such as messages about open quotations or outline agreements, search for customer-material info records, or credit limit checks.

> **Note**
>
> Activating checks can affect system performance. Adding a new sales document type is time consuming because many of the entities in Customizing depend on sales document type. I recommend that new sales documents be generated by copying existing ones that have similar functions.

The one referenced should be from the SAP standard delivered or one previously tested by your company. When you copy the document type, both the fields and the dependent entries are copied. Once the system has copied the document, it automatically generates a log that can be saved for documentation purposes.

When a document is changed after its initial creation, it goes through different determination procedures based on the change. While you are creating an inquiry, you might decide to change it to a quotation. You can also change a saved inquiry to a standard order.

Before you change the sales document type in the sales document, check that there are no subsequent documents, that the sales document is not a status-relevant subsequent document, and the document has not been created from a service notification or from contract. The item categories must be re-determined when the sales document type is changed, and the following requirements apply:

▶ The item category must be changeable (e.g., a make-to-order item for which the costs have already been posted can no longer be changed).

▶ If a listing exists for the new document type and you have already entered items, these items must also be contained in the list.

▶ If an item has been already entered, the new sales document type may not have an exclusion.

If you choose a new order type, the system checks for the following:

▶ Document determination procedure; if different, reruns the pricing

▶ Material determination procedure; if different, determines the material

▶ Listing/exclusion determination procedure; if different, re-determines the listings/exclusions

▶ For free goods procedure; if different, re-determines free goods

Note

If you change a document that has already been saved, both the new and the old document types must belong to the same number range.

You can define two alternative document types for each sales document type in Customizing (use **Alt. sales doc type1**, **Alt. sales doc type2**). Calling up **F4** (possible entries) will give you the list of sales document types that fulfill the necessary prerequisite.

During this process, the system checks the consistency of a number of Customizing items. The document types must have the same payment guarantee procedure, partner determination, text-determination procedure, status procedure, hierarchy category for pricing, billing plan type/invoice plan, payment card planning type, promotion/receiving point determination (setting in customizing for retail), commitment data, and checking group for payment cards. In addition, the sales document type must not be blocked, the sales document type must not have an indicator, and the settings in the item division fields must agree for both types.

Figure 2.12 displays the assignment of Sales Document Type to the Sales Area. The configuration related to sales document definition, related configuration and assignment can be found under Display IMG. While in display IMG, follow the menu path: **Sales and Distribution • Sales • Sales Documents • Sales Document Header**.

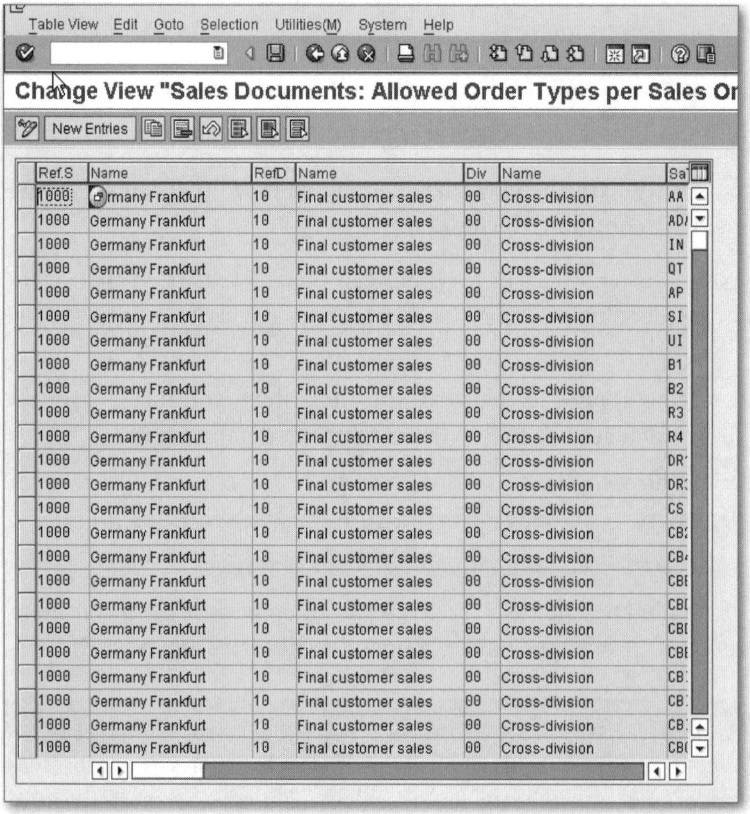

Ref.S	Name	RefD	Name	Div	Name	Sa
1000	Germany Frankfurt	10	Final customer sales	00	Cross-division	AA
1000	Germany Frankfurt	10	Final customer sales	00	Cross-division	AD/
1000	Germany Frankfurt	10	Final customer sales	00	Cross-division	IN
1000	Germany Frankfurt	10	Final customer sales	00	Cross-division	QT
1000	Germany Frankfurt	10	Final customer sales	00	Cross-division	AP
1000	Germany Frankfurt	10	Final customer sales	00	Cross-division	SI
1000	Germany Frankfurt	10	Final customer sales	00	Cross-division	UI
1000	Germany Frankfurt	10	Final customer sales	00	Cross-division	B1
1000	Germany Frankfurt	10	Final customer sales	00	Cross-division	B2
1000	Germany Frankfurt	10	Final customer sales	00	Cross-division	R3
1000	Germany Frankfurt	10	Final customer sales	00	Cross-division	R4
1000	Germany Frankfurt	10	Final customer sales	00	Cross-division	DR'
1000	Germany Frankfurt	10	Final customer sales	00	Cross-division	DR:
1000	Germany Frankfurt	10	Final customer sales	00	Cross-division	CS
1000	Germany Frankfurt	10	Final customer sales	00	Cross-division	CB:
1000	Germany Frankfurt	10	Final customer sales	00	Cross-division	CB·
1000	Germany Frankfurt	10	Final customer sales	00	Cross-division	CBE
1000	Germany Frankfurt	10	Final customer sales	00	Cross-division	CBI
1000	Germany Frankfurt	10	Final customer sales	00	Cross-division	CBI
1000	Germany Frankfurt	10	Final customer sales	00	Cross-division	CBE
1000	Germany Frankfurt	10	Final customer sales	00	Cross-division	CB:
1000	Germany Frankfurt	10	Final customer sales	00	Cross-division	CB:
1000	Germany Frankfurt	10	Final customer sales	00	Cross-division	CB:
1000	Germany Frankfurt	10	Final customer sales	00	Cross-division	CB(

Figure 2.12 Sales Organization and Sales Document Type Assignment

2.3.2 Controlling Sales Document with Item Category

Item category control allows many different types of products to be on the same order, and allows the same product to be treated differently depending on the sales document it is referencing. The SAP system provides different item categories to support the different business processes. You can use them as examples or as templates for creating your own item categories. The item category is defined with a four-digit key. Just as sales document types allow you to control the sales process at the order type level, item category allows you to define processes within the order type; e.g., you could have a free goods item along with a regular sale item, or one of item could be third-party item.

These keys are copied automatically from the original German keys, and are not translated. The first two characters provide a clue to the sales document type that was originally designed for these item categories. The last two characters indicate the use of the item category. Every item in a sales document is controlled through its item category. This enables you to do the following:

▶ Use different item categories in different sales document types

▶ Allow different business processes for each item in the sales document

Now we can see some of the essential characteristics of item category functions to consider in deciding to configure:

▶ Whether the business data in the item can be different from that of the document header (for example, free-of-charge delivery in a regular sales order)

▶ Whether pricing applies to the item (for a text item, you might want the pricing to be calculated or the system attempt to determine it)

▶ Whether and how the item is billed (whether you create bill out of the sales order or after you delivery based on the delivery document)

▶ Whether the item refers to an item or is just a text item

▶ Which incompleteness log is used to check the item data (an incompleteness function or procedure can be assigned to header or item level)

Note

The incompleteness check reminds you that data essential for processing is missing from the document. With configuration, you can define the fields you want to consider for incomplete in a document and the system creates a log in the status view listing all the missing data.

Item Category Definition

You can define new item categories based on your business needs. You should always copy an item category that already exists and has been tested, then change them to meet your requirements. The delivery relevance indicator is only for items without schedule lines. You can indicate that a text item is relevant for delivery so that the system copies this item from the sales order into the delivery document.

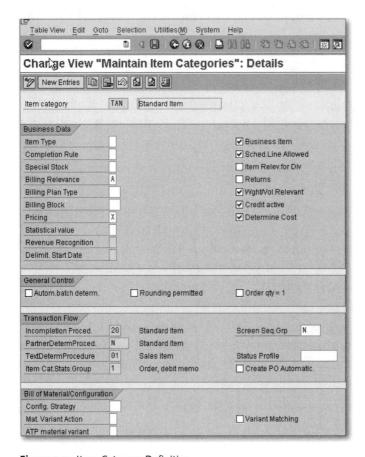

Figure 2.13 Item Category Definition

Let's look at some business examples, below:

▶ A text item for inquiry, which is not relevant for pricing and billing but allows schedule line (SAP standard delivered—AFTX)

▶ Standard item in quotation, for which pricing is relevant; schedule line is allowed but not relevant for billing (SAP Standard delivered—AGN)

▶ Standard item in order, relevant for pricing; schedule line is allowed and also relevant for billing (SAP standard delivered—TAN).

▶ Free of charge item in order, relevant for pricing; schedule line is allowed and also relevant for billing (SAP standard delivered—TANN)

The configuration related to item category definition, related settings, and assignment can be found under the Display IMG. While you are in display IMG, go to **Sales and Distribution • Sales • Sales Documents • Sales Document Item**. The configuration definition of an item category is shown in Figure 2.13 on the pevious page.

Item Category Assignment

Once you have configured the item category to your needs, you must assign it to the sales document type. The purpose of this assignment is to ensure the following:

▶ The system proposes an item category when you create a document based on sales document type.

▶ You can define and assign an alternative item categories to the system proposal.

▶ The item category group is maintained in the material master. The item category group allows you to group different materials that behave in a similar way during sales and distribution processes.

▶ Item usage indicator, which is a ABAP program. In certain cases, it is set internally in the program. The system usage type is TEXT, if the user enters an item in a sales document by entering data in the description field without entering the material number. Usage type FREE is used for controlling the free goods item.

▶ The item category of a higher level item, in case of a sub-item.

Figure 2.14 illustrates the influence of the assignment of item category on sales documents.

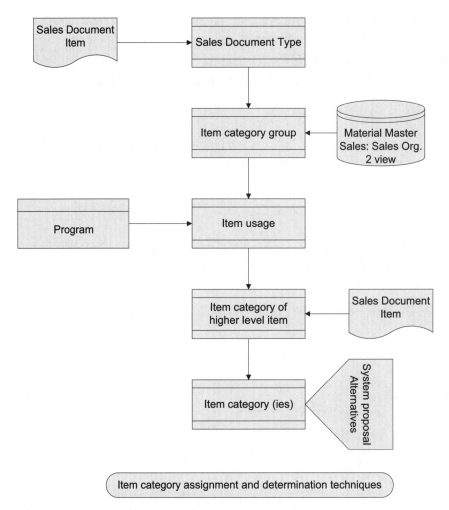

Figure 2.14 Item Category Assignment

2.3.3 Controlling Sales Documents with Schedule Line Category

Items within a sales document are further divided into schedule line categories. Schedule lines help you further control the item from the material management and planning aspect, like scheduling, and confirm the availability, delivery, and procurement of confirmed items. The schedule line category is the third Customizing object available for controlling sales documents. Sales document type, item category, and schedule line category allow you to control sales document at different levels to meet your business needs. Schedule line category is defined in two characters key. The standard system already includes keys that often indicate the usage of the schedule line category.

The first character—e.g., **A** or **B**—indicates the sales process in which the schedule line category is used. Table 2.5 lists the different characters and the sales processes they represent.

Character	Sales Processes
A	Inquiry
B	Quotation
C	Order
D	Returns

Table 2.5 Schedule Line Category Characters

The second character—e.g., **T**, **X**—in the key indicates what happens to the schedule line within logistics. Table 2.6 lists the second character of the schedule line and the logistic process each represents.

Character	Logistics Process
T	No inventory management
X	No inventory management with goods issue
N	No material planning
P	Material requirements planning
V	Consumption-based planning

Table 2.6 Schedule Line and Logistics Process

Schedule lines contain delivery dates and quantities, as well as information about requirements transfer and inventory management. Schedule lines are prerequisites for delivery materials. In Customizing for schedule line category, you decide whether you will allow schedule line for the item. Schedule line can be assigned to each item category. By defining a schedule line category, you can determine which schedule lines are actually relevant for delivery. You must activate the relevant to delivery indicator if you want the goods to be physically delivered.

Configuration allows you to deactivate requirements transfer and availability checks at the schedule-line level. If you activate a delivery block in the schedule line category, this block is automatically set at the schedule line level in the sales document. In the schedule line category, you can set up the movement type to control which changes to quantities and values are posted to

inventory accounting. Inventory management is responsible for maintaining the movement types.

Here are some business examples of how schedule line category control can be used:

▶ **Schedule Line in Quotation**
Not relevant for delivery; no requirements needs to be transferred to Materials Management and no movement type for account posting (standard delivered—BN). A quotation is used to inform a customer of a negotiated price, there is no order, and it is not relevant for delivery and no movement type for goods issue.

▶ **Requirement Planning in Order**
Not relevant for delivery; requirement transfer required and movement type determination for account posting (standard delivered—CP). With movement type also comes the goods movement (in this case issue) for delivery posting, and quantity is consumed from the unrestricted stock.

▶ **Schedule Line in Returns**
Relevant for delivery; no requirement transfer and movement type determination for account posting. If you want to return a return delivery to follow a return order, you need a schedule line category that is relevant for delivery.

You need to assign the schedule line categories to item categories because of the following reasons:

▶ The system proposes this automatically based on the assignment.

▶ You can manually determine a schedule line category that may be used instead of the one the system proposed.

Assignment is influenced by the Materials Requirement Planning (MRP) type in the material master record. Figure 2.15 depicts the two-step approach taken by the system in determining the schedule line category automatically. First, the system tries to determine the schedule line category using the key combination of item category and MRP type. If no schedule line category is found, the system searches the table in Customizing for key combinations of item category with no MRP type.

Figure 2.15 shows how the determination of schedule line category happens based on the assignment to item category.

Figure 2.16 displays the configuration screen for the schedule line category definition.

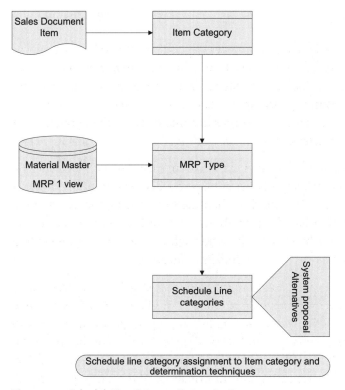

Figure 2.15 ScheduleLine Category Determination

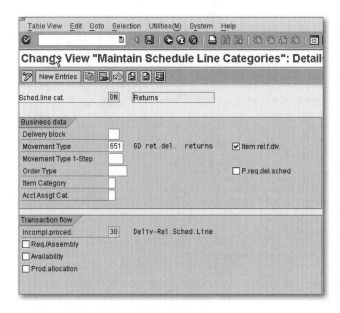

Figure 2.16 ScheduleLine Category Definition

2.4 Summary

This chapter explained the different ways data is determined in a sales document. During the data entry for sales document, the system gets information from various sources. Sources of master data are customer, material, and condition records. Existing document data can also be used for data determination when they are copied to another document; e.g., when you create a delivery note from a sales order.

We also saw the default values that can be set in Customizing. You can set a default value for the delivery date or configure a delivery or billing block in a sales document type. We also described the Customizing for determining document information based on combination criteria; e.g., the determination of shipping point. We also walked through the sales process, including order type, item category, and schedule line category.

Now that we have an understanding of Sales and Distribution master data and configuration, we can move on to Chapter 3. Chapter 3 addresses some of most popularly used functions within SD: key techniques as they apply to pricing, partner determination. and texts. Copy control is another powerful feature in SD, which is used to control your data transfer to subsequent documents, and to avoid repeating any information across the supply chain. These functions are the foundation of SD and apply to all the key areas within SD.

This chapter will cover the key (or most popular) techniques used in Sales and Distribution. You will become familiar with condition techniques as they are used in pricing. I will also go over some of the powerful determination techniques with partner function and text. Last but not least, you will learn about data transfer to the subsequent document from the preceding document.

3 Key Techniques in Sales and Distribution

SAP R/3, Enterprise version, and mySAP ERP use some common techniques to apply your business rules to the processes you are designing in the system. Let's say that in a sales transaction with a customer, you would like the final price to be based on the price of the material, any discount application, freight, and taxes. This determination depends on the business rules associated with that transaction.

Similarly, you might like to have some kind of text determined, based on the document; e.g., a sales order has a purchase order text, and a delivery note has the shipping instruction text. You would like some of the text items to be copied to subsequent documents; e.g., a special instruction for customer entered in the sales order copied to the delivery note.

Creating a delivery document involves copying information from the sales order, such as the materials and quantities. You can define control data for the flow of documents. Configuration allows you to define the specifications for copy requirements and data transfer.

Different customers can assume different roles in a business transaction. The customer who places the order doesn't necessarily have to be the same customer who receives the goods, or who is responsible for paying the invoice. Assigning partner roles in SAP Sales and Distribution (SD) determines the functions of particular partners in the sales process. We will examine the key configuration techniques involved in setting up partner functions and determinations.

3.1   Pricing Fundamentals

Pricing procedure is associated with the sales document and provides the different components needed to come to final agreements with customers on the price they will pay for the goods or service. Prices are stored as data within condition records. The values for condition could be for base price, surcharge, and discount. These are defined by condition types, which determine the category and describes how the condition is used.

Condition	Application	Condition Type	Control Data
Price	Price List Material Price Customer Specific	PRO1 PROO	Fixed amount based on time period.
Discount/ Surcharge	Customer Material Price Group Customer Material	KOO7 KO29	Calculation Type—Percentage, amount, or weight Scale Bases—value or weight

Table 3.1 Price Condition Application

Table 3.1 shows the condition for pricing and the different business application of this condition. These different business applications or categories of conditions are identified by their condition types. The control data provides the basis for calculation type and identifies any scale bases for value, weight, quantity, volume, or time period.

Price conditions are maintained through transaction under the menu path: **SAP Easy Access • Logistics • Sales and Distribution • Master Data • Conditions**. Condition type configuration can be accessed via the path: **Tools • Customizing • IMG • Execute Project • SAP Reference IMG • Sales and Distribution • Basic Functions • Pricing • Pricing Control • Define Condition Types**.

All condition types permitted in pricing are available in the pricing procedure. In the pricing procedure, you can define how the system should use the condition by specifying the requirements for each condition. The sequence in which the system accesses these conditions in the business document is also determined in the pricing procedure. Table 3.2 displays a typical pricing procedure. The reference level provides a method to specify a different basis to calculate the condition type and to group conditions for subtotal. The pricing procedure might contain any number of subtotals.

Step	Condition Type	Description	Reference Level	Manual	Requirement
1	PR00	Price	2	X	2
2	KA00	Gross Value	3—4		2
3	RA01	Offer Discount			2
4		Discount			2
5		Discount value			
6		Net Value			
7	HA00	Header discount	—	X	—
8	HD00	Freight			
9		Net Values 2			
10	MWST	Output tax	—	—	—
	SKTO	Cash disc. basis			
		Cash discount			

Table 3.2 Pricing Procedure

Pricing condition in the pricing procedure can be marked in the following ways:

- As a mandatory condition
- As a manually entered condition
- For statistical purpose only

Last but not least, we have the access sequence, which is assigned to the condition type (except for the condition types configured as header condition). Access sequence is the search that defines the sequence in which the system reads the condition records for a condition type. Figure 3.1 shows an access sequence overview. Access performed by access sequence is made using a condition table. A condition table is a combination of fields that form the key for a condition record. You can also make access dependent on certain requirements.

3.1.1 Pricing Overview

Let's take a typical example of how an item price is determined in a document. When item information is entered, the system runs a check for appropriate pricing procedures. The relevant pricing procedure is determined based on the sales area, customer, and sales document type (these are entered in the header of a sales document). Once it finds the right pricing procedure, the system reads the condition type listed in the pricing procedure sequentially, as maintained in the pricing procedure. Based on this condition type, it determines the access sequence.

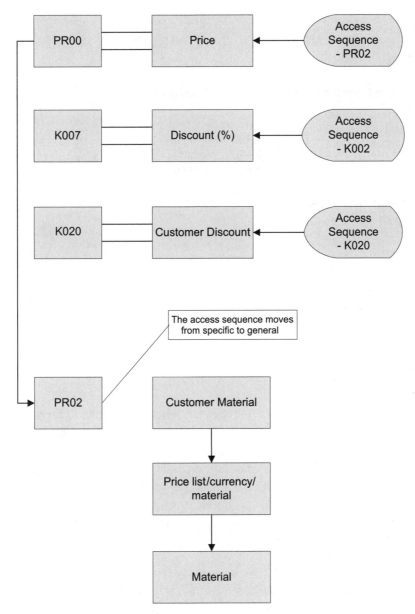

Figure 3.1 Access Sequence

The system reads the access sequence. The sequence of the condition tables represents the search strategy to find the relevant condition record. Each condition table represents an access, which can be made for a condition record with the specified key. The system searches for valid condition records with the key specified by the condition table (accesses). If the first

access does not find a valid condition record, then the system searches for the next access using the next condition table. Figure 3.2 gives a pricing overview.

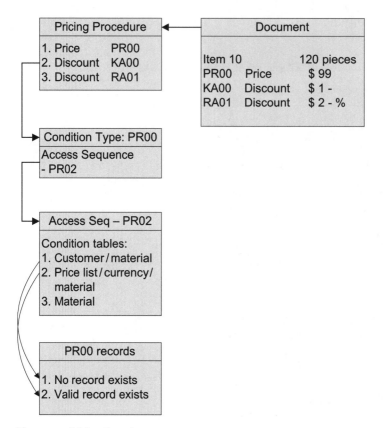

Figure 3.2 Pricing Overview

After the system finds a valid condition record for an access, the system reads the condition record and copies into the sales document the value that corresponds to the scale. The whole process is repeated for each condition type until the system has finished the entire pricing procedure.

> **Note**
>
> The prices, surcharges, and discounts determined automatically by the system can be changed manually and are then marked as manual changes. In condition records, you can specify limits within which a manual change can be made; e.g., for making a discount, which can only be changed between 1 % and 3 %. In addition to determining conditions automatically, conditions can be entered manually in sales documents. Conditions are marked as having been entered manually.

The condition maintenance screen can be accessed through SAP Easy Access, following the path: **Logistics • Sales and Distribution • Master Data • Conditions**. Figure 3.3 shows you the different condition maintenance options with the SAP Easy Access.

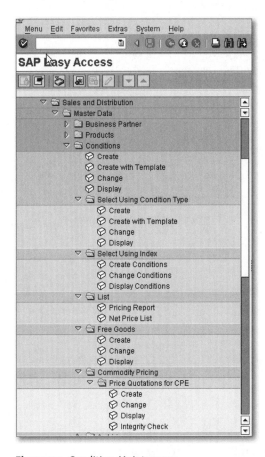

Figure 3.3 Condition Maintenance

3.1.2 Header Conditions

Conditions also can be entered at the document-header level, as header conditions, and are valid for all items. These header conditions are automatically distributed among the items based on net value. The basis of distributing the header conditions can be changed in the pricing procedure by selecting the appropriate routine; e.g., weight and volume, in the Alternative formula for Condition Base Value (**AltCBV**) field.

3.1.3 New Pricing

You can configure pricing behaviour in **Pricing Type**. With Release 4.5, you have the following two ways of controlling the new pricing function in the sales document:

▶ Update prices on the condition screens at the header and item levels. You can choose the pricing type in the dialog box that appears.

▶ To use the new pricing-document function for the sales document (menu path: **Edit · New Pricing documen**t), assign a pricing type to pricing procedure in Customizing. If you do not maintain an entry, the system uses pricing type B (Carry out new pricing). These functions are supported in the sales and billing documents.

Copy control makes it possible to handle re-pricing of billing documents based on several different scenarios. While all customers will not use every possible pricing type, the ability to specify what will happen to pricing calculation during billing is a decision each customer has to make.

3.1.4 Pricing Configurations

Condition tables contain the keys that can be used to create dependent condition records. You can add your own condition tables using tables from 501 through 999. Condition records are always created using specific keys. Condition tables are used to define the structure of the keys of a condition record. The SAP standard system provides most of the important fields used in pricing at the header and item levels. The key fields of a condition table must appear at the start of the table.

With release SAP R/3 4.5, you can also add non-key fields to the condition tables. This is explained in condition table 144, which is used in the price book (condition type PBUD).

3.1.5 Access Sequence

You can define prices, discounts, and surcharges at various levels. Each level is defined by a condition table. An access sequence consists of one or more condition tables. The order of the entries in an access sequence defines the hierarchy of the various levels. The system determines the condition records in the sequence specified.

Within each access of an access sequence, you can specify the document field or source field with which an access is performed. You can make access dependent on requirement to avoid unnecessary access, thus reducing the system load.

Document Field	Value	Access	Value	Condition Record key
Sales Organization	1000	Sales Organization	1000	1000
Distribution channel	10	Distribution channel	10	10
Price List type	02	Price List Type	02	02
Document Currency	USD	Document Currency	USD	USD
Material	M1	Material	M1	M1

Table 3.3 Source Field for Access

Table 3.3 displays the key fields of document used as a condition record key. So you could have a record value of $100 for a key combination of **Sales Organization** (1000), **Distribution Channel** (10), **Price List Type** (02), **Document Currency** (USD), and **Material** (M1), and $200 for a key combination of **Sales Organization** (1000), **Distribution Channel** (10), different **Price List Type** (01), **Document Currency** (USD), and **Material** (M1).

3.1.6 Condition Type

After the access sequence is created, it is then assigned to a condition type. You can also create your own condition type. You can determine the characteristics of each condition type; e.g., whether the condition type represents surcharges or discounts and whether the condition type should be dependent on values or quantities. The condition types are combined in the required sequence in the price procedure.

3.1.7 Procedure Determination

Remember that you also need to maintain the pricing procedure. The pricing procedure is determined according to the following factors:

- ► Sales Area
- ► Customer pricing procedure in the customer master
- ► Document pricing procedure field assigned to the sales document type

Figure 3.4 shows the pricing procedure determination process

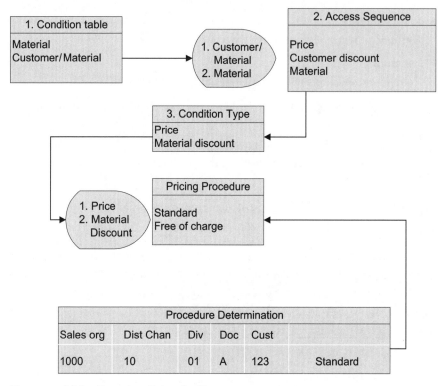

Figure 3.4 Pricing Procedure Determination

Putting it all together, the pricing component consists of the following:

- ► **Condition Table**
  Defines the key fields of the condition records
- ► **Access Sequence**
  Contains the hierarchy for condition record access
- ► **Condition Type**
  Represents the properties of the pricing conditions
- ► **Pricing Procedure**
  Defines how the condition types are linked

▶ **Procedure Determination**
Selects the correct pricing procedure

The following elements might be needed to implement complex scenarios:

▶ **Adding New Fields for Pricing**
Create new fields to meet customer requirement

▶ **Requirements**
Defines dependencies and improve performance

▶ **Formula**
Enables expanding the limits of standard configuration.

New fields may be added to the pricing field catalogue. This allows you to use the new field to define condition tables. Requirement routines and formulas make it possible to modify the standard pricing logic to meet unique user requirements. Figure 3.5 displays the configuration step screen for new field additions.

The screen shot in Figure 3.5 only displays access. To add a new field you need a special authorization object in your user profile S_TABU_CLI. Also be aware that this is a cross-client table and applies to all the clients in your system.

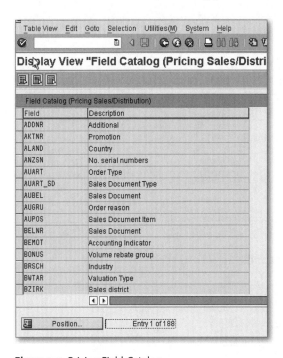

Figure 3.5 Pricing Field Catalog

Figure 3.6 displays the fields selected for the condition table from the list of the **Field Catalog**. We have selected the table for **Material** with the **Selected fields** on the left and the list of catalog fields (**FieldCatlg**) on the right.

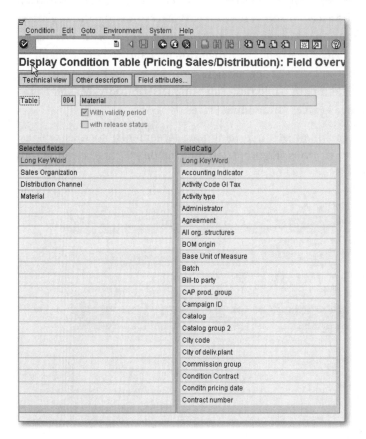

Figure 3.6 Field Catalog Selection

3.1.8 Working with Condition Records

Condition maintenance has two maintenance interfaces. You can mass maintain conditions based on characteristics like customers and material, which allows you to maintain condition records across all condition types and condition tables. The new condition maintenance function can be configured using the area menu. The standard area menu for condition maintenance is COND_AV. A user-specific area menu can be assigned by going to the menu path: **Environment • Assignment Area Menu**.

The user-specific area menus can be created using transaction code SE43; e.g., by copying the user menu, COND_AV, and changing it to meet specific

requirements. You can also follow this menu path through SAP Easy Access: **Tools • ABAP Workbench • Development • Other Tools • Area Menus**.

New condition records can be created with reference to existing condition records. This can be access through the SAP Easy Access menu path: **Logistics • Sales and Distribution • Master Data • Conditions Create with Template • Prices • Material Price**. The pricing change function allows you to maintain multiple condition records simultaneously. This can be reached through the SAP Easy Access menu path: **Logistics • Sales and Distribution • Master Data • Conditions • Change • Prices • Individual Prices**.

Long text can be maintained for pricing and agreements, such as rebates, sales deals, and promotions. Figure 3.7 shows the SAP Easy Access for condition maintenance.

Figure 3.7 Condition Maintenance

You can create and use condition indices to search for condition records that were created for a variety of condition types and condition tables. If you create your own indices, the system automatically activates each new index

when you generate it. You must also specify an update requirement for each condition index. You can configure for each condition type whether the system updates the condition indices when you post the condition records for the corresponding condition type.

You can allow a release procedure to be used when a condition table is created by selecting the **with release status** checkbox, as seen in Figure 3.6. This automatically adds the following fields to the condition table:

▶ **KFRST**
Release status as last key field

▶ **KBSTAT**
Processing status as a field of the variable data part (non-key field).

Release statuses are predefined as follows:

▶ Released

▶ Blocked

▶ Released for price simulation (net price list)

▶ Released for planning and price simulation (planning in CO-PA).

Calculation type for condition type is defined in Customizing. This calculation type determines how prices or discounts and surcharges are calculated for a condition. When creating a new condition record, you can select a calculation type that differs from the one set in Customizing.

3.1.9   Price Report

To provide an overview of existing condition records, you can generate a list of conditions for analysis. The layout of the lists and the conditions reported are set in Customizing. When creating a new program for pricing reports, you first decide the views in which you want to analyze the condition records. To do this, you need to select specific fields from the existing condition tables.

Depending on the fields selected, the system generates a list of tables, which contain at least one of the selected fields. From this list of tables, you can select specific tables that will appear in the report. The list layout is specified by positioning and sorting the fields that appear in the selected tables in one of the three following report sections:

▶ **Page Header**
A page break occurs when a value changes

- ▶ **Group Header**
  A new line heading is generated for each table analyzed.

- ▶ **Item**
  Detailed record information is provided.

Price reports can be accessed through SAP Easy Access by following the path: **Logistics • Sales and Distribution • Master Data • Conditions • List • Pricing Report.** You can create your own price report by configuring it as follows from the Display IMG: **Sales and Distribution • Basic Functions • Pricing • Maintain Pricing Report • Create Price Report.**

3.1.10 Special Functions

There are special pricing functions that include grouping conditions. These allow you to carry out pricing for several items in an order, compare condition types, and use condition updates. Remember that condition types are standard and delivered with pre-set business rules.

Group Conditions

In Customizing, you can set a condition type to be group condition. The condition base value, such as weight, is then calculated as the sum of the individual items within a group. The different type of group keys could be as follows:

- ▶ **Complete Document**
  All quantities with the same condition type are accumulated.

- ▶ **Condition Types**
  All quantities of condition types that have assigned group condition routine 2 are accumulated.

- ▶ **Material Pricing Group**
  All quantities with the same condition type and material pricing group are accumulated.

Excluding Conditions

Conditions can be linked to requirements in the pricing procedure. A requirement can evaluate the condition exclusion indicator and ignore the condition if the indicator is set. The condition-exclusion indicator can be set in either the condition type or the condition record. This can be applied in a

situation where more than one condition is used for pricing and you want the highest price to be selected.

Comparing Condition Types

Condition types to be compared are placed in an exclusion group. During pricing, the conditions—which result in the best price (lowest charge or highest discount—are selected from his group. All other conditions are deactivated. The following comparison methods are available:

▶ **A**

All conditions found within the first exclusion group are compared and the condition with the best price is chosen. All other conditions are deactivated.

▶ **B**

All condition records found for one condition are compared. The best price is chosen. All condition are deactivated. This method can be used with condition type PR00.

▶ **C**

The total of condition records found in the first exclusion group is compared to the total of comparison records found in the second exclusion group. The group that provides the best price is chosen. The conditions of the other groups are deactivated.

▶ **D**

If a condition record is determined for the condition types of the first exclusion group, all the condition records for the second exclusion group are deactivated.

▶ **E**

Similar to method B, except that the worst (highest charge or lowest discount) price is chosen.

▶ **F**

Similar to method C, except that the group with the worst overall price is chosen. The conditions of the other group are deactivated.

The condition type definition can be accessed through the SAP Easy Access by following the menu path: **Tools · Customizing · IMG · Execute Project · SAP Reference IMG · Sales and Distribution · Basic Functions · Pricing · Pricing Control · Define Condition Types**.

Hierarchy Pricing

Hierarchy accesses optimized pricing for hierarchy data structures, such as the product hierarchy. The functions in hierarchy accesses enable you to solve problems by using one access to a condition table. When you create the access sequence to use this condition table, you need to define at the field level whether each field is a fixed component of the key or whether the field is optional. Priorities are assigned to the optional fields in the next step. During pricing, the system sorts the records found with this single access according to priority and uses the record with the highest priority. Hierarchy accesses also provide clear and easy master data maintenance because the different condition records for a condition type can be created together in the quick entry screen for maintaining conditions.

3.1.11 Special Condition Types

The SAP standard system provides many condition types that can be used immediately. Referencing these condition types and creating your own condition types will help you meet the business requirement based on these standard delivered condition types.

Manual Pricing

The header condition type HM00 allows you to enter the order value manually. The new order value is then distributed proportionately among the items, taking into account the previous net item value. Taxes are determined again for each item. The PN00 condition in the standard system allows you to specify the net price for an item manually. The original conditions are deactivated.

Minimum Price Value

You can use the condition type AMIW for minimum order value. If the value in the order header is less than this minimal order value during pricing, the system automatically uses the minimum as the net order value. The minimum order value is a statistical condition.

Condition type AMIW is a group condition and is divided among the different items according to value. Calculation formula 13 is assigned to condition type AMIZ in the pricing procedure. This formula calculates the minimum value surcharge by subtracting the net item value from the minimum order value, AMIW.

You can use condition type PMIN for material minimum price. If the minimum price is not met during pricing, the system determines the difference using condition type PMIN.

You can maintain condition records with interval scales if the condition type is set to the scale type D in Customizing. Interval scales cannot be used for group conditions.

Hierarchy Pricing

Customer hierarchies are available in Sales Order Management so that you can create flexible hierarchies to reflect the structure of the customer organizations. These hierarchies could represent different groups within a company. You could use this hierarchy during the sales order and billing process in determining pricing and runtime statistics. Customer hierarchy consists of the following elements:

► Master record for each node

► Assignment of nodes

► Assignment of customer master record to node

With customer hierarchy, you can assign a price or rebate agreement to a higher-level node. The agreements are then valid for customers at all subordinate levels of this node. You can create pricing condition records for each node indicated as relevant for pricing. If one or more nodes in the hierarchy of a sales order contain pricing information, the system takes these nodes into account automatically during pricing according to the underlying access sequence.

Discount and Surcharges

KP00 condition type is controlled by formula 22 in the pricing procedure, which only takes the number of complete pallets into account to give a pallet-level discount. KP01 condition type uses formula 24 in the pricing procedure to charge customers with surcharges for incomplete pallets. The mixed pallet discount (KP02, group condition—X and unit of measure-PAL) accumulates the quantities of individual items and calculates the discount for a complete pallet. The mixed pallet surcharge is controlled by formula 23, which calculates the fractional proportion of the total mixed quantity for a full pallet.

Rounding Difference

You can maintain a rounding unit in Table T001R for each company code and currency. If the final amount in the order header differs from the rounding unit, the system rounds the amount up or down as specified. Condition type DIFF determines the difference amount. This is a group condition and is distributed among the items according to value.

Statistical Condition Types

You might have a requirement to determine prices for statistical purposes in a way that doesn't change the net value of the item. This can be achieved by marking the condition as statistical. For example, the material cost from the material master could be used for information purpose or as a statistical condition.

Condition type VPRS is used to retrieve the standard cost of the material and this is used as statistical condition. It uses the condition category G to access the valuation segment of material master for getting the standard cost or moving average cost, as specified in the material master. Condition category G accesses the standard cost, whereas condition category T always accesses the moving average cost. The profit margin is calculated using formula 11 in the pricing procedure; this subtracts the cost from the net value.

The condition type SKTO is used to retrieve the cash discount rate. The pricing procedure uses this condition type as a statistical value. Table T052 is accessed using condition category E, and an amount is calculated from the first percentage rate of the item payment terms.

Condition type EDI1 is used for comparing the net price with the customer expected price. You can use the EDI2 condition type to compare the overall item value, obtained by multiplying the net price and the quantity. When you copy the standard pricing procedure RVAA01, the system proposes the calculation formula 8 for condition type EDI1, with a maximum deviation of 0.05 currency units. There is an error in the SAP documentation, which refers to calculation formula 8 (SAP Note: 437780 talks about this documentation error). If the customer's expected price differs from the automatically determined price or value by more than the maximum difference price or value by more than the maximum difference allowed, the system considers this order incomplete when the order is saved.

3.1.12   Determining Taxes, Rebates, and Agreements

The criteria for determining taxes are departure country (the country of the delivering plant from the sales document), destination country (country from the ship-to party from the sales document), tax classification maintained in the customer master, and material tax classification accessed using departure country (maintained in the material master). The system determines a tax rate in the order/billing document on the basis of the following three criteria:

▶ Business transaction: domestic or export/import

▶ Tax liability of the ship-to party

▶ Tax liability of the material

You can define a promotion or general marketing plan for a product line for a certain period of time. You can then link this promotion with specific sales deals, which then are linked to special condition records used for promotional pricing or discounts.

A rebate is a discount, which is granted subsequently to a rebate recipient on the basis of a defined sales volume within a certain period. Rebate agreements are created to determine the values required for a rebate settlement with the validity period of the rebate agreement.

Determining Taxes

Taxes are calculated in SAP SD using the normal condition techniques. The condition type for tax is entered into the pricing procedure. Figure 3.8 on the next page displays the tax determination in pricing procedure. The access sequence is used to find the appropriate condition record for the current situation.

Tax procedure is assigned in the default for Financial Accounting by country. For example, for the United States there are the following options:

▶ TAXUS (taxes calculated in SD)

▶ TAXUSJ (taxes calculated in the central tax procedure using the tax jurisdiction value stored in the master data for the ship-to party)

▶ TAXUSX (taxes calculated through a remote function call (RFC) and a central tax procedure)

The jurisdictional and the third-party tax are calculated, after the procedure has been determined and the corresponding pricing procedure in SD uses

the appropriate condition types. If the tax procedure assigned is TAXUSJ, the pricing procedure RVAJUS uses the condition types UTXJ, JR1, JR2, JR3, and JR4. The condition type UTXJ initiates the tax calculation.

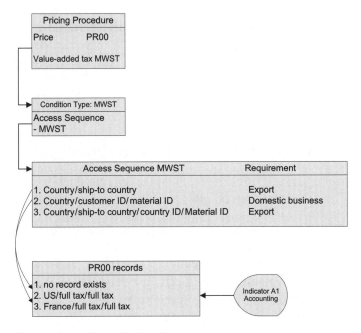

Figure 3.8 Tax Determination Procedure

Promotions and Sales Deals

You can maintain the sales deal through SAP Easy Access, following the menu path: **Logistics • Sales and Distribution • Master Data • Agreements • Promotion • Create**. You can also create condition records for discount and associate those with sales deals to represent the different process steps they go through. The possible values are given below:

▶ **_ > Released**
Assigned when a sales deal is released for processing

▶ **A > Blocked**
Asigned when a sales deal is blocked from processing

▶ **B > Released for price simulation**
Sales deal is specifically released for price simulation and not for processing it through.

▶ **C > (CO-PA)**
Released specifically for price simulation and planning (CO-PA)

Rebate Agreements

You can define rebates at as many levels as you want, similar to any other pricing condition. The SAP standard system provides the following agreement types:

- Material
- Customer
- Customer hierarchy
- Material group rebate
- Independent of sales volume

The rebate agreement is created with a specific rebate agreement type. The features of each rebate agreement type are set in Customizing. Table 3.4 displays the rebate agreement types delivered in the SAP system.

Agreement Type	Condition Table	Condition Type
0001	Customer/Material Customer/rebate group (percentage rebate)	B001 B001
0002	Customer/Material (absolute rebate)	B002
0003	Customer (percentage)	B003
0004	Customer hierarchy Customer hierarchy/material (percentage)	B004 B005
0005	Independent sales volume	B006

Table 3.4 Pricing Agreement

Condition records are linked to the rebate agreement specifying the rebate rate and the accrual rate. With the rebate agreement, you can specify the condition type to be used and the validity period.

The rebates are different from other discounts, as they are based on sales volumes. A settlement run creates the required credit memo request automatically. When the rebate-relevant billing documents are processed, accruals can be determined and posted automatically. You can use the rebate credit memo to reverse these accruals.

The rebate processing needs to be activated for the sales organization, payer master record, and billing document type. The rebate processing begins by

creating a rebate-relevant billing document. If it is not needed, rebate processing must be deactivated, as it might affect performance.

Rebate Settlement

The system uses the accumulated amounts in the rebate agreement to create a rebate settlement. The settlement can be performed manually, automatically, and in the background (batch programs RV15C001 and RV15C002). Accruals are reversed as soon as the rebate agreement is settled by credit memo. Partial rebate settlement can be limited for each rebate agreement type, such as:

- Up to the accumulated accrual amount
- Up to the calculated payment amount for the current date
- Unlimited

Retroactive rebate agreement allows you to take into account the billing documents created before the rebate agreement was created. Now let's look at the configuration steps in setting up the rebate agreement:

1. Follow the menu path: **Display IMG · Sales and Distribution· Billing · Rebate Processing · Activate Rebate Processing**.
2. Click on **Select billing documents for rebate processing**.
3. Navigate to the menu path: **Display IMG · Sales and Distribution · Billing · Rebate · Processing · Activate Rebate Processing**.
4. Click on **Activate rebate processing for sales organization**.
5. Maintain in the payer's customer master record.

Let me conclude the pricing discussion with a reference to some useful information. Table 3.5 displays the different conditions.

Table	Description
A001, A002, …, Annn	Condition tables
KONH	Condition header
KONA	Agreement
KONP	Condition item
KONM	Quality scale
KNOW	Value scale

Table 3.5 Condition Tables

You can also look at Figure 3.9 to see a typical pricing procedure.

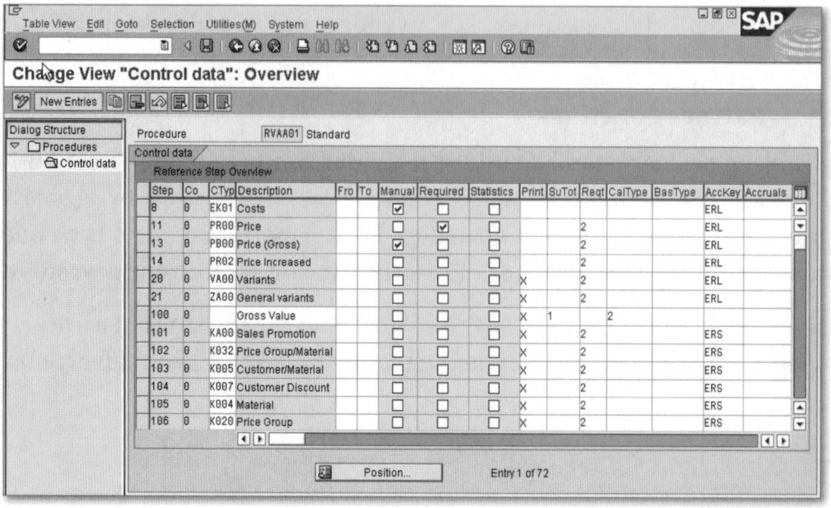

Figure 3.9 Pricing Procedure

Having learned the condition technique that is applied in pricing, let's see how partner determination works. Partner determination is used within the sales transactions for determining different business partners.

3.2 Making Partner Determination Work for Your Business

You might have different business relationships with different business partners, involving the roles of customer, vendor, employee, and contact person. Some examples are as follows:

▶ **Vendor-Customer**
The vendor acts as a forwarding agent to the customer.

▶ **Contact Person-Customer**
The contact person is employed at the customer's company, or is the customer's consultant, but doesn't work in the same company.

▶ **Customer-Customer**
The sold-to party and ship-to party are different parties.

▶ **Employee-Contact Person**
The contact person is looked after individually.

▶ **Employee-Customer**
This is the relationship you maintained with the Customer manager.

These business partners are represented by various partner types in the SAP R/3 or in the mySAP ERP system. Some examples of partner type are AP for contact person, KU for customer, LI for vendor, and PE for Personnel.

3.2.1 Partner Functions

While using partner types allows you to distinguish between different businesses partners, partner functions represent the roles played by business partners within the business transaction. For example, you could have one customer ordering the part, one who receives it, and another one pays for it.

Assigning partner functions in SAP SD determines the functions of particular partners in the sales processes. One partner might take on several functions, such as:

▶ **SP**
Sold-to-party

▶ **SH**
Ship-to-party

▶ **BP**
Bill-to-party

▶ **PY**
Payer

▶ **FA**
Forwarding agent

▶ **ER**
Employee responsible

In the simplest case, all the partner functions within the customer partner type would be assigned to one business partner. In other words, the same customer could be the sold-to party, ship-to party, payer, and bill-to party.

You can enter contact persons for a customer directly in the customer master, and this information will be automatically assigned to that customer. This contact person can be assigned to another customer; e.g., in a consultant role.

Transportation services are performed by the forwarding agent. These might include organizing the shipment, delivery and receipt of the goods, arranging carrier services, and handling custom issues. A vendor could take up this partner function role.

The SAP standard system delivers a set of partner functions, so before you create a new one, check the existing ones. The partner function configuration can be reached through the menu path: **Tools • Customizing • IMG • Edit Project • Select SAP Reference IMG.** Then configure as: Sales and Distribution → Basic Functions → Partner Determination. Click on **Set up Partner Determination.** This will provide a pop-up window with options for setting up partner determination for the following:

▶ Customer master

▶ Sales document header

▶ Sales document item

▶ Delivery

▶ Shipment

▶ Billing Header

▶ Billing Item

▶ Sales Activities

If Customizing allows, you can change or supplement these relationships manually by going to the partner screen and changing the function assignment. In Customizing, you can decide whether several partners can be assigned to one partner function in the customer master. If multiple partners of the same function are maintained, a selection list containing these partners appears when you enter the sales order. In the sales documents, the system has been configured so that only one partner can be assigned to each partner function. The only exception is for outline agreements (partner functions AA and AW). Figure 3.10 displays the configuration steps in partner function definition and determination.

You can also define partners at the item level in the sales documents. Business partners are only defined in the header and cannot be changed in the item. You can configure so as to prohibit anyone from changing the partner entered. It is possible to change the address of the partner, and this doesn't affect the master record.

The configuration starts with the partner function definition in the procedure along with other settings, as shown in Figure 3.10. As a next step, you need to assign the partner determination procedure to the appropriate sales document type. Within the Partner Functions configuration step you need to assign the partner type (whether it is a customer, vendor, or individual). The configuration step Account Groups-Function Assignment allows you to map the account group to the partner function.

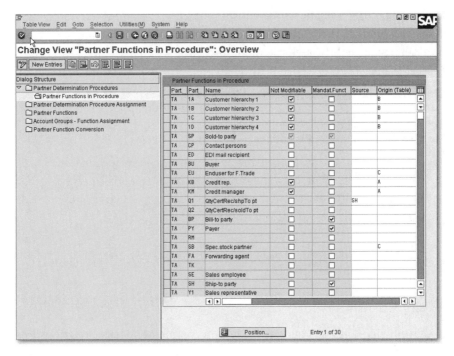

Figure 3.10 Partner Function Definition

3.2.2 Customer Master and Account Group

Partner function determines which partner assumes specific business function within the sales process and which account group controls the customer master record. Some examples of the account group are: 0001—Sold-to party, 0002—Ship-to party, 0003—payer, and so on. The following criteria are determined, while defining account groups:

▶ Data fields displayed and whether maintainance is mandatory, optional, or not possible.

▶ The number range

▶ A number of other control elements, for partners and texts of customer master records.

A ship-to party compared to another ship-to party might involve different customer master records. The billing information might not be required, and the correspondence fields are displayed.

Partner Function Specific to Account Group

You can restrict the allowed partner functions by account group in an organized sales processing. This control is accomplished by assigning partner functions to account groups. Examples include: Account groups 0002 (sold-to party), 0003 (payer) or 0004 (bill-to party).

Partner Determination Procedure

Partners appear in the system at different levels, such as the customer master, the sales document header, and the sales document items. You can define your own partner-determination procedures for each of these levels:

▶ Customer master

▶ Sales document header

▶ Sales document item

▶ Delivery

▶ Billing header

▶ Sales activity (CAS)

A partner-determination procedure is where you determine which partner functions should or must appear on the sales documents. You determine areas of validity by assigning procedures. The partner procedures are assigned to the partner objects as follows:

▶ Partner object to Assignment key

▶ Customer master to Account group

▶ Sales document header to Sales document type

▶ Sales document item to Item category in sales

▶ Delivery to Delivery type

▶ Shipment to Shipment type

▶ Billing header to Billing type

▶ Billing item to Billing type

▶ Sales activities (CAS) to Sales activity type

Figure 3.11 displays the partner determination procedure assignments set up for configurations.

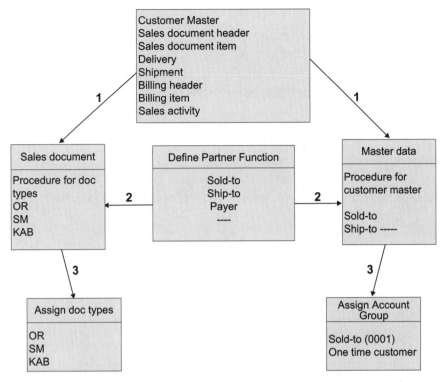

Figure 3.11 Partner Determination Procedure

Indirect Partner Functions

You can use other sources to automatically determine business partners in sales documents, such as the tables for customer hierarchy (KNVH), contact person (KNVK), credit representatives (T024P), and so on. Now that we have covered partner determination, we can move on to working with text items.

3.3 Working with Text Items

Information exchange is a key function within the logistics supply chain between business partners. This exchange of information is supported in SAP SD in the form of texts in master records and documents. Texts are available in the areas or functions of the logistics system (sales texts—notes for customer, shipping texts—shipping instructions in deliveries, internal notes, supplement texts, etc).

Text can be copied or carried through the document flow, from sales order to delivery. The copying of texts can be made language dependent. Based on the configuration setting, you can propose text from master data to the documents when they are created.

Text can be maintained at central locations, for accounting, marketing, external sales notes, partner notice, shipping, etc. These can be accessed in the customer master's create, change, or display transactions thus: **Extras • Texts**. For example, you can maintain notes for accounting in the customer master by branching out to accounting view in the customer master and then going to the menu path: **Extras • Texts**.

3.3.1 Text in Sales and Distribution Documents

Sales documents consist of inquiries, quotations and sales orders. The sales document text could reside in a header (header note, shipping requirement) or an item (material sales text, packing note). With deliveries, you could have a text referenced from the preceding document or without reference for header and item. Similarly, you can have header and item text for billing.

Header text refers to the entire document and can be found in the header document. The header text of the SAP standard system appears in the top of the text and should be reserved for important information. Another important standard text of SAP standard system is supplementary text, which appears in the bottom of all the texts.

Item texts are specific to the item and can be maintained separately for each item. The material sales text is an important item text copied from the material sales text and carried forward. You can also overwrite the text as you can other texts.

Not all the texts are activated for sales and distribution forms; some are meant for internal purposes. These are individually maintained in the customizing setting. The three main configuration steps are:

▶ Define text types

▶ Define the access sequence for determining texts (which uses the condition techniques)

▶ Define and assign the text-determination procedure

Figure 3.12 displays the configuration steps for customizing text determination.

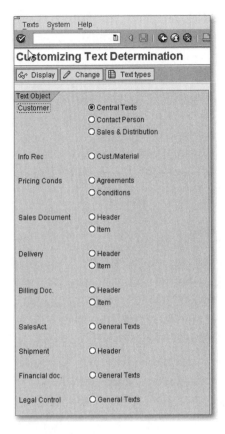

Figure 3.12 Text Determination

In the Figure 3.12 icon bar there are three icons: **Display**, **Change**, and **Text types**. You can display the text types in the system by clicking on **Text types**. Text types are client independent, so if you want to create a new one, you need to have the specific authorization: S_TABU_CLI. To maintain the text determination, select the specific object and the text area under which it falls.

Figure 3.13 displays the sales header text-determination procedure. We see the text determination procedure for sales header. If you select that and double-click on the Text IDs in the **Textprocedure**, you will see Text IDs listed in the sequence with the indicator for reference or duplication, followed by access sequence. If you create a new procedure, you need to maintain a similar entry here. The folder within the access sequence provides the details behind access sequence, search sequence, text application object, and the mapped **Text ID**. The last folder lists the assignment of text-determination procedure to sales document type.

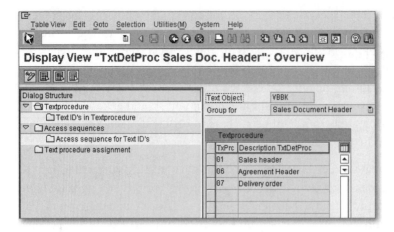

Figure 3.13 Sales Header Text Determination Procedure

3.3.2 Copying and Referencing Sales Texts

Text can be copied from the preceding document. This copying requirement uses the access sequence of condition techniques. Some text might be carried forward to the end of the logistics chain without being changed or altered. SAP SD provides you two options, one to reference the text from the original and one to duplicate it.

With duplication, the changes in the specific document don't affect the preceding document. Reference documents use less space, as they are not copied to the follow-on documents. We can now move on to copy control and requirements.

3.4 Copy Control and Requirements

In copy control, you determine which document types can be copied to other document types. Copy control helps you control the movement of data or information from the source document to target. SAP uses documents to identify business transactions. Sales orders, deliveries, shipping memos, billing, etc. within the logistic chains have information copied over or carried forward to the next process or document in the SAP system.

Another important function of the copy control is to check the prerequisite for the process before it can be processed. For example, creating a delivery might require a purchase order number or availability of the material, and these are checked during the copy control dynamically.

As we know, the sales cycle flows from inquiry to quotation to sales order to delivery (to transport order for warehouse management) to billing document or invoice. Copy control applies individually for each source and target combination; e.g., inquiry to quotation, quotation to sales order, sales order to delivery. For billing documents created out of the sales orders directly, the copy control from sales order to billing document should be maintained. For sales orders created from contracts, the copy control from contact to sales order should be maintained.

You could create a sales order copy from another existing sales order, for reference purposes or to reduce the date-entry time. For this you need to maintain copy control from a sales document to a sales document type. If you don't maintain the copy control from a source document type to a target document type and try to create the target document copying from the source, the system will prompt you with an error.

3.4.1 Configuring Copy Control in SD

You can define control data for a flow of documents. You can specify, for a particular sales document type, which document type is to be assigned to copied reference documents, and which item categories or schedule line categories are to be copied. You also must set the requirement specifications for copying requirements and data transfer, as well as quantity and value updates in the document flow. This must be done for each copying procedure at header, item and—if necessary—schedule-line level.

When you define a new sales document type by copying with reference, the SAP system copies all the specification of the reference original document. You can make specific changes to these settings based on your business requirement.

As mentioned earlier, copy control can be defined in different process steps of the supply chain (sales order to delivery to billing). The configuration for copy control from quotation to sales order can be found under the section sales document to sales document. Copy control from sales order to delivery can be found under sales document to delivery. Copy control from sales document to billing can be found under sales document to billing while copy control from delivery document to billing document can be found under delivery document to billing document. Copy control for creating billing document with reference to another billing document can be found under billing document to billing document. An example of this is the credit memo from invoice.

Configuration can be accessed through SAP Easy Access, following the menu path: **Tools · Customizing · IMG · Edit Project · Select SAP Reference IMG · Sales and Distribution · Sales · Maintain Copy Control for Sales documents**. Then choose copy control. Figure 3.14 displays the copy control from source to target document type options. Let's take the example of sales document to sales document. In Figure 3.14 you can see the copy control from a quotation to a sales order.

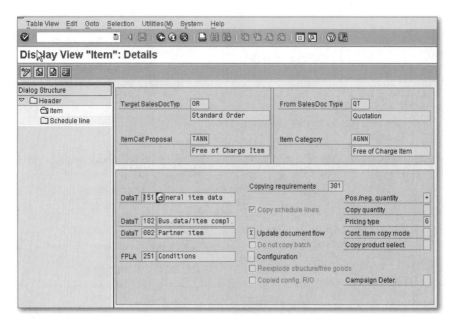

Figure 3.14 Copy Control

Copy controls in shipping can be found in the Display IMG by following this path: **Logistics Execution · Shipping · Copy Control**. Copy control for billing can be found under Display IMG by following the path: **Sales and Distribution · Billing · Billing Documents · Maintain Copy Control for Billing documents**.

In Figure 3.14 you can see the data transfer routines for header, item, and partner, **DataT**. The copy requirement is an ABAP code, which checks if specific requirements are met before copying. Here you define the target sales document type and the associated item category, source document type, and associated item category. The FPLA routine is meant for transferring condition records. If you check the copy schedule lines, the system will carry the schedule line information from source document to target.

If you want the document flow to be updated, you need to check the configuration. Pricing type setting allows you to set the pricing re-determination or re-calculation in the document. You have configuration options for copying quantity, pricing type, etc. Figure 3.15 displays the source-to-target configuration steps needed to match the sales structure.

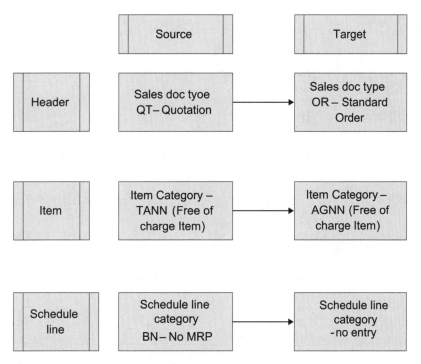

Figure 3.15 Source-to-Target Configuration Steps

3.4.2 Data Transfer Routines and Requirements

Data transfer routines control the way fields are copied from the reference document. With the copy requirement, you define requirements that are checked when a document is created with reference to another. If these requirements are not met, the system issues a warning or error and, if necessary, terminates processing.

You can define indicators or switches for setting specific controls for each transaction. For example, you can activate or deactivate the transfer of item numbers. As we saw in Figure 3.14, the copy requirement can be defined for each level, as follows:

▶ **Header**

Copy requirement at this level can check the instance to see whether the sold-to party and the sales area in the source and target document are the same.

▶ **Item Level**

Copy requirement at this level can check by instance whether the item that is used as a copy has a reason for rejection or status completed.

▶ **Schedule Line Category**

Copying requirement at this level for instance can check whether only a schedule line with an open quantity greater than zero is copied.

Routine and requirements are written in ABAP/4 code and can be processed in Customizing in SD under system-modifications transaction VOFM. The recommended approach would be to copy the standard and make necessary changes to the code by adding or deleting the line of code to meet the requirement.

3.5 Summary

In this chapter, I covered some key techniques of Sales and Distribution. Because pricing is one of the important functions, we went over the fundamentals, as well as, some additional features of this powerful functionality. Partner determination is another important functionality, which helps the organization define its business relationship within the transaction. Text is used as an information-sharing placeholder, and we saw how this information flows from one document to another through text types and procedures. The logistical or supply-chain processes are represented by the functions within the process and in SAP they are represented by document flow. Copy control helps you control the data flow from one process to another.

In Chapter 4, we will explore sales and distribution's influence on materials management. When you create a sales order, material availability is checked against the inventory and this function crosses SD and performs the function within SAP Materials Management (MM). We will learn how these are carried out. We will look at different sales transactions that use the materials-management functions, with Cross-Company Sales and Intercompany Sales. Similarly, there are functions within MM that use the SD functionality, such as the stock transport orders for shipping, delivery, and goods movement. Third-party processing is used in sales orders, which use MM functions for

processing. Similarly the subcontracting purchase order uses many SD functions. Finally, we will touch on the agreements initiated in SD and processed through the MM functions.

Processes triggered from Sales and Distribution (SD) cross other functions, such as Materials Management (MM). To confirm a line item with the due date, the availability check has to be invoked, which is part of the MM process. Similarly, processes initiated in MM use SD functions. You will gain insight into the inter-company and cross-company transfer order, cross-company sales, third-party processing, subcontracting, and scheduling agreements. These processes are initiated and driven by SD and support and use the MM functionality.

4 Influence of SD on Materials Management

Sales-order processing involves the commitment of the delivery of goods or services. To do that, you would like to check the available stock and may require information on the earliest possible delivery date, if the stock is not available. Generally, an availability check is carried out during sales-order processing, if the material is set for availability check and based on the appropriate check set in Customizing. When stock is not available in the plant within the company code indicating where the sales order is being processed, you might want to get the part delivered from a plant represented by a different company code, if that part is available. This is accomplished by cross-company sales, where the sales order is delivered from the plant with another company code.

Another method would be to transfer the stock from the plant in one company code to another plant in another company code. This process involves bringing the stock in the internal price into the company code's plant and delivering it to the customer within that company code. This is accomplished by a cross-company stock transfer order. You can also transfer stock between plants within the same company code starting with Material Requirements Planning (MRP), using purchase orders to trigger stock transfer, and making use of SD's shipping function for goods movement.

With third-party processing, the delivery of material request is forwarded to an external vendor. The vendor sends the material to the customer and

charges you for the material. The subcontracting procurement process involves providing the vendor with the component or material, which is used to manufacture the finished product. The shipping process can be used to send the components to the subcontractor. A scheduling agreement is an outline agreement between you and a sold-to party that is valid for a certain period of time. A contract is an outline agreement between you and your customer that is valid for a certain time. We can now move on to the subject of availability of materials.

4.1 Availability

Availability checks for material are identified by the availability check field in the **Sales: General/Plant** screen in the material master. You also indicate what type of availability check is carried out for the material. Figure 4.1 shows the value **ZZ**, customer-defined in the material master's **Availability check** field.

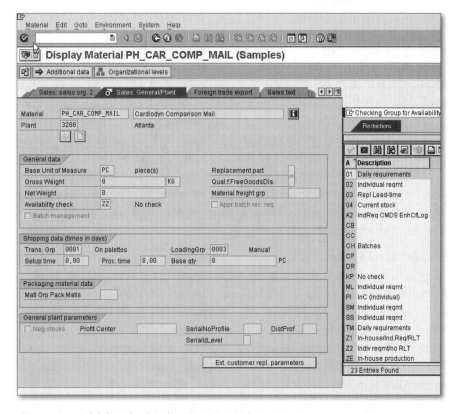

Figure 4.1 Availability Check Indicator in Material Master

Availability is checked on the material availability date and is checked against the various dates based on your Customizing settings, as follows:

- Order Date
- Material Staging
- Transportation Planning
- Picking and Packing
- Loading
- Goods Issue
- Required Delivery Date

Delivery scheduling is based on having enough material available in time for delivery to the customer on the requested delivery date. The system calculates this date, working backwards from the customer's requested delivery date.

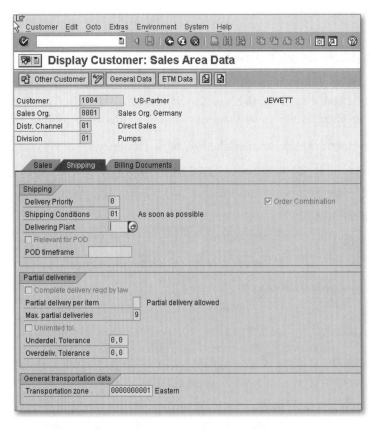

Figure 4.2 Delivery Plant Field Within Customer Master

The availability check is carried out based on the delivery plant. The standard delivery plant is accessed by the system in the following order:

1. Customer-Material Information
2. Ship-to Party Customer Master Record
3. Material Master Record

When you enter a plant manually, this overwrites the default plant proposed. Plant information can be found in customer-material info record **Sales: Sales Org. 1 Delivery** on the plant tab page or in the customer master shipping tab page.

Figure 4.2 displays the delivering plant field in the customer master. The customer master display can be found, while you are in SAP Easy Access, by following the menu path: **Logistics • Sales and Distribution • Master Data • Business Partner • Customer • Display • Sales and Distribution**. Then select the **Sales Area Data: Shipping** tab.

4.1.1 Availability Check Control

Customizing allows you to configure the different elements that influence the availability check based on the various transactions you use. You can define the different rules for inward and outward movements, as follows:

- Inward movement checks occur in the following sequence:
  - Stock (e.g., safety stock, stock in transfer, stock in inspection)
  - Purchase order or production order
  - Purchase requisition
  - Planned order
- Outward movement checks occur, take into consideration, the following:
  - Availability check with sales requirements
  - Orders
  - Reservations

Figure 4.3 shows the control of availability for inward and outward movements.

SAP SD communicates with MM and with Planning in terms of requirements for internal production or external procurement. Transfer of requirement type influences the availability check. Depending on the agreement for par-

tial/complete delivery in the customer sales order, you can deliver an order in one complete delivery or several partial deliveries.

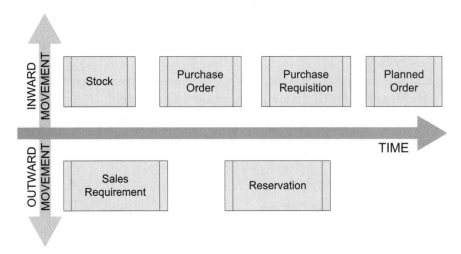

Figure 4.3 Availability Control

The partial/complete delivery proposal is maintained in the customer master record. The customer material info record also maintains the material agreement for item level. You can use the following agreements:

▶ _

   Partial delivery permitted

▶ **A**

   Enter delivery with quantity not equal to 0

▶ **B**

   Only create a delivery (also with quantity 0)

▶ **C**

   Only complete delivery can be carried out

▶ **D**

   Preferred subsequent delivery

4.1.2 Back-Order Processing

Back-order processing occurs when an order is backdated. This because the quantity of an order item is not totally confirmed, and the required delivery date for an order item cannot be kept. There are two types of back-order processing, as discussed below:

▸ **Manual with Back-order Processing**
You can use back-order processing to list sales documents materials and to process them manually with reference to the confirmation. This means Available to Promise (ATP) quantities can be reassigned and any shortfall can be cleared.

▸ **Rescheduling**
You can use the delivery priority (proposed from the customer master record) as a sorting criterion in automatic rescheduling.

The menu path for rescheduling can be found under SAP Easy access: **Logistics ▸ Sales and Distribution ▸ Sales ▸ Backorders ▸ Backorder processing and Rescheduling**.

4.1.3   Configuration Setting

Configuration setting starts with defining requirement classes for which the availability check and/or transfer of requirement should be carried out. The global settings at requirements class level can be differentiated at schedule line level. Figure 4.4 displays the configuration settings required for **Requirements Classes**.

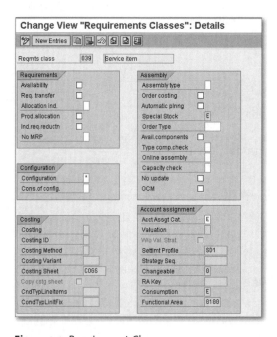

Figure 4.4 Requirement Class

Within **Requirements**, the **Availability** indicator enables the SD availability check. There is also the **Req. transfer** indicator used for the transfer of requirements. In **Allocation ind.,** you can indicate the allocation strategy, if there is any.

As a next step, you need to assign the requirement type to the requirement class (**Reqmts class**), as seen in Figure 4.5. The requirement type identifies different requirements, such as sales order, delivery requirement, which can be changed to represent customer-specific terms. An allocation to the individual transaction in sales and distribution is carried out by means of requirement type, together with item category and **MRP Type**.

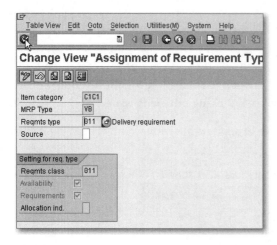

Figure 4.5 Requirement Type Assignment

4.1.4 MRP Types

MRP types are maintained in the material master. This assignment is maintained in the **Determination of Requirement Types to Using Transaction** under the **Transfer of Requirement** configuration settings. Figure 4.5 displays the details behind this assignment. What you see in this figure is item category (C1C1). MRP type (VB) provides the assignment of requirement type-011 (Field name **Reqmts type** displayed in the screen shot), and the Requirement Class-011 within the section **Setting for req. type. Availability** and **Requirements** indicators are already checked here, as they are defaulted from the definition of **Requirement Class**.

Now you need to maintain the define procedure for each schedule-line category. Here you define whether the schedule line category has an availability

check for sales, activate the transfer at schedule line level, and determine if you want to have product allocation active. The configuration steps can be found within Display IMG, follow this menu path: **Sales and Distribution** • **Basic Functions** • **Availability Check and Transfer of Requirements**.

You can define the system reaction to the confirmed quantity when it is blocked for any reason. When requirements are transferred to MRP, the confirmed quantities are also reserved and the stock cannot be used elsewhere. You can define the system so that this stock can be used by other requirements; e.g., priority sales order, rush order, etc. In that case, the requirement does get transferred but the stock is not reserved, so that it is available for other priority orders.

When the block is removed, it carries out an availability check. For this, you first define the delivery blocking reason or criteria and then the reason for transferring the block. Figure 4.6 shows the different block reasons and the different points of the process: order (**Order**), confirmation (**Conf.**), print (**Print.**), delivery due list (**DdueList**), **Picking** or **Goods issue**.

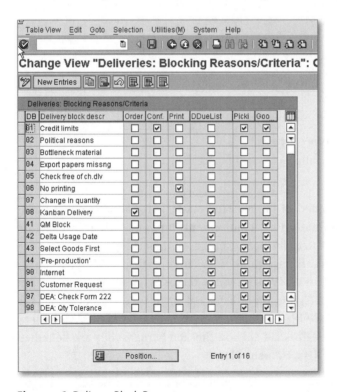

Figure 4.6 Delivery Block Reasons

4.1.5 Transfer Requirements

The SAP system allows you to maintain your own requirements for the transfer of requirements. Requirements are essentially ABAP code written to meet your specific requirements, since the standard system cannot meet them. Requirements are coded for easy identification and assignment to the appropriate configuration settings or parameters. They are basically ABAP programs encapsulated in the form of requirements, and can be called when needed based on where they are placed.

By now, you should understand the transfer of requirement configuration setting. Let's go over the configuration steps for availability check controls. The availability check is controlled by means of the same elements as the transfer of requirements, as seen below:

▸ Requirement Class

▸ Requirement Type

▸ Checking Group

▸ Checking Rule

▸ Scehdule Line Category

▸ Strategy Group

▸ Planning Strategy

There are three settings within the availability check:

▸ Availability Check with ATP or against Planning

▸ Availability Check againsts Product Allocation

▸ Rule-based Availability Check

Within the availability check with ATP are the following settings or definitions:

▸ Checking Group is determined based on the material type and plant and is proposed in the material master record. Together with the checking rule, the checking group determines the scope of the availability check, as seen below:

  ▸ Material block for other users is where you can define here whether you would like to block the material for other orders during the availability check. If it is blocked, you cannot create two orders for the same material at the same time.

  ▸ You can indicate where you would like this block to be activated, during order, delivery, or reservation.

- ▸ Default checking group by material type is where you can define a default value for checking group by material type and plant
- ▸ Availability check control

Here you map the availability check to the checking rule. Figure 4.7 displays the different stocks that need to be considered. You can choose to check without the replenishment lead time or storage location inspection. You can check the inward and outward movements to be considered for availability check.

You can define settings to include dependent, released, planned, and production orders. You can define past and future receipts you would like to include and checking period for goods receipt in case of missing-part processing as follows:

- ▸ Procedure by requirement class is where you indicate for each requirement class whether an availability check and/or transfer of requirement should be carried out.
- ▸ Procedure for schedule line category is where you can fine-tune or further control the availability check and/or transfer of requirements based on schedule line category.
- ▸ Procedure for delivery item category allows you to switch off the availability check based on a particular item category. An example is return delivery, where you would like to deactivate the check.
- ▸ Check rule for updating back-order needs you to be explicit so that these don't conflict with the sales order (A) and Delivery (B) availability checking rule.
- ▸ Some default settings can be defined for availability check based on the sales area, such as the fixed data and quantity indicator, and availability check rule.

Availability check against product allocation allows you to allocate and control goods that are in short supply early on. The check is performed during order requirement and confirmed via the product allocation to the customer. If the product is not allocated or confirmed, then—as soon as the order is placed and the check is performed—it might be consumed by another order, and the commitment you gave to the customer might be missed.

Rule-based availability check allows you to activate availability based on defined rules; e.g., to carry out availability check in several plants and with different alternative materials. The availability check takes place in the stan-

dalone SAP system Advanced Planner and Optimizer (APO). The results are returned to the source system, be it ERP-SAP R/3 or mySAP ERP.

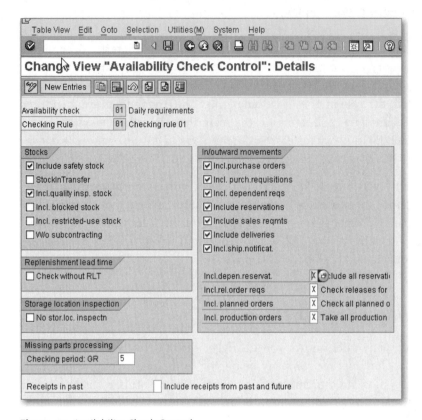

Figure 4.7 Availability Check Control

4.1.6 Batches

For material managed in batches, if you enter the batch in the sales document the system checks to determine whether its availability and expiration dates are valid. The availability of materials managed in batches is checked in two stages. The quantity that can be confirmed is the minimum quantity determined by the two separate checks: Check # 1 batch level, and Check # 2 Plant level. While displaying a delivery (or while creating and change), you can view the batch split by going to the menu item: **Item • Batch Split**. Typical transactions for display, change and create are VL03, VL02 and VL01 respectively. You can use the suffix N—e.g., VL01N—for a newer version of these transactions with release 4.6C.

4.1.7 Bill of Material

If there is a bill of material (BOM) master record, it can be expanded in the sales document. You can control the function of each item category when you define it. In the sales document, the material that has a BOM is entered in the order and becomes the main item of the bill of material. Second, the item category of the main item is determined; this item category controls whether and how BOM is expanded. Third, if the BOM needs to be expanded, the system does it automatically. The components are then listed in the document as sub-items for the main item. Fourth, the system determines an item category for each sub-item. You can create, change, or display an order BOM by using the transaction code CS61/CS62/CS63.

Availability was one of key impacts of sales process on materials management. There are processes initiated by the sales process that trigger subsequent materials management processes for material movement and inventory replenishment. We will see how different selling models or processes affect your materials management processes.

4.2 Cross-Company Sales

Cross-company sales allows you to trigger direct delivery to the customer from stocks of another company belonging to the sales group, without the goods shipping via the enterprise's own warehouse. This is made possible through the configuration option of assigning plants to sales organizations with different company codes, which essentially allows you to do cross-business-area sales orders.

Figure 4.8 displays a typical example of cross-company sales process. Let's say the customer's purchase order is received, and a sales order is created in the selling sales organization (**2000**). This sales organization belongs to the ordering company code **2100**. The delivering plant (**1100**) is assigned to the supplying company code **1000**. The shipping process creates outbound delivery from the delivering plant **1100**, and goods are transported to the customer. An invoice is created for the end customer in the sales order **2000** and ordering company code **2100**.

The supplying company code creates an internal invoice for the ordering company code via the sales organization **1200**. The invoice receipt can be entered automatically or manually in the financial accounting of the ordering company code **2100**.

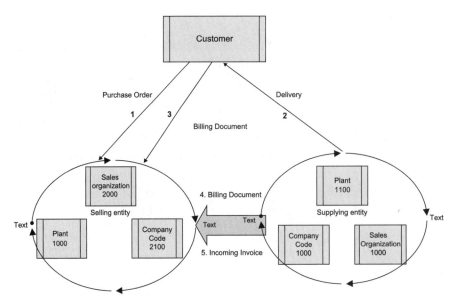

Figure 4.8 Cross-Company Sales Process

4.2.1 Sales Order for Cross-Company Sales

When a sales order is created, the system checks whether the combination of sales organization, distribution channel, and delivering plant is permitted. Based on your distribution model, you can set up the plants that are permitted to deliver products; i.e., that associate themselves with the selling entity or sales organization.

Note

As you know, the sales organization belongs to one company code, so that plants also belong to one company code. However, the plants and sales organization are assigned to one another, so the combinations become complex. These plants and sales organizations assigned to each other need not belong to same company code or in other words assigned to different company codes. As an example, plant 1000 could be assigned to company code 2000, sales organization 3000 could be assigned to company code 4000, and sales organization 3000 could be assigned to plant 1000 for a sales transaction.

The sales organization and plant assignments makes it possible to have sales from the assigned plants only. When creating a sales order, if a plant is proposed or entered manually with the company code assignment different from the one for the sales organization, the system recognizes this as a cross-company sale.

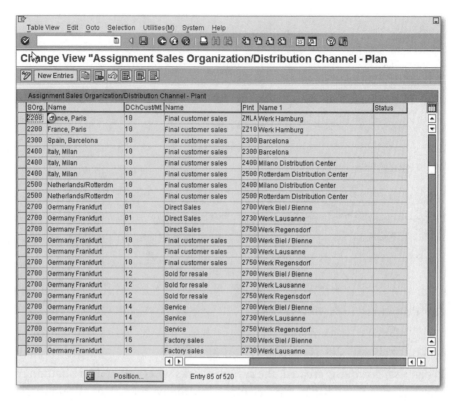

Figure 4.9 Sales Organization and Distribution Channel Assignment

The price for sales revenue is proposed by the price condition maintained for the pricing procedure determination (sales organization). Typically, the PR00 price would be the customer billing price. Subtracting the internal price (PI02), gives the profit margin for that sale to the customer. The inter-company price (internal price) appears as a statistical value.

The customizing for assignment of plants to the sales organization can be accessed through the SAP Easy Access menu, by following this path: **Tools • Customizing • IMG • Execute Project • SAP Reference IMG**. You can also use transaction code SPRO to bring up Display IMG. Within the Display IMG you can use the following path: **Enterprise Structure • Assignment • Sales and Distribution • Assign sales organization-distribution channel-plant**.

Figure 4.9 displays the assignment for Sales Organization, Distribution Channel to Plant, which can be seen as **Assignment Sales Organization/Distribution Channel-Plan**.

4.2.2　Inter-Company Billing

As described earlier, for the purpose of inter-company billing for the service or goods provided to the customer of the selling sales organization 2000, the delivering company code creates an internal invoice for the ordering company code 2100. The sales organization of the delivering plant (1200) creates an internal invoice. An internal invoice pays for the goods delivery by the supply plant, and accounting requires that this be cleared and accounted for. The sales organization will use its customer invoice to bill the customer directly.

Billing type IV is used as a default for inter-company invoices. The payer of the internal invoice here corresponds to the ordering company code, which looks like a customer to the supplying company code. You need to create a customer master record in the supplying company code. You enter the relevant data for billing in this customer master record. The customer master record must contain at least all the information relevant for the role of payer (address, control account, for example). You need to maintain the currency in which the inter-company billing will be carried out.

In organizing the ordering company code, you need to assign this customer. Figure 4.10 displays this configuration step assignment. This configuration step can be reached while you are in the Display IMG, follow the path: **Enterprise Structure • Definition • Sales and Distribution**.

1. Click on **Define, copy, check sales organization**

2. Click on **Define Sales Organization**

The company code in the inter-company invoice is determined based on the company code assigned to the delivering or the supplying plant. You need to maintain the sales area for the supplying plants. Therefore, the sales organization, distribution channel, and division assigned to the supplying company code must be assigned to form a sales area.

There are two invoices generated in a cross-company sales processing, an invoice for the customer and another internal one for the ordering company code. An internal price, which is agreed by the supplying and ordering company codes, is displayed in both the billing document for the customer and in the internal invoice. You can see how to define the sales organization in Figure 4.10. The standard delivered pricing condition in configuration is **PI01**, seen in Figure 4.11. Figure 4.11 also displays the definition behind the condition.

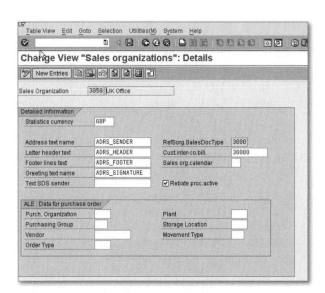

Figure 4.10 Define Sales Organization

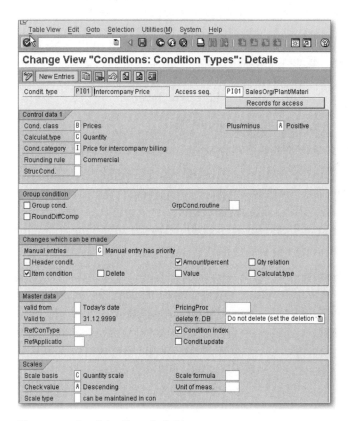

Figure 4.11 Condition Type Definition

> **Note**
>
> The pricing procedure or calculation scheme for inter-company transactions is determined based on the document pricing procedure (the document type of the internal invoice), the sales area (based on the supplying plant assignment), and the customer pricing procedure. The customer pricing procedure is based on the customer master created to represent the ordering sales organization.

The outgoing invoice from the supply plants needs to be completed with an incoming invoice to the ordering company. This can be entered manually or set for automatic entry. If the ordering company code wants to enter it manually, the supply plant can print the invoice using the message type RD00 (we will talk about message type in Section). For automatic invoice receipt, the message type RD04 is triggered based on the message determination scheme V40000.

This output determination can be triggered through the SAP Easy Access or the screen you see, as you log on to SAP system. Follow the menu path: **Logistics • Sales and Distribution • Billing • Output • Issue Billing Documents**. Technical conversion takes place using Electronic Data Interchange (EDI) techniques. This enables cross-company, electronic data exchange between business partners that deploy different hardware, software and communication services, or it could be data exchanged between two partners within one system. We will review the EDI techniques later.

The billing configuration steps can be accessed through the Display IMG if you follow this menu path: **Sales and Distribution • Billing • Intercompany Billing**. The following list details the configuration steps within the intercompany billing settings:

▶ **Define Order Types for Inter-company Billing**
Here you assign billing type to the sales order types that you would use in cross-company sales.

▶ **Assign Organizational Units by Plant**
Here you assign the distribution channel and the division to the plant.

▶ **Define Internal Customer Number by Sales Organization**
This is another place you can assign the customer number to the sales organization. Note that if you maintain it in one place, it will be reflected in the other.

▶ **Automatic Posting to Vendor Account (SAP-EDI)**

This has three configuration sub-steps, which are the configuration settings for automatic posting of the incoming invoice in the ordering company:

▶ Maintain output types

▶ Assign vendor

▶ Activate account assignment

As we saw, cross-company sales initiated within the SD module use the MM module for execution. With inter-company and cross-company stock transfer, the process is initiated or triggered from MM and uses the SD functions.

4.3   Inter-Company and Cross-Company Stock Transfer

An enterprise might have one centralized and several decentralized warehouses providing support and services to customers within various regions. Stock needs to be transferred from a central warehouse to one in a particular region. Stock transfer involves physical movement of goods between plants. Associated with the stock transfer, you will hear the term *transfer posting*. Transfer posting is not connected with actual goods movement, but involves the change of stock ID or stock type of material.

A stock transfer between two plants can be executed using different procedures. You could do the stock transfer without the Logistics Execution (LE) outbound delivery functionality by just using the MM functionality, or you can use a combination of MM and SD, which involves the use of stock transfer orders. I will show you how we can make use of Logistics Execution functionality with stock transfer, which makes use of the functionality combination of SD and MM. The stock transfer could happen between plants assigned to the same company code (stock transport order with LE outbound delivery for intra-company code) or between plants located in different company codes (stock transport order with LE outbound delivery and SD billing document for cross-company-code stock transfers).

4.3.1   Stock Transport Orders

Stock transfer involves the movement of goods from one plant to another. The plant ordering the part is called the receiving plant and the plant delivering the goods is the supplying plant. Some advantages of using stock transport orders are as follows:

- ▸ The receipt can be planned in the receiving plant
- ▸ It is possible to use a vendor in the stock transport order
- ▸ Delivery cost can be planned
- ▸ MRP can be used
- ▸ The shipping process can be used
- ▸ Goods receipt can be posted directly to consumption
- ▸ The complete process can be followed in the purchase order history

There two procedures available with stock transport orders—two-step procedure and one step procedure—examined below:

- ▸ **Two-step Procedure**

  In a two-step process, you issue the goods out of the supplying plant. Stock in transit is monitored and can be displayed in the stock overview for the materials. This stock is valuated and not assigned for unrestricted use at the receiving plant. When the goods arrive at the receiving plant, the goods are posted. You can transfer this stock according to your choice: unrestricted use, blocked, or quality.

- ▸ **One-step Procedure**

  In this procedure, there is no stock in transit and instead you define in the order item where the receipt should occur: unrestricted, stock in quality inspection, or blocked stock. Manual goods receipt posting is not needed in the receiving plant. This one step might make sense if two plants are situated near to each other.

With Customizing, you can define to work with one-step or two-step procedures depending on the supplying plant and receiving plant. We will go over all the steps required for setting up a stock transport order later in this section.

4.3.2 Materials Resource Planning

You can define a special procurement key to the materials maintained in the receiving plant that are predominantly procured via stock transport order from another plant. This key is set up in Customizing and is plant-dependent; you need to define this key for each supplying plant. In case of a shortage, the program can generate purchase requisitions with item category stock transfer (U) for these materials. These requirements will also appear in the supplying plant.

4.3.3 Document Type

Stock transport orders created for stock transfer between plants within the same company code uses UB document type in the default and NB document type for plants assigned to different company codes.

4.3.4 Configurations Steps for Stock Transport Order

The configuration steps to set up stock transport order can be found through the Display IMG by following this path: **Material Management • Purchasing • Purchase Order • Set Up Stock Transport Order**. Let's now take a look at the configuration steps related to stock transport order:

► **Define Shipping Data for Plants**
Here you assign the customer number and sales area to the supplying plant.

► **Create Checking Rule**
This is defined for the availability check for stock transport orders.

► **Define Checking Rule**
This allows you to define the checking rule; e.g., the receiving plant requiremnt is checked against the supplying plant replenishment.

► **Assign Delivery Type and Checking Rule**
Here you assign the stock transport order document type, delivery type to checking rule, and other related indicators, such as shipment scheduling and route scheduling. Figure 4.12 displays the screen for this configuration step.

► **Assign Document TypeOne-Step Procedure, Underdelivery Tolerance**
Here you define the mapping berween supplying plant, receiving plant, document type. Check if this is a one-step procedure, and check for any undelivery tolerance.

► **Set up Stock Transfer Between Storage Locations**
These settings are for activating stock transfer between the following storage locations:

  ▻ Activate Stock Transfer Between Storage Locations

  ▻ Assign Delivery Type and Checking Rule According to Storage Location

  ▻ Business Add-In for Determining of Issuing Storage Locations

  ▻ Define Shipping Data for Stock Transfer Between Storage Location

▶ Set Up Storage Location Dependent Shipping Point Determination

▶ Define Rule for Determination of Shipping Point

▶ Assign Shipping Points According to Storage Location

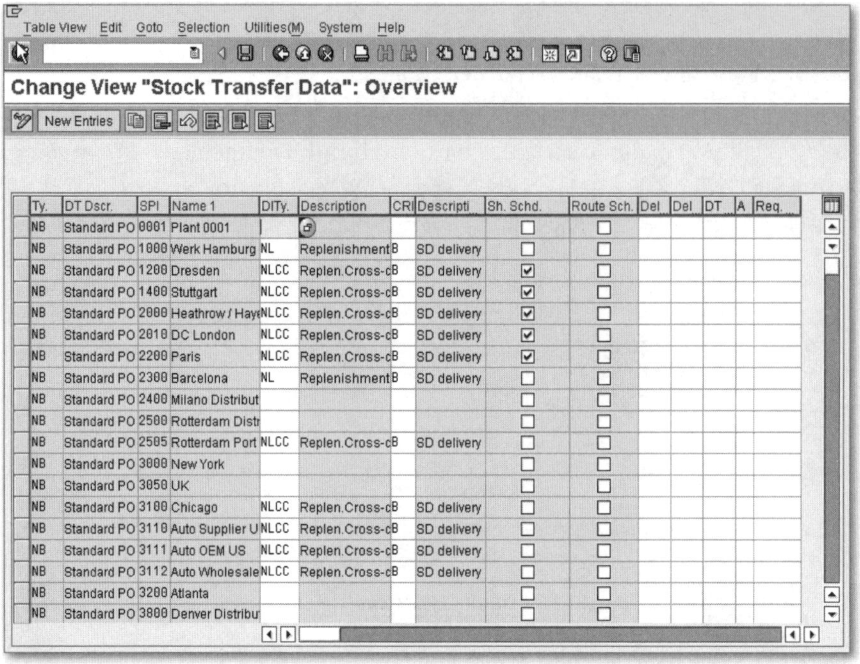

Ty.	DT Dscr.	SPl	Name 1	DITy.	Description	CRl	Descripti	Sh. Schd.	Route Sch.	Del	Del	DT	A	Req.
NB	Standard PO	0001	Plant 0001					☐	☐					
NB	Standard PO	1000	Werk Hamburg	NL	Replenishment	B	SD delivery	☐	☐					
NB	Standard PO	1200	Dresden	NLCC	Replen.Cross-c	B	SD delivery	☑	☐					
NB	Standard PO	1400	Stuttgart	NLCC	Replen.Cross-c	B	SD delivery	☑	☐					
NB	Standard PO	2000	Heathrow / Hay	NLCC	Replen.Cross-c	B	SD delivery	☑	☑					
NB	Standard PO	2010	DC London	NLCC	Replen.Cross-c	B	SD delivery	☑	☐					
NB	Standard PO	2200	Paris	NLCC	Replen.Cross-c	B	SD delivery	☑	☐					
NB	Standard PO	2300	Barcelona	NL	Replenishment	B	SD delivery	☐	☐					
NB	Standard PO	2400	Milano Distribut					☐	☐					
NB	Standard PO	2500	Rotterdam Distr					☐	☐					
NB	Standard PO	2505	Rotterdam Port	NLCC	Replen.Cross-c	B	SD delivery	☐	☐					
NB	Standard PO	3000	New York					☐	☐					
NB	Standard PO	3050	UK					☐	☐					
NB	Standard PO	3100	Chicago	NLCC	Replen.Cross-c	B	SD delivery	☐	☐					
NB	Standard PO	3110	Auto Supplier U	NLCC	Replen.Cross-c	B	SD delivery	☐	☐					
NB	Standard PO	3111	Auto OEM US	NLCC	Replen.Cross-c	B	SD delivery	☐	☐					
NB	Standard PO	3112	Auto Wholesale	NLCC	Replen.Cross-c	B	SD delivery	☐	☐					
NB	Standard PO	3200	Atlanta					☐	☐					
NB	Standard PO	3800	Denver Distribu					☐	☐					

Figure 4.12 Stock Transport Document Assignment

4.3.5 Shipping Process

The supplying plant might create an outbound delivery or replenishment delivery to ship the goods out. To process this outbound delivery, a relevant customer master record must exist. The customer master is created in the sales area. The customer number and sales area data are mapped to the supplying plant. Figure 4.13 on the next page displays the mapping of sales area and customer to the plant. When you create a stock transport order, it will use the customer number assigned to the supply plant to identify the business partner and ship-to party. The sales organizations are for the customer against which the business party is created.

The default delivery type associated with the intra-company stock transport order is NL and default item category being NLN. The delivery type for the cross-company stock transport order is NLCC, and the default item category

is NLC. Shipping point determination is based on the supplying plant, the shipping condition of the customer master record that belongs to the receiving plant, and the loading group of the material.

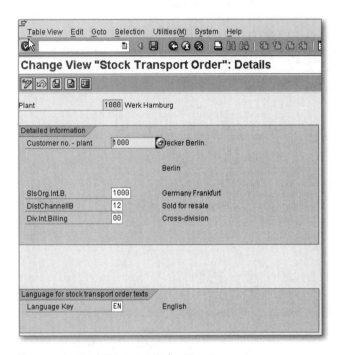

Figure 4.13 Stock Transport Order Mappings

With the material master record in the shipping data (**Gen. Sales/Plant data**), accounting data for the material must be maintained in the material master record of the supplying plant. Purchasing and accounting data from the material master record is needed for the receiving plant. Sales area data for sales organization for inter-company also must be maintained for the material.

4.3.6 Goods Movement

The system creates a material document during the goods-issue posting in MM inventory management. This one-step procedure results in a quantity of stock that is booked in the supplying plant. Simultaneously, the quantity of stock is booked in the relevant stock type of the receiving plant.

However, if you use the two-step procedure, the stock in transit is created in the receiving plant. This is then reduced or cancelled out when the goods are received. If the plants belong to different valuation areas, an accounting doc-

ument is created along with material document. The transfer posting with the valuation price of the material is valuated in the issuing plant.

The movement types for goods issues for the delivery are taken from the schedule line category. Schedule line is determined based on the item category and the MRP type maintained in the material master (these assignments are maintained in the configurations). Table 4.1 defines the mapping of the movement types based on the assignment of stock transfer order (STO) type, delivery type, item category, and schedule line category.

Stock Transfer	Delivery Type	Item Category	Schedule Line category	Movement Types
Intra-Company	NL	NLN	NN	647—one step 641—two step
Cross-company	NLCC	NLC	NC	645—one step 643—two step

Table 4.1 Movement-Type Mapping for STOs

Figure 4.14 displays the configuration definition of the schedule line category. This configuration step can be quickly accessed through the transaction code VOV6.

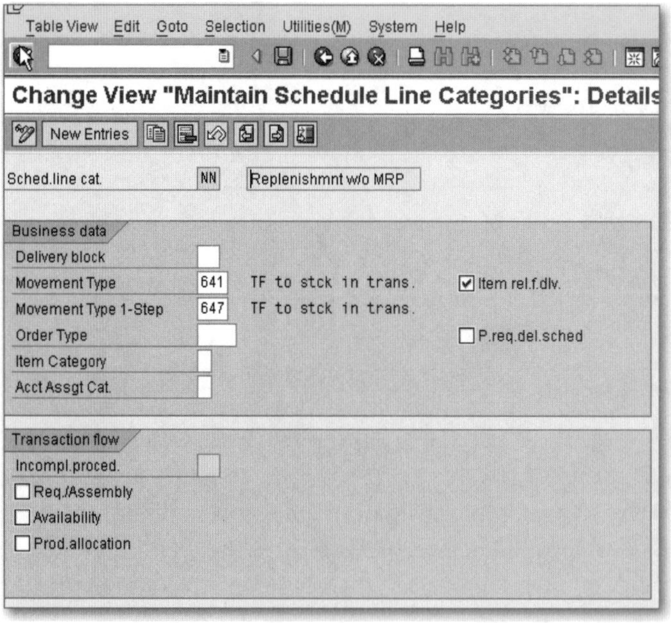

Figure 4.14 Schedule-Line Configuration

We have seen how the sales process can also be triggered by a materials management function, like stock transport order. In this case, it uses the sales function to accomplish this task. We will proceed now to another process, where MM processes are triggered based on a sales activity, third-party processing.

4.4 Third-Party Processing

If you use an external vendor to deliver goods and services directly to the customer, you might want to use third-party processing. In this process, the sales area passes the order to an external vendor, and the customer will receive an invoice from the sales area. The process starts with the customer purchase order entered as sales order in the sales organization of your enterprise SD application. This triggers an automatic creation of a purchase requisition. This purchase requisition is converted into a purchase order in your MM application.

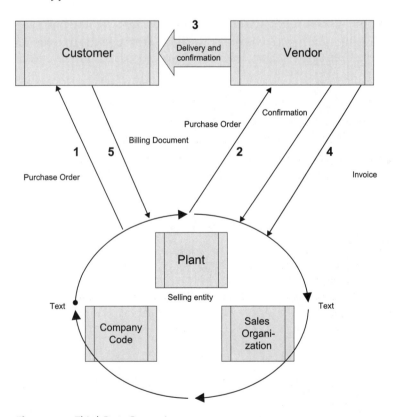

Figure 4.15 Third-Party Processing

The vendor is notified that the goods need to be delivered directly to the customer. Once the vendor notifies the company that ordered the outbound delivery of the goods, you can post the goods receipt in your system. An invoice detailing the payment to the vendor is entered in the MM invoice verification system. The customer is the billed from your SD system. Figure 4.15 shows this third-party processing flow.

4.4.1 Ordering Through Third-Party Processing

A sales order with third-party items triggers third-party processing. You can have a complete sales order transferred for third-party processing or a partial one. Customization allows you to set the determination for third-party automatic (automatic third-party) processing. While creating a sales order, you can set the default to a standard item category, in which you normally deliver the part yourself. You can than change it manually to third-party processing item category if you would like the vendor to deliver it for you. This is called manual third-party processing.

In Chapter 3, we saw that a sales order has a header and a number of items. Each item contains a schedule line item. Procurement and shipping data are parts of the schedule line category determination and are found within the schedule line level l.

The item category code TAS is provided by the SAP system with a default setting for third-party items. This item category determines the schedule line category CS. The TAS item category is not set for automatic creation of purchase requisition. If you want to have automatic creation of purchase requisition and order, you might want use another standard-delivered item category: ALES.

> **Note**
>
> Item category determination is based on the sales document type and the item category group maintained in the material master. This configuration step can be found through the Display IMG. When you are in Display IMG, follow this menu path: **Sales and Distribution • Sales • Sales Documents • Sales Document Item • Assign Item Categories**. The item category group allows you to group material with similar processing. Third-party item could have an assignment of third-party item group (BANS).

A related purchase requisition is created for each third-party item in the sales order. This is achieved by setting up the schedule line category in the configuration. Figure 4.16 displays the definition behind the schedule line cate-

gory, **CS**. This can be accessed through Display IMG by following this path: **Sales and Distribution** • **Sales** • **Sales Documents** • **Schedule line** • **Define Schedule Line Categories**. With the schedule line category **CS**, as shown in Figure 4.16, item relevant for delivery (**Item rel.f.dlv**) is not checked. This setting ensures that delivery is not carried out by your company. Rather, the vendor will do it on your behalf.

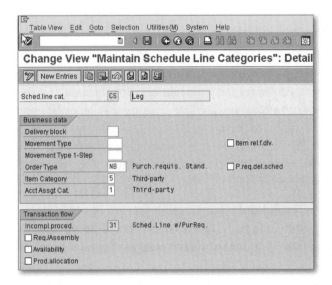

Figure 4.16 Schedule Line Category Definition

The configuration setting also defines the specific purchase requisition and the purchase item category along with account assignment category. If the third-party item has more than one schedule line with confirm quantity (greater than zero) assigned, then a purchase requisition item is created for each schedule line. The system branches to display the purchase requisition item created out of the schedule line of the sales order. The automatically created purchase requisition already contains a fixed source of supply based on the MM configuration settings.

The planned delivery times are derived from the purchasing info record maintained in the purchasing function for the vendor or an existing contract between you and the vendor. The system determines the delivery proposal based on this maintained information. You can subsequently change the delivery date and quantity for a third-party item in the sales document. The changes are automatically copied to the purchase requisition, as long as the processing status of the purchase requisition permits this. The account assignment cannot be changed in the purchase requisition.

The delivery address of the third-party item contains the address data from the related customer master record. Changes in quantities and dates, which you make in purchase order are transferred to the sales order automatically. The requested delivery date from the sales order is transferred to the purchase requisition and purchase order, based on the forward and backward scheduling; the final delivery date determined in purchasing is transferred to the sales document.

4.4.2 Goods Receipt

When goods arrive at your company, you need to acknowledge receiving them into your inventory. This process is carried out by the goods receipt functionality in the system. Account assignment category X is set for the following indicators:

▶ Goods receipt for the item provided/possible or not

▶ Goods-receipt posting valuated or not

▶ Goods-receipt related invoice verification planned or not

The configuration setting for the account assignment category can be reached through Display IMG via this menu path: **Material Master • Purchasing • Account Assignment • Maintain Account Assignment Categories**. Figure 4.17 (see next page) displays the settings of the account-assignment category.

The system allows the creation of a third-party item without a material master record. Also, goods receipt with reference to the order item can be entered. An invoice receipt that refers to the order item must be entered.

Since third-party processing portrays goods movement directly from the vendor to the customer, inventory management is not affected by this event. The effects of goods receipt are as follows:

▶ The warehouse stock is not updated.

▶ The goods receipt is posted directly to consumption, and the consumption quantity in updated.

▶ The order value is posted to a GR/IR clearing account for invoice verification purpose.

▶ The goods receipt can be traced in the purchase-order history.

You can either post the goods receipt when the vendor confirms the delivery of the goods or when the customer confirms the receipt.

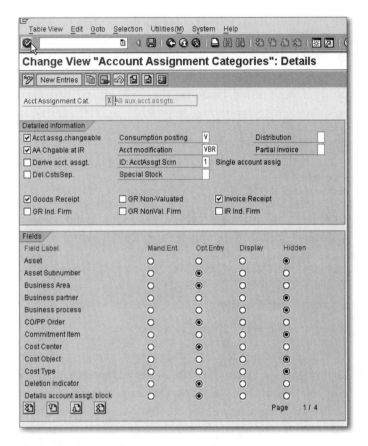

Figure 4.17 Account Assignment Categories

4.4.3 Invoice Receipt

When the invoice arrives, you can enter the invoice in logistics invoice verification and make a reference to the vendor purchase order number. If the indicator for the goods receipt has been set in the order item, the system proposes the goods receipt quantity that has already been posted, as well as the value of the goods received.

Variance between the invoice price and the purchase order price can lead to the invoice being automatically blocked for payment. These variances are also used to determine the profit margin in the sales order.

4.4.4 Customer Billing

Once the invoice receipt has been entered, the customer is billed. The default setting for the third-party item category in the copying control for sales doc-

ument to billing document determines that the quantity from the invoice receipt document is transferred to the billing document. Figure 4.18 displays the configuration setting in the copy control. The billing quantity setting is set to **F**, which is **Invoice receipt quantity less invoiced quantity**.

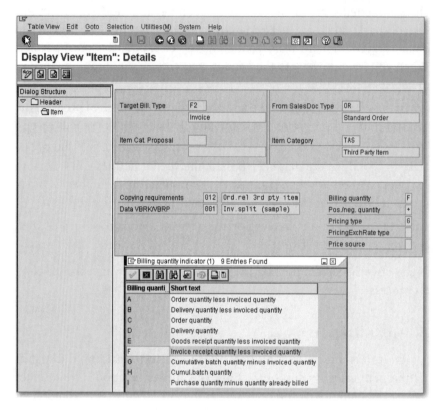

Figure 4.18 Billing Quantity Settings With Copy Control

Having looked at the third-party processing, lets see how a subcontracting process triggered within the MM module uses the SD support functions such as delivery, shipping, and so on.

4.5 Subcontracting

With subcontracting, the company orders the finished product from vendor by supplying them with the components. Your company could partially or fully make the components needed for the production of the material available to the vendor. Let's look at the steps involved in a typical subcontracting process. These occur in the following sequence:

1. The company orders the end product via a subcontract order (purchase order). The component the vendor would receive to create this product is listed/or named in the subcontracting PO. You can use a BOM, which can contain further component that the vendor receives.

2. The components are delivered to the vendor and stocked as vendor-related special stock or stock provided to vendor (type O). The vendor can obtain this component from your company or another business partner. When you send the part to the vendor, you can use the shipping function in Logistics Execution.

3. When the vendor completes the task and delivers the finished product, the comsumption of the product is automatically booked using goods receipt posting.

4. Once the goods receipt has been posted, the vendor notifies you that more or fewer components than planned were consumed and whether the stock needs to be updated (subsequent adjustment).

5. The vendor issues an invoice for the service rendered, which is then checked in invoice verification.

Let's see how the subcontracting function is triggered through the procurement process.

4.5.1   Procurement Process

You indicate the subcontracting items (SC item) in purchasing documents using the item category subcontracting. This means that you have to enter one or several sub-items for each subcontracting item for the component that are provided. If the BOM exists for the material that is to be procured, then the components are copied from the BOM to the subcontracting item. The system will allow you to enter the component manually or add further components to the bill of material.

If a material for a plant is procured via subcontracting, you could control this through a special procurement key in the material master. This indicator translates to purchase requisition for these materials in MRP. This indicator (special procurement−30) is maintained in the MRP 2 view along with the procurement type F (external procurement).The purchase requisition generated with an item category L (subcontracting). In the BOM, dependent requirements are created for the component.

> **Note**
>
> The subcontracting purchase order type default available in the system is the document type NB, with the associated item category being L for subcontracting. You can also use a scheduling agreement for the procurement of materials via subcontracting. The components themselves are determined in the scheduling agreement schedule line, or they have to be entered manually.

You can display the current stock/requirement list for your components through the SAP Easy Access via the path: **Logistics • Materials Management • Inventory Management • Environment • Stock • Stock/Requirement List**. The purchase order for subcontracting can be created through SAP Easy Access by navigating to the path: **Logistics • Materials Management • Purchasing • Purchase Order • Create • Vendor/Supplying Plant Known**.

4.5.2 Goods Movement

The stocks of the components that are to be made available to the vendor for carrying out the operations needed to deliver the finished goods are entered in the stock of the material provided to vendor. The stock has the following characteristics:

- It is administered as part of the total valuated stock and is available for material requirement planning.
- It is only adminstered at plant level, as it is not stored in your company, but with the vendor.
- It carries out the inventory of the stock of material provided to the vendor.
- Two types of stock are possible, as seen below:
  - Unrestricted use
  - Stock in quality inspection. Stock can be transferred from one to another of these two categories, but material withdrawal can only be posted from the unrestricted-use stock.

From release 4.0 onwards, you can create MM transfer postings with movement type 541, using an LE outbound delivery for a subcontracting process. The advantage of this procedure is that shipping documents and delivery notes are available when you ship the material provided by a customer. This allows you to use the standard function of shipment and transportation processing such as picking, packing, and dispatching in shipments.

4.5.3 Sales and Distribution Delivery

You can create delivery via shipping from subcontracting stock monitoring for the vendor list. The following data needs to be maintained in the system to create a delivery:

▶ A sales organization, a distribution channel and a division need to be assigned to a plant. This configuration is the same as for the stock transport order.

▶ A delivery type needs to be defined for the plant from which you deliver. This customizing step can be reached through the Display IMG by following the path: **Material Master • Purchasing• Purchase Order• Set Up Subcontract Order**.

▶ If you want to refer to a reservation when creating a delivery, then set the indicator Predecessor essential to **L** (provision of materials for subcontract order essential) when defining the respective delivery type. Therefore, the reservations can be correctly offset against the orders created. Figure 4.19 displays the delivery type definiton for subcontracting. The configuration setting for the delivery type definition can reached though the Display IMG via the path: **Logistics Execution • Shipping • Deliveries • Define Delivery Types**.

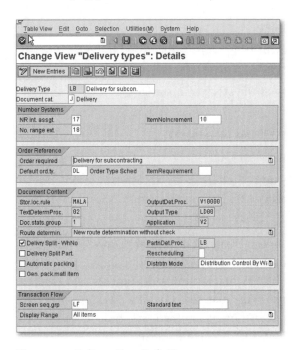

Figure 4.19 Delivery Type Definition

When deliveries are created, these should refer to a customer (also called Debtor) in the organization unit's sales organization, distribution channel, and division of the supplying plant. This customer is assgined to the vendor master record. Figure 4.20 displays the control screen of vendor master record where the customer assignment is maintained.

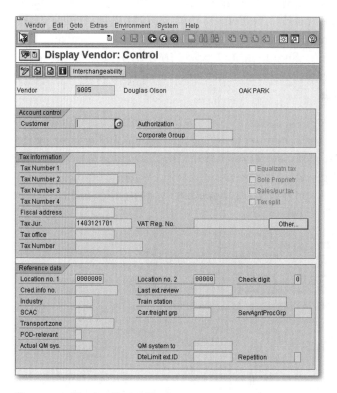

Figure 4.20 Vendor Master Display

The material provided to the customer must be created in the organizational unit sales organization, distribution channel, and division of the supplying plant. A shipping point must be assigned to the combination of shipping condition (from subcontracting customer master record), loading group (from the material master record of the subcontracting component), and plant. As we have seen before these assignment are maintained in the Customizing step for assigning shipping points within Logistics Execution.

The default delivery type available in the system is LB. The item category assigned is LBN. The MRP type and item category determined that the schedule line category assigned is LB, and the schedule line category determines the movement type 541.

4.5.4 Serial Numbers

Serial numbers can be used to uniquely identify material or product during goods movement; e.g., when you ship them to a customer. Serial numbers are also used as the basis for routine maintenance and plant maintenance, providing that equipment master records exist for the individual product.

Serial number profiles need to be defined in Customizing, and these determine whether serial numbers can be used during sales-order processing. This Customizing step can be found within Display IMG by following the menu path: **Sales and Distribution** • **Basic Function** • **Serial Numbers** • **Determine Serial Number Profile**.

Figure 4.21 shows you the screen of the material master view **Sales: general/plant** where the serial number profile is maintained. In the same figure, within **General plant parameters,** you can see the field name **SerialNoProfil**, where by using a drop-down menu you can select values from the possible entries. On the right-hand side you can see the list of profiles maintained in the system with **28 Entries**.

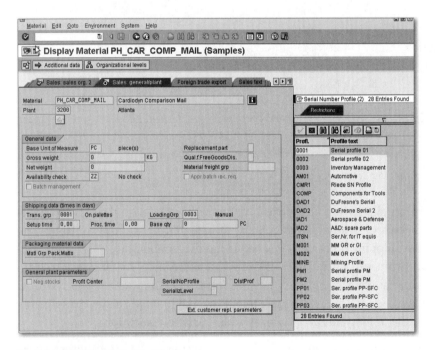

Figure 4.21 Material Master Display

If you have maintained the master data for the serial number, you can enter the serial number for each item in the delivery. The system will then display

a dialogue box where the number needs to be entered. You can also go to item and serial number fields to enter serial numbers. In this dialogue box, you have the choice to automatically create the serial number by selecting **Create serial numbers automatically**.

4.6 Agreements

Outline agreements, as do sales document types, play an important role in nearly all business processes. Customers and vendors agree on goods to be provided under certain conditions and within specific time frames. The two main outline agreements are scheduling agreements and contracts. Examples of standard SAP supplied outline agreements are discussed in the following sub-sections.

4.6.1 Scheduling Agreements

The scheduling agreement contains fixed delivery dates and quantities. These dates are contained in the schedule lines. Once scheduling agreements are due for delivery, you can create delivery as a normal process. When you enter schedule line for an item in the scheduling agreement, the system adds up the quantities that have already been entered and compares them to both the target and the quantity shipped. Based on the agreement, you can process invoice periodically or when agreed upon. All deliveries due for billing are then combined in a collective invoice. The types of scheduling agreements are listed below:

- ▶ **DS**
  Scheduling agreement

- ▶ **BL**
  Scheduling agreement with delivery schedule

- ▶ **DEL**
  Scheduling agreement for external agent

4.6.2 Contracts

The contract doesn't contain any schedule line, delivery quantities, or delivery dates, but you can agree on special price agreements or delivery times. Schedule lines are created in the release order when it is placed. The release order is then processed like standard order. Any special agreements regarding prices or delivery deadlines are copied from the contract. Release orders

are created with reference to a contract. This generates a document flow record that allows you to update release quantities and values in the contract. In the configuration, you can maintain a copy control for creating release order out of contract document type.

While maintaining the document type, you can specify if the system prompts you to list or search the outline agreement when you use the option to create with reference to contract. You need to also configure a place-holder for contract data with the option **Contract data allowed** field. Figure 4.22 displays this configuration setting. The types of contracts are listed here:

▸ **QC**
Quantity contract

▸ **WK1**
General value contract

▸ **WK2**
Material-related value contract

▸ **QP**
Rental contract

▸ **SC**
Service and Maintenance

4.6.3 Scheduling Agreements vs. Contracts

When you create a contract, the system proposes the start and end dates of the contract. You define the date determination rules in Customizing. If you specify a duration category, the system automatically generates the duration of the contract. If you assign a contract profile to the sales document type, the system automatically determines default values specific to the contract. These could be rules for determining start and end of contract, duration category; subsequent activities, or cancellation procedure. Value contracts are covered in Chapter 6.

For creating contracts you use the menu path: **Logistics • Sales and Distribution • Sales • Contract • Create**. After releasing the order, configure **Sales document • Create** subsequent order to create sales orders.

For creating sales orders, follow this menu path: **Logistics • Sales and Distribution • Sales • Order • Create**. Similarly for creating scheduling agreements follow the menu path: **Logistics • Sales and Distribution • Sales • Scheduling Agreement • Create**.

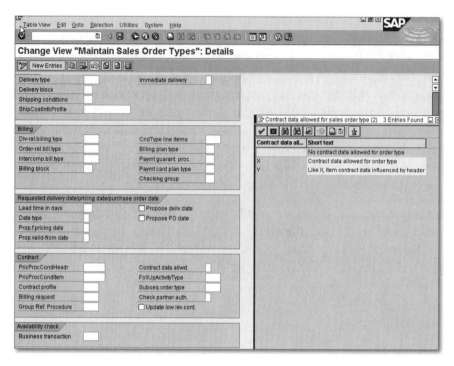

Figure 4.22 Sales Order Type Maintenance

For creating deliveries out of these scheduling agreements, you can follow the path: **Logistics • Sales and Distribution • Shipping and Transportation • Outbound Delivery • Create • Single Document • With Reference to Sales Order**.

4.7 Summary

In this chapter, I examined the different cross-function processes between MM and SD. We could see the SD processes making use of MM function, in cross-company-code sales and third-party processing. In the case of cross-company-code sales, delivery of material required by the customer doesn't take place from one's own company code, but from a plant of another company code. With third-party processing, delivery of the material required by the customer is not carried out by your company. Instead, you forward the request to an external vendor, who then sends the material directly to the customer and charges you for the material.

We tracked the MM process, which makes use of the SD functionality for shipping and delivery. With intra-company-code stock transfer, material is transferred between plants that have the same company code. Starting with material requirements planning, you can trigger the stock transfer via a purchase order and use shipping for the goods movement. With subcontract procurement processing, the vendor is provided with material or components of manufacture the material required to manufacture the finished product. You can use shipping to send the components from your company to the subcontractor. We covered the basics of the scheduling agreement and the customizing required for outline agreements.

Now that we understand the closest interface to SD, let's move on to the other functions that are influenced by the SD processes. These can be considered more of SD supply chain extension. We will look at the Logistics Execution and Warehouse Management functions in detail in Chapter 5.

A sales order is delivered by picking goods, packing them, loading them, and finally transporting them to the receiving party. This chapter will discuss the supply chain extensions process, including the execution of your shipment, planning of transportation, warehouse management, and the features behind the decentralized warehouse management.

5 Supply Chain Extension of Sales and Distribution

Logistics Execution (LE) is a link between procurement and distribution, whether the process is internal or involves third parties. The logistics involved include the goods receipt process, goods issue process, internal warehouse process, and transportation process. Transportation involves inbound and outbound shipments and shipment cost calculation and settlement. A shipment is a collection of inbound or outbound deliveries that are shipped together. The inbound or outbound shipments therefore have the same shipping conditions.

Warehouse processes include processes for inbound and outbound deliveries. We will explore the basics of Warehouse Management, and also touch briefly on the decentralized warehouse management to explain the application and concept behind this system. An enterprise resource planning (ERP) system processes delivery through all partial activities and functions that are in preparation for a subsequent processing of activities in the warehouse. These include the creation of sales or purchasing documents for different checks and subsequent invoice handling. The Warehouse Management System (WMS) includes functions that handle warehouse processes, such as picking, packing, and material movement with warehousing implemented. These functions include planning, goods receipt, storing, goods issue, and monitoring warehouse activities.

5.1 Transportation with Logistics Execution and Shipment Execution

Inbound shipments are an integral part of the process chain in procurement (represented in the SAP system by MM Purchasing) and are processed-based on inbound deliveries. The basis of the procurement process is the purchase order. The subsequent document is the inbound delivery notice that is used by the vendor to confirm the delivery.

The inbound delivery is an R/3 or a mySAP ERP ECC document and is created with reference to a purchase order. The inbound delivery document is the basis for creating the inbound shipment; that is, the shipment of the ordered goods from vendor to the company's plant. Transportation processing refers to the shipment of goods. Following are the different types of shipments with the different business parties involved:

▶ Goods coming from vendor to plant refers to inbound shipments

▶ Goods shipped out from plant to customer refers to outbound shipments

▶ Goods moving from plant to plant refers to shipment for stock transfer

Figure 5.1 displays the flow of shipments in Logistics Execution.

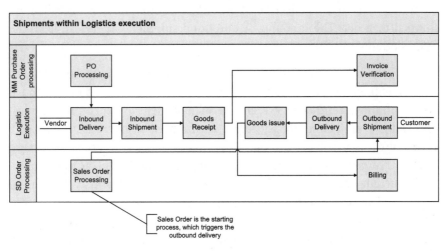

Figure 5.1 Shipment Process Within Logistics Execution

Outbound shipments are part of the Sales and Distribution (SD) process and are processed based on outbound deliveries. The basis of SD, as we know, is the sales order. The subsequently created document is for the outbound delivery and documents the shipping of goods. The outbound delivery document

is the basis for creating the outbound shipment; that is, the shipment of the goods from the company's plant to the customer. Goods issue is then posted and the invoice created. Figure 5.2 displays the screen with a standard order under the **Shipping** tab, where the shipping information is maintained.

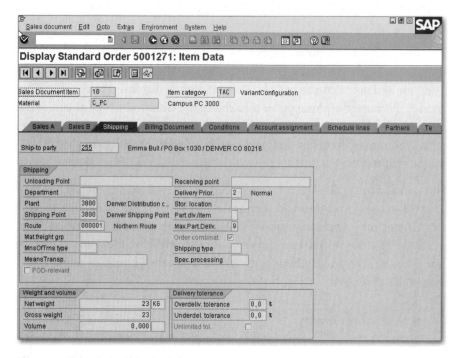

Figure 5.2 Sales Order Shipping Information

5.1.1   Shipment Documents

The shipment document is the central document used for processing shipments in the SAP R/3 or the mySAP ERP systems. It contains all information necessary for organizing necessary for organizing and carrying out a shipment. The shipment document provides the following functions:

► Combining inbound deliveries to form inbound shipments

► Combining outbound deliveries to form outbound shipments

► Assigning service agents, mode of transport, shipment types, and so on

► Planning and monitoring deadlines

► Specifying shipment stages

► Cross-delivery packing and creation of handling units

▶ Creating output and shipping papers

▶ Recording shipment-relevant texts

▶ Recording partner information

▶ Freight cost estimate

▶ Shipment tendering

The shipment document contains general data that applies to the whole document, such as shipment type, transportation planning point, route, deadlines, and status information. This information is displayed in the shipment header. Because the shipment is a collection of inbound or outbound deliveries that are shipped together, the items of the shipment correspond exactly to the inbound shipments, and to the outbound deliveries in the case of outbound shipments.

Shipments can be displayed through the SAP Easy Access or the SAP screen you see when you log on and then follow this menu path: **Logistics • Logistics Execution • Transportation • Transportation Planning • Display**. You need to enter the shipment number or choose one from the list of shipment numbers, which can be displayed by hitting **F4** in the Shipment number field and in the appropriate selection.

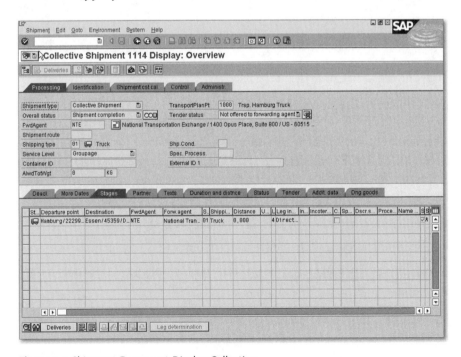

Figure 5.3 Shipment Document Display-Collective

Figure 5.3 displays the collective shipment document, which consists of several views, including **Processing**, **Identification**, **Shipment cst cal** (Shipment cost calculation), **Control** and **Administr.** (Administration). Each view has general information in the top section and a sub-folder of information within itself. You can see this in Figure 5.3, in which I have taken **Processing** as an example. Take note of the **Stages** folder information.

5.1.2 Individual vs. Collective Shipments

Shipments can be individual or collective. An individual shipment has the following characteristics:

- One or more inbound or outbound deliveries involved in the shipment
- One single point of departure and one single destination
- In most cases, only one mode of transport used
- Shipment document is created

A collective shipment has the following characteristics:

- One or more inbound or outbound deliveries involved in the shipment
- One or more points of departure and one or more destinations
- In most cases, only one mode of transport is used
- Shipment document created

Shipments are collections of inbound or outbound deliveries that are shipped together. The inbound or outbound deliveries therefore have the same shipping conditions. Since these shipping conditions may differ according to companies' requirements, there are numerous criteria in the SAP R/3 or mySAP ERP systems that you can use to group inbound or outbound deliveries to form shipments. These are called selection criteria. Table 5.1 displays a few selection criteria and some examples.

Selection Criteria	Business Example
Destination	Indicated by ship-to-party, location, zip code, country, plant, etc.
Point of departure	Indicated by shipping point, warehouse number, dock door, vendor, etc.
Due date	Indicated by transportation planning point, date, delivery date, loading date, delivery priority, etc.

Table 5.1 Shipment Selection Criteria

Selection Criteria	Business Example
Transportation planning	Route, incoterm, shipping type, forwarding agent, etc.
Other information	Means of transport, means of transport category, shipping units, etc.

Table 5.1 Shipment Selection Criteria (cont.)

The menu path through SAP Easy access or the SAP screen after you log on to create a shipment manually is: **Logistics Execution · Transportation · Transportation Planning · Create · Single Documents · Shipment and Deliveries**. For collective processing, use the menu path: **Logistics · Logistics Execution · Transportation · Transportation Planning · Create · Collective Processing**.

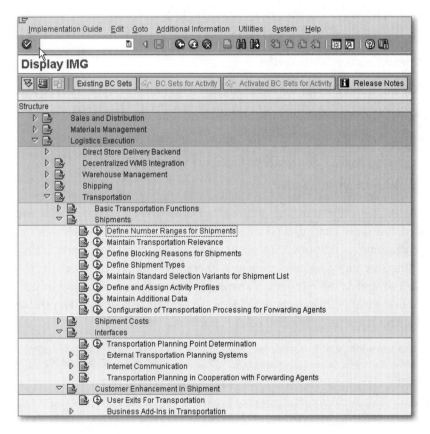

Figure 5.4 Shipment Configuration Steps

Whether a shipment can be created is determined by the transportation relevance of the delivery type, the delivery item category, and the route set in

Customizing. The outbound delivery must contain a route that is relevant for transportation (this does not apply to inbound deliveries). A route is defined as the connection between a point of departure and a destination point with several possible points in between.

The configuration step for transportation relevance can be found within the Display IMG. While you in the Display IMG, follow this menu path: **Logistics Execution · Transportation · Shipments · Maintain transportation Relevance**.

For configurations steps specific to shipments within Display IMG, follow this path: **Logistics Execution · Transportation · Shipments**. Figure 5.4 displays the configuration steps. We will explain the configuration steps, as they apply in below sections. When you create a shipment, the shipment is identified by a system generated sequence number based on the number range defined in the configuration step **Define Number Ranges for Shipments**.

5.1.3   Stages of Shipments

Shipment stages contain information on the geographical characteristics of a shipment. This information is frequently used as a basis for calculating shipment costs. The system differentiates between the following stage types:

▶ **Leg**
This is the connection between starting point and end points.

▶ **Load Transfer Point**
This is where a shipment is loaded, unloaded, or transferred from one means of transport to another.

Stages can be determined manually or automatically. Manually, the stages are determined based on one of the following.

▶ **Simple Rules**
Using this, the system generates legs only, determining the point of departure, the destinations, and some leg-related data, such as shipping type, service agent, leg indicator, and shipment cost relevance.

▶ **Determine Legs Parameter**
Using this in Customizing for the shipment type, you can control the type of leg determination used.

Automatic determination makes use of route, from which stages are adopted by using the option to adopt route parameter in the shipment type.

5.1.4 Delivery Split

You may need to divide a delivery to form several shipments if, for instance, the whole delivery cannot be loaded onto a truck. Using the delivery split function, you can call up a list from which you can select delivery items, partial quantities of items, or handling units that need to be removed from existing deliveries, and then split them. The subsequent outbound-delivery split function simplifies this process by accomplishing the same thing in one step. An existing delivery can be split whenever you discover that the delivery contains too many items or is too large to be processed in subsequent functions (picking, goods issue, transportation planning, etc.).

To use the subsequent delivery function, you must first make the necessary settings in the Implementation Guide (IMG). While you are in Display IMG, follow this path: **Logistics Execution • Shipping • Deliveries • Subsequent Delivery Split**.

Figure 5.5 displays the screen shot for this configuration step. During the subsequent outbound-deliveries split, the system checks the status (no goods movements or billing documents, etc.), confirms characteristics (delivery groups and correlation), copies data (text), calculates attributes (volume and weight), and carries out determination (outputs). The split result controls which delivery items are grouped together in the same delivery. All remaining items make up the split reminder.

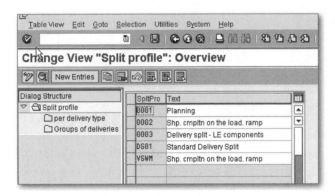

Figure 5.5 Split Function

Shipment documents are used for transportation planning and processing the deliveries. Let's now gain an understanding of the transportation functions within Logistics Execution.

5.1.5 Transportation

Transportation processing requires several organizational units. These units reflect the organizational structure of the company. As we know, a company code is a self-contained unit with its own financial accounting. *Plants* are elements that subdivide a company code from a logistics point of view. A plant produces goods or provides goods for distribution (e.g., production plant, distribution center). In terms of the Inventory Management (IM) application, plants are sub-divided into one or more storage locations (e.g., raw material storage area, finished products storage area, etc.). By assigning plant-storage location combination(s) to a warehouse number, you establish a link between Inventory Management and Warehouse Management.

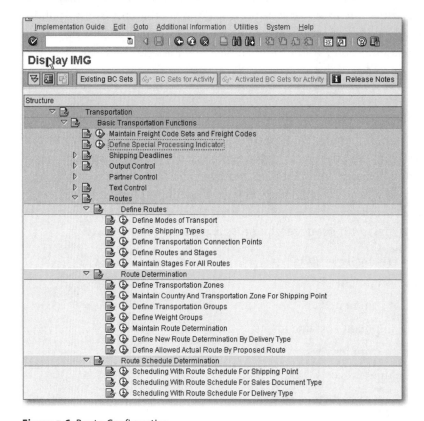

Figure 5.6 Route Configuration

The most important organizational element for shipping is the *shipping point*. It reflects the location or the group of people responsible for carrying out shipping activities. Each delivery is processed by a single shipping point. A shipping point can be assigned to one or more plants. A shipping point can

be further divided into loading points. The transportation planning point processes shipments. They are assigned to one company code and are not linked to the other organizational units. Figure 5.6 displays the organizational structure in **Transportation**.

Transportation Planning Point

The transportation planning point is the central point within the company that plans, processes, and monitors shipments. It can be a location or a group of people responsible for processing. Each shipment is created and processed by a single transportation planning point. You can freely define the transportation planning points to meet your corporate requirements; e.g., in terms of the location or the mode of transport. The transportation planning point is defined specifically for the company code in Customizing. This assignment of the planning point to the company code is important for shipment cost calculation and settlement.

Controlling Transportation

Transportation planning and execution are controlled by the shipment process. The shipment document captures the essence of the transportation process. From delivery, information is retrieved and formulated for transportation. When you create a delivery, you are initiating a physical movement of the goods from your company's premise. The typical steps involved in the transportation with goods receipt or issue process are as follows:

1. Create shipment document

2. Process shipment

3. Monitor shipment

4. Create shipment cost document

5. Calculate shipment costs

6. Settle shipment costs

7. Bill shipment costs to customer

Typical transportation scenarios could be one of the following:

- Shipment by truck from one plant to one customer
- Shipment using several trucks from one plant to several customers
- Shipment by rail from the vendor to the plant

▸ Empty return shipment from the customer to the plant

▸ Shipment using different modes of transportation from several plants to several customers

A company can use different transportation scenarios, which will be characterized by different processing types or means of transport. To process these different kinds of shipments, you can define shipment types in Customizing. The shipment type controls elements in the shipment document and therefore represents a particular processing type for a shipment. Figure 5.5 displays the shipment type definition in configuration.

Shipment types control the elements in the shipment document, therefore representing a particular processing type for shipment. The shipment type settings include:

▸ Leg determination type (e.g., automatic leg determination)

▸ Completion type (e.g., loaded outbound shipment, inbound shipment)

▸ Processing control (e.g., collective shipment using one mode of transport)

▸ Service level (e.g., general cargo, grouped load)

▸ Shipment type (e.g., truck, train, mail)

▸ Leg indicator (e.g., preliminary leg, subsequent leg, direct leg)

▸ Copying data from preceeding documents (forwarding agent, route, etc)

▸ Output, text, and partner determination procedures (picking and packing slips through output, partner determination for carrier and shipment parties profile or data).

▸ Default values for the shipment document (e.g., weight and volume unit, planning profile)

▸ Setting to cause automatic generation of items in a delivery document for handling units created within a shipment

The configuration step for shipment type definitions can be accessed through IMG by following the menu path: **Logistics Execution • Transportation • Shipments • Define Shipment Types**.

Transportation Chain

A transportation chain supports the shipment of inbound or outbound deliveries. Inbound and outbound deliveries consist of several modes of transport, like planning, execution, and routing. This means that the deliveries are

involved in subsequent shipments for different processes, such as consolidation, or splits. For example, you might want to consolidate deliveries for a particular destination or customer and split it for actual delivery to the end customer. A transportation chain is an important aspect of the leg determination and planning. A transportation chain has the following characteristics:

▶ One or more deliveries involved in several shipments

▶ One or more points of departure and one or more destinations

▶ Various mode of transport used

▶ Several shipment documents created: preliminary legs, main leg, and subsequent legs

Route

A route can be defined in great detail and can consist of individual stages. However, a route can also be a general description or even simply a destination area. You need to define routes in Customizing. A route can contain many pieces of information that are important for the shipment. Examples include distance, transportation lead-time, travel duration, shipping type, service agent, and so on. If you define stages for the route, you first need to create starting points and destination points for the legs, and then load transfer points and border crossing points in order to provide transportation connection points.

At the stage level, you can also define information such as distance, service agent, leg indicator, shipping type, travel duration, and total duration. A transportation connection point could be an airport, a railway station, a harbor, or a border crossing. However, you can use the connection point to refer to a plant, a shipping point, a customer, or a vendor.

> **Note**
>
> Stages contain information about the geographical factors for a shipment. If you want to adopt stages from route into shipment header, the configuration parameters must be set for the shipment type, and the route stages are copied as shipment stages. Shipment stages might include legs, load transfer points, and border crossing points.

Table 5.2 gives you an idea of how the system determines the route.

Business Question	System Determination parameter
From where?	Transportation zone: shipping point
How?	Shipping condition
What?	Transportation group
To where?	Transportation zone: ship-to-party

Table 5.2 Route Determination Rule

The configuration step for defining routes can be found under Display IMG by following the menu path: **Logistics Execution • Transportation • Basic Transportation Functions • Routes • Define Routes • Define Routes and Stages**.

Let me make this clearer by describing a business case where the Internet can be used to save money and time by supporting collaboration between the shipper and the carrier. Where a carrier works primarily for a particular shipper, the shipper can determine which planning functions are to be performed by the carrier and which are to be retained by the shipper. The entire planning process occurs in the Internet through Web transactions. A typical scenario, seen in sequence below, would be:

1. Shipper offers deliveries to the carrier through the Internet using IDocs.

2. Carrier creates shipments on the basis of these deliveries and transmits the planned shipments back to the shipper using Easy Web transaction.

3. Shipper then decides whether to accept the planned shipments from the carrier or to tender the shipments to a different carrier.

4. Shipper sets tendering status to *confirmed*, thereby triggering an automatic email message sent to the carrier, using output controls.

5. Internet tracking function allows you to exchange data between shipper, forwarding agent, and customer.

The configurations steps for basic transportation can be found within the Display IMG, if you follow this path: **Logistics Execution • Transportation**.

You will find a set of configuration settings for setting up shipping deadlines. **Output**, **Partner** and **Text** control are similar to the other functions or areas, as the use the same techniques. The next important configuration element being the route definition, route determination, and route schedule determination. Figure 5.7 displays the organizational elements and structure with inventory management, shipping, and transportation.

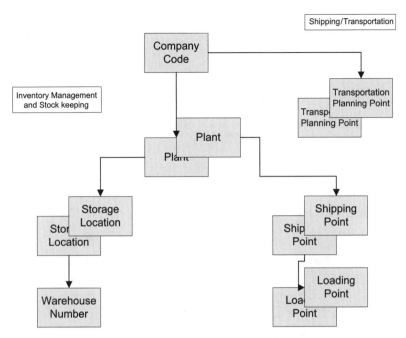

Figure 5.7 Shipping and Transportation Organizational Structure

Having looked at shipping and transportation, let's move to the Warehouse Management System. WMS allows you to map your entire warehouse complex in detail, down to the storage-bin level.

5.2 Warehouse Management Basics and Business Process Outsourcing

Goods movement processes, inbound and outbound, are mapped by goods receipts and goods issues within the Logistics Execution functions. Materials produced in-house and procured externally are put away and removed from storage using WMS. This inventory taken away could be used to supply the enterprise's own production or to deliver to retailers or end users, through goods issues and receipts.

Figure 5.8 displays the process overview of Logistics Execution with the goods receipt and issue postings within it. A transfer order is the document used to execute all material movements in the warehouse. If you work with deliveries, WMS activities (creating and confirming a transfer order) are completed before posting in IM. However, the IM posting also can occur at

the beginning of the process. The goods receipt/goods issue posting then generates a transfer requirement, which forms the basis for warehouse activities in terms of planning and posting. A put-away of picking activity with the transfer order completes the process.

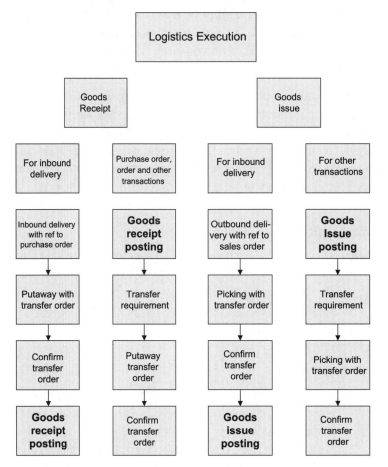

Figure 5.8 LE Goods Issue and Receipt Process Flow

5.2.1 Basic Functions of Warehouse Management

Warehouse Management in SAP ECC fulfills the following five basic functions:

▶ Inventory management exact to the storage-bin level

▶ Mapping and control of all goods movements

▶ Monitoring of the processing of these goods movements

▸ Connection to mobile data entry as part of the integrated radio frequency solution

▸ Connection to specialist external system using an interface

While Inventory Management, as part of Materials Management, can only provide information on the total quantity of material in stock. Warehouse Management enables you to locate the exact location of a particular quantity of material and informs you whether this quantity is currently in a storage bin or on the move.

These movements of storage bin stocks are generally triggered by goods receipts and goods issue, or by stock transfer. Warehouse Management uses a special document, the transfer order, to map and control warehouse movements. When you create a transfer order, the system checks all the relevant settings at master data or Customizing level and use this data to determine suitable storage bins to put away or pick stock.

5.2.2 Interfaces with Other Applications

Warehouse Management can also exchange data with other application components via interfaces. There are connections to the following components:

▸ Inventory Management (MM-IM)

▸ Delivery Processing (LE-SHP)

▸ Production Planning and Control (PP)

▸ Quality Management (QM)

The interface to IM is most important when using Warehouse Management. The connection to delivery processing within Logistics Execution plays a particularly significant role in sales order processing. Generally, goods are picked on the basis of outbound deliveries. If you want to provide regular supply of components to production, you can use the interface to PP. Using the QM component; you can configure the interface to Warehouse Management to control how goods are dealt with inside the warehouse if they have to undergo quality inspection.

5.2.3 Organizational Structure

The warehouse number is the organizational unit at the highest level in Warehouse Management. In practice, the warehouse often corresponds to a physical building or a distribution center (DC). Figure 5.9 displays the substructure below the warehouse number.

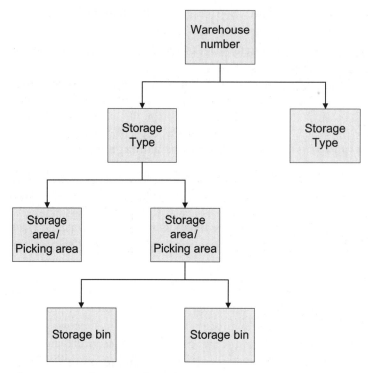

Figure 5.9 Warehouse Number Sub-Structure

Each warehouse number contains several subordinate organizational units (depending on the setting in Customizing): storage types, storage section, and picking areas. The storage type is used to map a storage space that forms a separate unit within a warehouse number, spatially and/or organizationally. A standard system already contains a certain set of pre-configured storage types; e.g., high rack, fixed bin, and bulk storage types.

The interim storage areas play a special role and can generally be recognized at first glance in the standard system by their key (a number beginning with a 9). The storage areas form a sort of bridge to Inventory Management. Goods receipt areas and goods issue areas are typical examples of interim storage areas. Every goods movement that affects both Warehouse Management and Inventory Management is processed using an interim storage area. An everyday example is a goods receipt for a purchase order, which is first posted in Inventory Management. Then the goods are brought into the warehouse via an interim storage area, the goods receipt area.

Storage sections are created within storage type to further subdivide the storage space. There can be various criteria for creating various storage sections.

Often, the material to be stored in the storage type plays an important role. The system only takes storage sections into account during put-away. The picking area is on the same hierarchy level as the storage section and can be used to subdivide the area of a storage type to control stock removal. The picking area is an optional organizational unit. Storage bins are represented in master data and are created within a storage section.

5.2.4   Delivery Processes with Warehouse Management

The goods receipt process with inbound or incoming deliveries, maps very accurately to normal procedures in many enterprises. The vendor sends notification of the goods receipt in the form of a shipping notification. The inbound delivery then can be created either manually or automatically on the basis of the shipping notification. The inbound delivery references for subsequent put-away with a transfer order.

A transfer order is required to put away goods that have been delivered. This transfer order is based on the inbound delivery and takes most of the data from inbound delivery for further processing. During the creation of the transfer order, the system determines the storage types, sections, and bins for put-away on the basis of master data maintained and Customizing setting defined. The process is complete when the goods receipt is posted in Inventory Management. Inbound delivery is a document used to receive the goods from your vendor or supplier into your stock. It prepares for goods receipt, and the warehouse management uses all the information within the delivery to process the inventory into your stock.

Stock Removal for Outbound Delivery

Generally, a sales order occurs at the beginning of the goods-issue process with outbound deliveries. The outbound delivery, which is at the center of the process, is created with reference to the sales order. The transfer order used to remove stock from storage is, in turn, based upon the outbound delivery. You need to let the system know that the picking process is complete by confirming the transfer order. Only then can you post the goods for the outbound delivery in Inventory Management.

Upon creation of the outbound delivery, the system attempts to determine a picking location for each document item. The picking location is actually the storage location. You set up the picking location determination for shipping in Customizing. A prerequisite is that the picking location determination has

been activated for the corresponding delivery item category. The system takes the following factors into consideration during the determination:

▸ Shipping point

▸ Supplying plant

▸ Material storage conditions

To create an outbound delivery against a sales order through application menu, use SAP Easy Access or the screen you see when you log on and follow this path: **Logistics • Logistics Execution • Outbound Process • Goods Issue for Outbound Delivery • Outbound Delivery • Create • Single Document • With Reference to Sales Order**.

When the location determination is selected, the system checks to see whether the determined storage location is assigned to a warehouse number in Customizing. If it is assigned to a warehouse number, a transfer order has to be created to remove the material from storage. Along with the warehouse number, the outbound delivery displays two statuses, which are:

▸ Total picking status

▸ Total status of transfer order

Upon the creation of a transfer order for an outbound delivery, the system determines a storage type for stock removal for each delivery item. The system then searches for stock according to the stock removal strategy that is valid for this storage type. You can influence or change the result manually.

To pick the delivery quantity with transfer order in background, use the menu path within the SAP Easy access or the screen you see when you log on to the SAP system and follow this path: **Logistics • Logistics Execution • Outbound Process • Goods Issue for Outbound Delivery • Picking • Create Transfer Order • Single Document**.

Once transfer orders are created, the stocks are removed from the bin and put away. The transfer orders need to be confirmed for the physical movement of the parts out of the bin. This process confirms the system's proposed quantity and actual picked quantity. While you are in the initial screen for confirming transfer orders, two control options are available: **Adopt pick quantity field** or **Option 2**. **Option 2** not only corrects the delivery quantity, but also triggers the goods issue posting directly after the correction, if any based on your actual picked quantity.

You can define the default values for the adjustment quantity in Customizing for Warehouse Management by following this path in Display IMG: **Logistic Execution • Warehouse Management • Interfaces • Shipping • Define Shipping Control**.

Pick and Pack

If you want to map the packing process of picked materials in the SAP ECC system or in SAP R/3, you can use the packing dialog for the outbound delivery. Delivery items are assigned to packaging materials to form packages. These packages are described as handling units in the system. This term was introduced in SAP R/3 4.6C, and it replaces the previous description of shipping unit. Often, the goods are picked for an outbound delivery and placed directly in the shipping container. This process is carried out in Warehouse Management in SAP ECC by the pick-and-pack function.

Collective Processing of Outbound Deliveries

Collective processing of deliveries allows you to process several deliveries instead of individual, based on some common criteria, such as end destination, route, or delivery date. This might help in planning, load distribution, and so on. Apart from the manual creation of single transfer orders for single outbound delivery, there are several options for collective processing, such as:

▶ Automatic creation of transfer orders with report RLAUTA20

▶ Group creation in the outbound delivery monitor and subsequent transfer order creation for the group

▶ Two-step picking

Two-step picking can also be used for groups of transfer requirements. The Customizing setting for two-step picking can be found in Display IMG by following the path: **Logistics Execution • Warehouse Management • Activities • Transfers • Set Up 2 step Picking for Transfer Requirement**.

If you use the two-step picking procedure, you can preset this by defining step 1 as withdrawal, and step 2 as allocation. To use two-step picking, you have to consolidate outbound deliveries into groups. The outbound delivery monitoring transaction code VL060 is the most suitable transaction for doing this. You can use the transaction VG01 to group outbound deliveries for processing.

> **Note**
>
> Wave picking is a special form of collective processing used in transfer order creation. Again, the outbound deliveries are grouped together for further processing. However, this time the selection takes into account time-based criteria, for example a common goods-issue time. In Customizing for shipping, you define when picking takes place during the work day. For each warehouse number, you also specify the compare time the system should take into account during the selection of the outbound deliveries. You can use the wave profile to set limits for weight and volume, and a maximum processing duration for each wave.

Return Transfer for Outbound Delivery

Sometimes a customer cancels an order at the last minute or wants to postpone the delivery. If goods have been picked and taken to the goods issue area, they have to be returned to storage. Up to and including SAP R/3 4.0, stock removals could only be reversed using a transfer order without reference. As of SAP R/3 4.5A, the transaction **Return to Stock for Delivery** (transaction code LT0G) makes this process much easier.

Whether you want to return all or some of the picked materials to storage, you can choose between the following options:

▸ Return transfer of the picked quantity to the picking bin

▸ Put away in another storage bin, possibly in another storage type

You can only return the materials to the picking bin if the storage type for the stock removal allows addition to stock, or if the storage bin was emptied as a result of the last picking activity.

Features Introduced with SAP R/3 4.7 Enterprise

You can create a group with WMS reference in the outbound delivery monitor as usual, in the following manner:

1. Set the Transfer Order (TO) for Multiple Delivery Indicator (**Mult.Del.**).

2. Navigate via this menu path: **Logistics · Logistics Execution · Goods Receipt Process · Goods Issue for Outbound Delivery · Picking · Create Transfer Order · For Multiple Deliveries**.

3. You can also use the transaction code LT0S.

The second feature introduced in SAP R/3 Enterprise was the option of delayed update of stock removal data in the outbound delivery during trans-

fer order confirmation. This feature was added to reduce system locks during the update process and to improve general system performance. This functionality is accomplished as follows:

▶ Updating the outbound delivery after confirming a tranfer order item

▶ Cumulated updating of the outbound after confirmation of the last item in the transfer order

▶ Updating the outbound delivery after confirming the last transfer order if there was an order split (several transfer order per outbound delivery).

Having understood the concepts of warehouse management, let's look at how this functionality is applied to a distributed environment or how you could use a decentralized WMS system with multiple ERP systems.

5.3   Decentralized Warehouse Management

If your company wants to separate warehouse processes from central processes, so as to make the warehouse processes run independently of the core system, you might want to evaluate the Decentralized Warehouse Management System with the SAP LE. You can use the ERP system for processes such as sales, material management, etc., and use a separate WMS for warehouse activities. The communication between ERP and WMS takes place via Business Application Programming Interfaces (BAPIs). Figure 5.10 displays an overview of the distributed WMS process.

5.3.1   WMS Applications

For incoming and outgoing processes, inbound or outbound delivery serves as a basis for activities in the warehouse. A BAPI is called when the delivery is saved. This BAPI starts the creation of an intermediate document (IDoc) and sends the delivery to the WMS, where the replication of delivery is done. This replication serves as a basis for subsequent processes in the warehouse, such as creation and confirmation of transfer orders, printing shipping documents, and posting goods movements.

Posting the goods issue (or goods receipt) clears the interim storage bin and calls a BAPI. This BAPI confirms to the ERP system the data that was created or changed in the WMS (such as, quantities, weight, packaging, and batches). When confirmation is received in the ERP system, the goods movement is executed in Inventory Management.

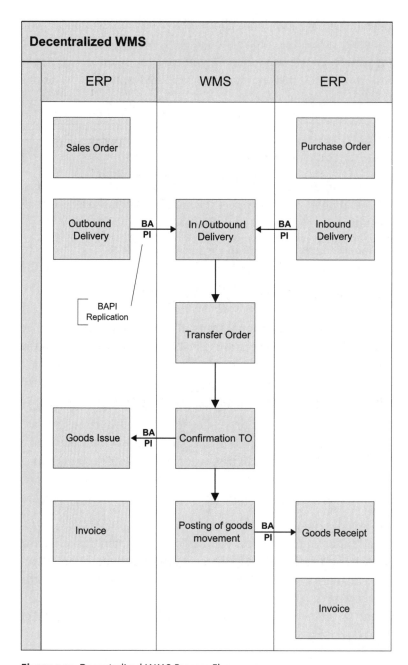

Figure 5.10 Decentralized WMS Process Flow

During the creation of a delivery, the system establishes whether the delivery is relevant for distribution. The delivery is only relevant for distribution when all delivery items match in plant and storage location, and the combi-

nation of plant and storage location is allocated to a warehouse number. The warehouse number carries the information about a decentralized warehouse management system. To use this function, you have to use the delivery split by warehouse number. A delivery can be distributed only if all items are determined for this warehouse.

5.3.2 Prerequisites for Connecting Decentralized WMS to an ERP System

You could use your decentralized WMS system to connect to several ERP systems, both SAP and non-SAP. To connect several ERP systems to a decentralized WMS, you need to consider the following:

▶ **Unique Numbers for Master Data in Decentralized WMS**
The various customer master records and vendor master records from the various ERP systems have unique numbers so that a master records can always be read clearly in the decentralized WMS.

▶ **Unique Numbers for Organizational Units in Decentralized WMS**
The various plants and storage locations must have unique numbers in the decentralized WMS.

▶ **Unique Delivery Numbers in Decentralized WMS**
In the decentralized WMS, the deliveries from the various ERP systems must be unique. Make sure that on replication of the deliveries, they are unique in the decentralized system. If the same delivery numbers come from several ERP systems, you can use customer exit V50S0001 and function module EXIT_SAPLV50S_001 to reassign the numbers. In this way, you can ensure that the delivery numbers in the decentralized system are unique.

In inbound and outbound deliveries, you can change certain data after the deliveries have been distributed from the central ERP system to the decentralized WMS. Changes can be made either in the central system or in the decentralized system.

5.3.3 Inbound and Outbound Deliveries

In contrast with the integrated scenario, inventory postings in the ERP system are not performed immediately. With the creation of the IM posting, an inbound delivery or outbound delivery is created and communicated to the WMS. With the confirmation of the delivery from the WMS, the posting in Inventory Management is executed automatically. Stock movements are pos-

sible where material is moved out of or into WMS. Posting changes are yet not possible. Stock movement is possible only in two steps. One-step movements are not possible in this scenario.

In the decentralized scenario, the delivery is the major means of communication between the systems. To reconstruct the status of the inbound or outbound delivery in the ERP system, a distributed status is used. This status indicates whether there is a decentralized scenario. If this is case, the status indicates whether delivery is relevant for distribution, distributed, or already confirmed by the WMS.

If the delivery has the status relevant for a decentralized scenario, the delivery can be changed. When the delivery is saved, the distribution to the decentralized system takes place. An ERP delivery with the status distributed can be changed only to a limited degree. The delivery can be changed in the WMS only. With the goods-movement postings in the WMS delivery, there is an automatic confirmation to the ERP system where the goods movements are executed in Inventory Management. To record this step, the distribution status is set to confirm and the goods movement status is set to Completely Processed. Invoicing can then be processed.

Deliveries in the ERP system are usually created with reference to a purchase order or sales order. This reference gets lost when the delivery is sent to WMS because the previous documents are not distributed. A delivery item reference provides information about the previous documents, using selected data from the purchase order or the sales order that is relevant for the WMS.

5.3.4 Distributed Model

Communication between the two systems takes place asynchronously. To enable this communication, a distributed model must be generated that contains all objects for the information flow.

The distribution differs in each installation. Therefore, you should create your own message types; e.g., sending master data, such as customer, vendor and material. So that WMS can work efficiently, only required master data should be distributed. Data that has local significance is maintained in the WMS; e.g., the WMS view in the material master. The following master data is distributed from ERP to WMS, based on need:

▸ Material
▸ Customer

- ▶ Vendor
- ▶ Classification
- ▶ Inbound and outbound deliveries

From WMS to ERP, the following master data and transaction data are distributed:

- ▶ Batches master
- ▶ Confirmation of inbound/outbound deliveries
- ▶ Inventory posting

Let's take a brief look at the procedure for setting up the distributed model, seen in the sequenced steps below:

1. Define a logical system to represent ERP and WMS in the ERP and WMS.

2. Before generating the distributed model, the reduced message type for material master, customer master, and vendor must be created. The generation can be set per warehouse number.

3. Use the filter to distribute certain views of the material or customer master. This is useful if the material master is maintained for different organizational units, but data in the WMS is only needed for one organizational unit.

4. If you need the address file, the distribution of the address is intended as an independent object. Therefore, you have a separate generation function to the final screen of the generation of the WMS distribution. After the generation, it is possible to generate the necessary parner profile for all messages and methods in the created model view.

5. The model view can be introduced to the WMS. The distributed model itself is sent to the WMS. With this step, the communication channels are known in the WMS.

6. Generate the partner profile in the WMS.

5.4   Summary

Logistics Execution offers you two basic means of mapping processes for goods receipts and goods issues. You can either make delivery creation or an inventory management posting, each with reference to the preceding document. The Logistics Execution component maps the logistics processes of a company. It covers the entire process chain from the vendor through the

warehouses, production facilities, and distribution centers, to the customers. Delivery represents the shipping and transportation function within the logistic execution.

If your company has warehouse management for stock movement, the delivery will be processed through Warehouse Management. We described the differences from the basic Inventory Management process and what additional process steps needs to be followed. One business scenario could be that your company wants to separate the warehouse processes from the central processes, to make the warehouse processes run independently from the core system. This is accomplished by the decentralized WMS.

Once you have delivered the goods or product to your customer, through these supply chain process, you want to bill your customer. Billing documents are generated within the SD process, but interface with the Financials component to transfer the data into the Financials and Controlling. In Chapter 6, we will look at the Financials and Controlling interface with SD.

When an order has been settled effectively, all services related to the customer are run as an integrated process. This interfaces with the Financials and Controlling component of the SAP ERP system. In this chapter, I will help you understand the tracking of sales process from the accounting point of view, provide an overview of the order-to-cash process, and explain the role of the interface between billing in Sales and Distribution (SD) and accounts receivable in Financials Accounting.

6 Financials and Controlling: Key Influence and Interface

During a sale, costs and revenues related to the sale are planned in the sale order item and are updated later in actual revenue. The planned revenues are calculated using pricing in the sales order. Planned revenues are compared to the planned costs. For stock products, these generally originate from a material master. The actual revenues are posted when invoicing takes place, whereby the evaluation of the cost of sales is also posted with the costing.

For made-to-order products, especially in the generation of services, plan costs can also be calculated individually on the sales order item. Base-object costing can, therefore, serve as a template. The actual costs result from the material removals, production orders, internal activity allocations, and surcharges that can be offset directly on the sale order item. The actual revenues and actual costs are settled in Profitability Analysis to determine profitability in conjunction with other sales characteristics.

To balance the planned consumption rates with the actual expenditure in Financials Accounting, you must carry out a period and closing for the cost centers. For sales-order items, the revenues are also posted directly to the order during invoicing. When the order is settled, you can transfer the costs and revenues directly to Profitability Analysis. This settlement is not necessary for Financials Accounting, since the costs and revenues have already been updated to the cost object from a Financials Accounting perspective.

The document defined in the SAP system make sale order administration easier for you and your customers. When you post data in SD, line items are created for delivery and billing in Financials Accounting as well as in Profitability Analysis. When you create the invoice, data from the sales order and the delivery is transferred to invoicing.

Sales process ends with billing of the customer for goods and service provided. Billing documents are used to interface the sales process with the finance and controlling.

6.1 Integration of Billing in SD Processes

The billing document represents the final function in the SD process chain. Billing is an important part of the financials interface. This allows documents to be created automatically in Financials Accounting and Controlling when you create billing documents. A billing document has structure similar to that of a sales document, with header and item. The billing type controls the billing document. The following is a list of billing types in the SAP system:

▶ **F2**
  Invoice, used for final customer invoice

▶ **F8**
  Pro forma invoice, used for printing documents without having to post to the invoice

▶ **G2**
  Credit memo, used for issuing credit for any returns to the customer

▶ **L2**
  Debit memo, used to issue debit for getting money not received from customer

▶ **RE**
  Returns, for generating any return document

▶ **S1**
  Cancellation invoice, if you want to cancel an invoice and issue a new one

▶ **S2**
  Cancellation credit memo

▶ **LR**
  Invoice list, to generate a list from multiple invoice

- ▶ **LG**

  Credit memo list, to list all the credit memos to a customer for a specific period

- ▶ **IV**

  Inter-company billing (invoice), used to post financial data between company codes, for inter-company goods movement

- ▶ **IG**

  Inter-company billing (credit memo), to issue credit between company codes

- ▶ **CS**

  Cash sale, for issuing invoice any sale made through without any delivery involved

Figure 6.1 displays the different types of control for which these billing types can be configured.

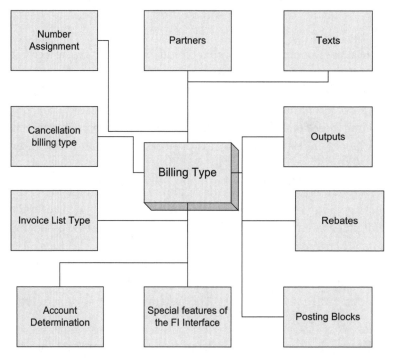

Figure 6.1 Billing Type Functions

The next important role is played by the item category, as it determines whether a billing can be carried out against sales order or delivery. The menu path for billing type definition can be found within Display IMG by follow-

ing this menu path: **Sales and Distribution • Billing • Billing Documents • Define Billing Types**.

The item category for billing relevance is maintained under this path: **Sales and Distribution • Sales • Sales and Distribution • Sales • Sales Documents • Sales Document Item • Define Item Categories**.

Choose item category **TAN,** and then click on the detail icon (magnifying glass), for TAN. In the Business Data screen, update Billing Relevance with **A** (= Delivery related billing document).

6.1.1 Special Billing

You might want to cancel an invoice, to correct any mistakes, in terms of wrong pricing or quantity, or some other error. To cancel a billing document, you must first create a cancellation document. The system copies data from the reference document into the cancellation and offsets the entry in accounting. The reference document of the billing document can now be billed again.

You can create a credit memo or debit memo request and than create a credit memo or debit memo based on this request, if your company has an approval process. If you prefer, you can create a credit memo and debit memo directly with reference to a billing document. With Customizing you can set a billing block automatically for a credit memo or debit memo request. This helps you establish a process of releasing a credit memo after review.

The invoice correction request represents a combination of credit and debit memo requests. On the one side, credit is granted fully for the incorrect billing item while it is simultaneously debited (automatically created as a debit memo item). When creating an invoice correction request, the items are automatically duplicated; this means that for every item in the billing document, a second item is created. The resulting item categories must have opposite positive or negative +/- values. The system delivery document type for invoice correction request is RK.

Quantity difference is used when processing a customer complaint for any quantity discrepancy caused by damaged or sub-standard goods. The system corrects the quantity to be billed via the debit memo item. If other item pairs arise from the relevant billing document and these item pairs are unchanged, they can be deleted in one step, using the **Delete unchanged** items function.

Price difference is used when a customer compliant is being processed for the incorrect pricing of goods. A correction of the pricing elements must be carried out in the debit memo.

Billing types for pro forma invoices are available for export transactions. You can create a pro forma invoice with reference to an order or deliveries. You do not need to post the goods issue before creating a delivery related pro forma invoice. You can create as many pro forma invoices as required, because the billing status in the reference document is not updated. Data from pro forma is not transferred to accounting.

For cash sales, payment is made when the goods are ordered. The invoice is also printed at this time. The SAP system offers a cash sale transaction for business transactions of this type. With cash sales, the order and delivery are created with one step, and goods issue is posted with different transaction. The order type is CS and it has its own output type RD03, which allows printing an invoice from the order. Figure 6.2 displays the billing type configuration setting for cash sale.

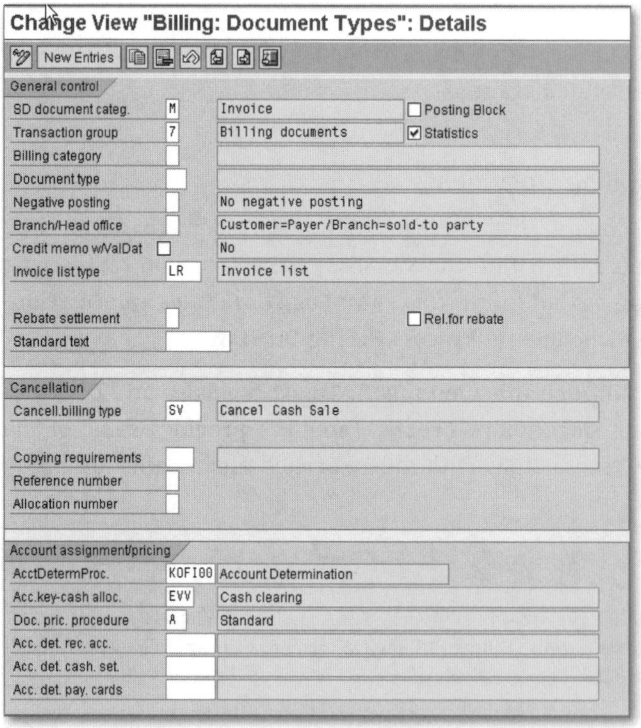

Figure 6.2 Billing Type Definition for Cash Sale

Pricing in the billing document carries the financial values and is used for posting into the appropriate account. At the time of billing, the following possible pricing types may be set for the items:

▶ **A**

The pricing elements are copied from the reference document and updated according to a scale.

▶ **B**

Pricing is carried out again.

▶ **C**

The manual pricing elements are copied, and pricing is carried out again for others.

▶ **D**

The pricing elements are copied unchanged from the reference document

▶ **G**

The pricing elements are copied unchanged from the reference document. The tax conditions are determined again.

▶ **H**

The pricing elements are copied unchanged from reference document. The freight is determined again.

6.1.2 Creating Billing Documents

You can use the billing-due list to create billing document (based on due date) using the menu path within the SAP Easy Access, or you can use the SAP screen as you log on and follow this path: **Logistics • Sales and Distribution • Billing • Billing Document • Process Billing Due List**.

The other option is through this menu path: **Logistics • Sales and Distribution • Billing • Billing Document • Create**. Table 6.1 provides some of the most popularly used transactions with the associated menu paths for billing documents.

Transaction Code	Menu Path	Function/Description
VF01/VF02/VF03	**SAP Easy Access • Logistics • Sales and Distribution • Billing • Billing Document • Create /Change/Display**	Create, display or change billing document

Table 6.1 Commonly Used Transactions in Billing Functions

Transaction Code	Menu Path	Function/Description
VF11	**SAP Easy Access • Logistics • Sales and Distribution • Billing • Billing Document • Cancel**	Cancel billing document
VF06	**SAP Easy Access • Logistics • Sales and Distribution • Billing • Billing Document • Background processing**	Create background job for billing
VFRB	**SAP Easy Access • Logistics • Sales and Distribution • Billing • Billing Document • Retro-Billing**	Allows you to evaluate the effect of new pricing on the billing document that have been already processed and settled
VSB1	**SAP Easy Access • Logistics • Sales and Distribution • Billing • Billing Document • Self-Billing Proceed**	Inbound monitor: SD self-billing procedure, status window
CMP_PROCESSING	**SAP Easy Access • Logistics • Sales and Distribution • Billing • Billing Document • Complaints Processing**	Complaint processing
VFX3	**SAP Easy Access • Logistics • Sales and Distribution • Billing • Billing Document • Blocked Billing Docs**	Displays billing document that are blocked for transfer to accounting
VF21 / VF22 / VF23	**SAP Easy Access • Logistics • Sales and Distribution • Billing • Invoice List • Create/Change/Display**	Create, change or display invoice list
VF26	**SAP Easy Access • Logistics • Sales and Distribution • Billing • Invoice List • Cancel/Reverse**	Cancel invoice list
VF24	**SAP Easy Access • Logistics • Sales and Distribution • Billing • Invoice List • Work List for Invoice Lists**	Creates work list for invoice list

Table 6.1 Commonly Used Transactions in Billing Functions (cont.)

Note

The self-billing procedure allows you to settle shipment costs without needing to receive an invoice. The Complaints Processing function allows you to enter a reason and create sales or billing document with reference to a billing document. You can change the quantity, unit of measure, material, and certain conditions in the items you create. You can also display credit memos and returns already generated for a billing document.

You need to define reason for complaints in Display IMG by following this path: **Sales and Distribution • Billing • Billing Documents • Define Reasons for Complaint.**

Invoice Split

As a rule, the system attempts to combine all compatible transactions in a single billing document. In the SAP system, you can include both order-related and delivery-related items in the same billing document. If the header partners or the data in the header fields are not identical, the system will automatically perform an invoice split. This split helps you separate the invoice based on the specific billing criteria and generate an invoice to the end customer from where the actual payment will be received. You can also define additional split requirements in Customizing for copying control to prevent the system from combining sales documents in a billing document. Field VBRK-ZUKRI is used in the billing header to store these additional split criteria. Fields that cause a split are displayed in the split analysis.

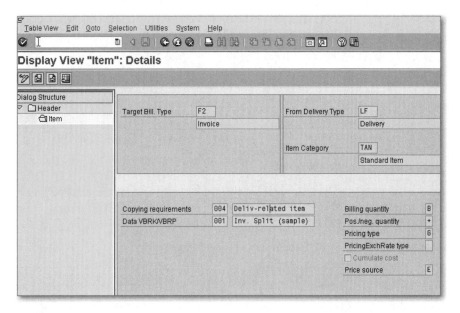

Figure 6.3 Copy Control

Let's say you want a restriction whereby you create one billing document per sales order. To do that, you need to code in the data transfer routine by setting the field ZUKRI in the table VBRK. Figure 6.3 displays the copy control where the data transfer routine is defined. In Figure 6.3 the routine, **001** –

Inv. Split (sample) is defined in the field **Data VBRK/VBRP. VNRK** is the header and **VBRP** is defined in the item table.

Invoice List

Invoices lists contain various billing documents (invoices and credit and debit memos) and can be sent to the payer on specified days or at certain intervals. The following Customizing step needs to be maintained within the Display IMG by following the path: **Sales and Distribution · Billing for Invoice List**. Keep the following in mind, while doing this:

▸ If you agreed for upon a factoring dicount, maintain condition type RL00 (factoring discount) as well as condition type MW15.

▸ Each billing type to be included in an invoice list must be assigned an invoice list type. The SAP standard version includes two invoice list types: LR for invoices and debit memos, and LG for credit memos.

The following are also the master data prerequisites for the invoice list:

▸ Define a factory calendar, which specifies when invoice lists are to be created. Enter this factory calendar in the payer customer master record (Billing screen, **Invoice list sched.** Field).

▸ Maintain condition records for condition type, RL00, for the payer.

▸ Create output condition records for condition types, LR00 and RD01.

Periodic and Milestone Billing

Periodic billing is often used for rental and service agreements, in order to bill the full amount periodically at certain dates. Milestone billing is often used in plant engineering and construction, in order to spread billing of the full amount over several dates within a billing plan.

Periodic billing is used for rental contracts. The start and end dates define the duration of the billing plan. During milestone billing, the total value to be billed is distributed among the individual dates according to certain rules. Billing plan dates are blocked for billing. A typical example of milestones is the billing of projects in plant engineering.

The billing plan may consist of rules that help define the billing process. A billing rule can be created for each billing plan date. This rule determines how the value to be billed on a particular date is determined. This allows you to define, for instance, whether a fixed amount or a percentage of the total

amount is to be billed. The differentiation of periodic billing and milestone billing with the relevant controlling parameters is carried out via the billing plan type. Billing type plan are configuration setting for maintaining the controlling parameter.

This is set up in Customizing within Display IMG via the following path: **Sales and Distribution • Billing • Billing Plan • Define and Assign Date Categories • Maintain Date Category for Billing Plan Type**.

Figure 6.4 displays a typical date category billing type plan. In this figure you can see that for **BillingPlanType 01**, the **Billing rule** is **4**.

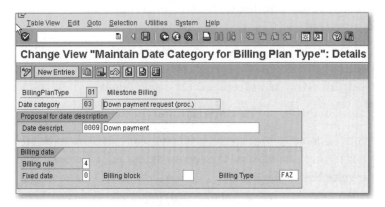

Figure 6.4 Billing Plan Type Definition

6.1.3 Payment Processing

When you get a payment from a customer that needs to be processed in the system, there are different ways of acknowledging this. If the payment is not processed or entered, it will appear in the accounts receivable as the payment to be processed or posted.

Down Payment Processing

Down payments are usually arranged with the customer when dealing with plant engineering and construction or capital goods. At the corresponding due date, a down-payment request is send to the customer. The down-payment request is automatically posted as such in Financials Accounting (FI). The item has a special General Ledger (G/L) indicator **F**, which ensures that posting is statistical. Posting is made to a different reconciliation account, which allows you to differentiate down-payment requests from other receivables.

When posting an incoming payment for a down payment, the incoming payment is assigned to the down-payment request. The item has a special G/L indicator A. Within FI, the down payments are deducted from the special reconciliation account and entered in the standard reconciliation account. Billing type FAZ is used to create the down-payment request.

Installment Payments

An installment payment allows the customer to pay in installments. Only one billing document is created for all the installment payments. The printed invoice is created on the basis of this billing document and includes a list of individual payment dates and exact amounts. Each installment payment creates an accounts receivable line item posting in Financials Accounting.

You must define installment payment terms in Customizing. For installment payment terms, you must specify the number and amount of the installment in percentage and payment terms for each installment payment. When you post an invoice with installment payment terms, the system will generate the appropriate number of postings in the accounting document, based on these specifications.

6.1.4 Reference Data for Account Posting

The system sends billing data in invoices, credit memos, and debit memos to FI and posts them to the correct accounts. Normally, the system automatically transfers accounting-related data to FI. However, you might not want the data to be transferred automatically for certain billing types. In that case you can set a posting block for the billing type concerned. The system will then generate the accounting documents only after you have released the billing documents. This allows you to generate SD billing documents first, then print out the billing documents and finally, transfer them to FI.

The system either generates all or none of the accounting documents. This means that if the posting is active, or errors have occurred during account determination, the system will not create Controlling (CO) documents. The accounting documents will not be created until you have deactivated the block or corrected the error. The following data can be changed before an accounting document is created:

- Billing date
- Pricing

▸ Account determination

▸ Output determination data

However, once the billing document has been released to accounts, you can only change output data.

Figure 6.5 displays the document flow and the document links between the reference numbers and allocation numbers. You can automatically fill in the **Reference number** and **Allocation number** field in the **Accounting Document** with numbers from SD documents. The reference number is the header of the accounting document and is used for clearing. The allocation number is in the customer line item and is used for sorting line numbers. In Customizing for copy control in billing, you can define the number that needs to be copied as reference or allocation number (A—Purchase order number, B—Sales order number, C—Delivery number, D—External delivery number, E—Billing document number, and F—External delivery number or—if available otherwise—delivery number).

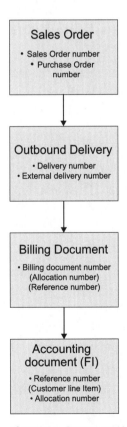

Figure 6.5 Document Link Between Different SD Documents

With reference to the invoice list, you must create billing documents and post them to FI before combining them in an invoice list. When the invoice list is created, the reference number from the invoice list overwrites the reference numbers from the individual billing documents. This enables you post incoming payment with the invoice list number.

Customer line items can be viewed with the SAP Easy Access or the SAP screen as you log on and follow this menu path: **Logistics • Sales and Distribution • Billing • Environment • Accounts Receivable or Accounting • Financials Accounting • Customers • Account • Display/Change Line Items**.

Billing documents help you carry the SD information or close the SD interface to Financials. The Financials interface calls for posting of invoice value, these invoice values are determined by the pricing and other condition values determined in the document. In the next section, we'll look at how account determination happens so that these values are posted to the right account.

6.2   Account Determination

Account determination helps the system find the right account to be determined based on the procedure and Customizing that are defined. With the goods issue or delivery document, the product or stock account is credited and offset as a change in stock. The invoice is the SD document that supports you when you are creating bills. It is used as a data source for FI to support you in monitoring and handling payments. If you create an invoice document, the G/L accounts are generally automatically updated. The SAP system executes a debit posting on the cash account of the customer and a credit memo on the receivable account of the customer. Table 6.1 illustrates the accounting part of the sales process.

Transaction	Delivery	Billing	Payment
Products	Credit	—	—
Stock Comparison	Debit	—	—
Customer	—	Debit	Credit
Revenue	—	Credit	—
Bank	—	—	Debit

Table 6.2 Account Postings for Sales Processes

6.2.1 Ex Stock Sale Process

To understand account determination more fully, look first at the activity output of the product. An expenditure (e.g., costs of the production order), that is paid through bank accounts) precedes both the external procurement of services and in-house production.

The outbound delivery in the order to cash process withdraws from this produced stock (thus reducing the stock account) and posts the delivery quantity multiplied by the material valuation price to the stock change account. Billing creates the income and the corresponding receivables, leading to a debit posting on your bank account.

6.2.2 Sale of Services

With the sale of a service, SAP recommends that a sales order item be used as a cost object. An example of service could be providing a repairing a part under warranty. An order-specific preliminary costing can be created for the cost unit. In this case, we are dealing with a sales-order calculation whose profits can be saved for the sales order as plan values. The actual cost incurred by rendering a service are changed directly to the order item; e.g., the service utilized by a cost center, use of materials by the warehouse, or externally procured goods and external services.

In comparison to the ex-stock sale process, the delivery of goods does not apply here. Billing creates the income and the corresponding receivable vis-à-vis the customer. The payment settles these receivables, leading to a credit memo on your bank account. In the ideal case, all accounts are settled exactly, except with an adjusted, higher bank balance. This occurs because the income is higher than the expenditure, which is also shown in the profit-and-loss statement by a corresponding profit.

6.2.3 Account Assignment Criteria

The system allows you to automatically post to the relevant accounts in FI for sales revenues, deductions, taxes, etc. The sales-revenue accounts are created in FI, to receive certain evaluations and to be able to carry out reconciliation with the Profitability Analysis. Therefore, you can set different criteria for account determination of the relevant accounts. Table 6.2 lists the criteria in the standard SAP system account-determination procedure.

Account Determination Element in Billing Document	How it Gets this Information?
Chart of accounts	Company code
Sales Organization	Assignment to the company code
Account Assignment Group for Customer	Payer master record
Account Assignment Group Material	Material master record
Account key	Assigned to the condition types in the pricing procedure. Example: ERL—sales revenue; ERS—sales reduction.

Table 6.3 Account Determination

You must ensure that the configurations you make for account determination match the configurations in FI and CO. Figure 6.6 displays a typical account-determination procedure. Account determination is carried out using the condition technique. An account determination procedure is assigned to bulling type, which in turn determines the G/L account (G/L). This determination procedure contains one or more condition types, and to these condition types access sequences are assigned. Access sequence is composed of individual accesses in the form of condition tables. The condition tables contain the fields and field combinations upon which revenue account determination depends. In Figure 6.6, you can see the steps and condition types.

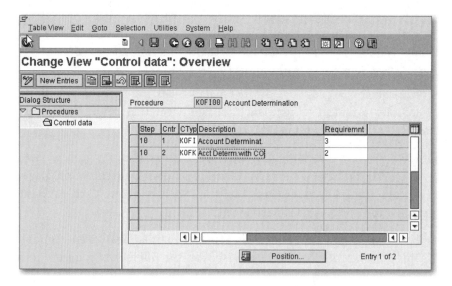

Figure 6.6 Steps and Condition Types for Revenue Account Determination

The key fields are filled with document data, so that the system can search for corresponding G/L accounts for the relevant combination. If an access determines a G/L account, then it is set in the accounting document and the search is terminated.

The following are the Customizing settings for Account determination set up and their menu paths in IMG:

▶ For Customer Accounts use the path: **Sales and Distribution • Basic Functions • Account Assignment/Costing • Revenue Account Determination • Check Master Data Relevant for Account Assignment • Customers Account Assignment Groups**.

▶ For Assign Account Keys use the menu path: **Sales and Distribution • Basic Functions • Account Assignment/Costing • Revenue Account Determination • Define and Assign Account Keys • Assign Account Keys**. Then, click on the appropriate pricing procedure and seach for the condition type, for which the account key is maintained.

▶ For Access Sequence use the menu path: **Sales and Distribution • Basic Functions • Account Assignment/Costing • Revenue Account Determination • Define Access Sequence and Account Determination Types • Maintain Access Sequences for Account Determination**.

▶ For Assign G/L Account use the menu path: **Sales and Distribution • Basic Functions • Account Assignment/Costing • Revenue Account Determination • Assign G/L Accounts**.

Figure 6.7 displays the configuration steps within account assignment/costing area. Here you have sections for **Revenue Account Determination, Revenue Recognition, Reconciliation Account Determination, Cash Account Determination** and **Business Account Assignment**.

There are processes within Financials Management that help you streamline the supply chain processes. In the next section, we will look at some of these processes.

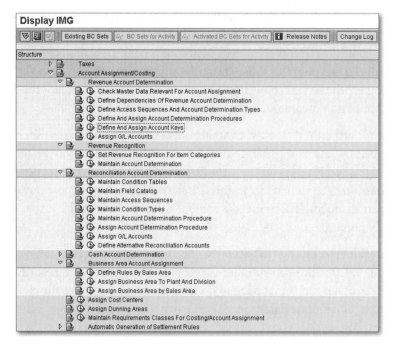

Figure 6.7 Account Assignment/Costing Configuration

6.3 Financials Supply Chain Management

Financials Supply Chain Management (FSCM) makes it possible to optimize the order-to-cash process during the pre-transaction phase and after contract fulfilment. The functions in FSCM are closely integrated with existing SAP R/3 functions and complement and/or optimize these.

Credit Management is a process management function in the FSCM. Credit Management enables cross-company credit-limit check and variable monitoring of a customer on all distribution channels. You can analyze customer credit limits, taking into account the credit policy of your company. Another available process is electronic bill payment, which helps you automate the payment receipt and posting process. Before we explore these processes in detail, let's understand the basic concepts of FI.

6.3.1 Financials Accounting

Financials Accounting focuses on the main ledger, the processing of receivables, payables, and asset accounting. Important tasks of FI are the recording of monetary and value flows as well as the evaluation of the inventories. The

G/L contains the recording of all accounting-relevant business transaction on to G/L account from business point of view. Every G/L is structured in accordance with a chart of accounts. The chart of accounts contains structured definitions of all G/L accounts in G/L. These definitions basically include the account number, the G/L account determination, and the categorization of the G/L account as an income statement or balance sheet account.

For reasons of clarity, the G/L often contains only collective postings. In such cases, the posting data is represented in a more differentiated way in so-called subledgers, which pass on their compressed data to the G/L. Reconciliation accounts link the subledgers to the G/L in real time. As soon as a posting is made to a subledger account, the same posting is made to the respective reconciliation account in the G/L.

Accounts Payable Accounting (AP) records all business transactions that have to do with the relationships to suppliers. Accounts Receivables (AR) records all the business transactions that have to do with the relationships to the customers. It takes much of its data from SD. The bank accounting supports the booking of cash flows.

6.3.2 Electronic Bill Presentment and Payment

Most bills still reach customers by mail. The traditional way of sending bills by post has various disadvantages, including, some that are listed below:

▶ Both the biller and the customer have to go through numerous individual steps to process the transaction. The biller prepares the bill and then sends it. The customer receives the bills and checks the content. This takes a lot of time and is subject to error.

▶ Creating a bill for mailing is expensive.

▶ Processing incoming payments can be very time-consuming, especially if only part of the bill is paid or if you cannot assign payments.

Electronic Bill Presentment and Payment enables you to prepare and display bills within different scenarios from B2B (Business-to-Business) and B2C (Business-to-Customer) using the Internet. Using Electronic Bill Presentment and Payment makes several individual processing steps superfluous. This reduces the amount of time required to forward the bill information to customer.

Electronic Bill Presentment and Payment can be implemented to show customers their billing information via the Web (Electronic Bill Presentment). The customer receives the billing information and can then carries out vari-

ous actions: The customer can arrange payments—e.g., by credit card or direct debit—or submit questions and complaints.

There is complete integration with the open items and bill data. Electronic Bill Presentment and Payment can also be integrated into industry-specific portals. These portals are also known as business packages. Figure 6.8 displays the Electronic Bill Presentment and Payment flow vs. traditional Invoicing. A traditional billing process will start with creating a bill, printing it, enclosure to mail it for payment. If the payment is not received, the company will send multiple reminders, and once the payment is received, it is posted and cleared.

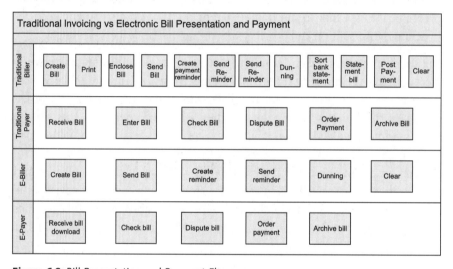

Figure 6.8 Bill Presentation and Payment Flow

You might want to sort out the statement to view the payment details. This is much simplified by receiving the bill, entering and checking it. There is definite added value in these processes, as you can focus your time on validating the bills before sending them. You can use the dispute bill for any dispute management and post the payment by order payment. Finally you can archive the bill.

There are three Electronic Bill Presentment and Payment Models, which we will now discuss below:

▶ **Biller Direct Model**
   In this model, the billers exchange their bills with several customers directly via the Internet (1: n relationship).

▶ **Thick Consolidator Model**

In this model, several billers exchange bills with several customers (n: n relationship) via consolidator. In both consolidator models, you can decide whether data is exchanged exclusively with the Thick Consolidator (complete use) or whether data is only partially exchanged with the Thin Consolidator (partial use). With the thick consolidator model, the invoicing party sends his or her invoices with all the detailed information.

▶ **Thin Consolidator Model**

In this model, the invoicing party supplies only the most important data (invoice header information). The invoice receipt is presented with only the invoice overview in the Consolidator Portal. For further details, the invoice receipt clicks a link to the home page of the invoicing party and receives detailed information and possibly marketing materials (cross-selling).

The Biller Direct model is defined so that there is no consolidator between the biller and the bill recipient. Once the purchase, order, and delivery have taken place, the bill is created. Purchase and order take place in the usual way; i.e., the bill is sent via the Internet. The customer then logs on the biller's home page and sees his bills displayed. The customer can either pay the bills directly from there, or transfer the information to his own system. The customer can download the information in Excel, and then upload it and convert it into incoming bills in the SAP system. If the customer pays via the Internet, the customer checks the collection authorization, or the customer sends payment notification to his bank, and the bank forwards the transfer to the biller's bank.

6.3.3 Credit and Risk Management

Credit Management helps you manage risk caused by outstanding receivables or bad debts. You can define credit limit to the customers you deal with, which helps you access the financial situation of a customer, based on your assessment or group of customers and get early warnings. Credit Management is part of the component of Accounts Receivables (FI-AR). Some features of credit management are as follows:

▶ Credit check can be automatic by the system, based on your company's requirement.

▶ Credit check can be part of your supply chain process:during order entry, delivery, goods issue, and so on.

▶ You can choose to notify the credit representative and employee automatically while the credit limit process unfolds during order processing.

▶ Credit representatives can take appropriate action following the warning, if they want to grant the credit or reject the credit.

▶ Credit Management can be used in a centralized financials system with the sales and distribution in several connected ERP systems.

Like Credit Management, you can run Risk Management via guaranteed-payment methods such as letters of credit, credit insurance, and payment cards. These forms of payment help you control payment of the sales document item You can use a secure form of payment such as letter of credit to try and minimize the payment risk. Beyond this, you can run Credit Management to create a credit limit to restrict the risk. Figure 6.9 shows how risk can be minimized by this approach, moving up from step to step in terms of security.

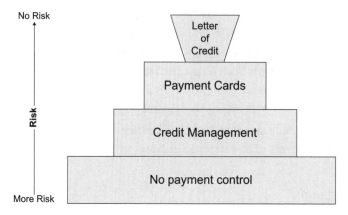

Figure 6.9 Risk Management

6.3.4 Settings

As a prerequisite for Credit and Risk Management, you should have already implemented FI-AR and SD. The master data for the customers whose credit you want to monitor needs to be maintained for SD and FI.

You define the credit limit for customer through the menu path: **Accounting • Financials accounting • Accounts receivable • Credit management • Master data • Change**. In the Customizing for Enterprise Structure you need to define one or more credit control areas and assign it to one or more company code, as follows:

▶ For Definition use the menu path: **Display IMG · Enterprise Structure · Structure maintenance · Définition · Financials Accounting · Maintain Credit Control Area**

▶ For Assignment use the menu path: **IMG · Enterprise Structure · Structure maintenance · Assignment · Financials Accounting · Assign Company Code to Credit Control Area and IMG · Financials Accounting · Accounts Receivable and Accounts Payable · Credit Management · Credit Control Account · Assign Permitted Control Areas to Company Code**

▶ For Assignment you can also use the menu path: **IMG · Structure maintenance · Assignment · Sales and Distribution · Assign Sales Organization to Company Code**

Here are other configuration steps to help you manage risk.

▶ For Risk Category use the menu path: **IMG · Financials Accounting · Account Receivables and Accounts Payable · Credit Management · Credit Control Account · Define Risk Categories**

▶ For Credit Limit use the menu path: **IMG · Sales and Distribution · Basic Functions · Credit Management/Risk Management · Credit Management · Define Automatic Credit Control**

▶ For Payment Guarantee use the menu path: **IMG · Sales and Distribution · Basic Functions · Credit Management/Risk Management · Receivables risk management · Define Forms of Payment Guarantee**

6.3.5 Value Contract

A value contract is a legal agreement entered into with a customer. It contains the materials and services that the customer receives within a specified time period, for a value up to a specified amount. A value contract can contain certain materials or group of materials. It states that your customer agrees to purchase a fixed-dollar amount of goods and services during the defined period. The value contract can contain other agreement between you and your customer that are checked in the release order, such as price agreements, customer restrictions, or material restrictions.

In SAP R/3 SD, you can list the materials that can be released in a value contract as a product hierarchy or as a list of valid materials (assortment module). An assortment module can be created within the products themselves and can be found under the SAP Easy Access or the SAP screen by following this path: **Logistics · Sales and Distribution · Master Data · Products · Value contract · Assortment module · Create.**

Normally, you create a release order with reference to a contract. Several functions exist for searching for relevant contract. Delivery quantities and times are stored in the schedule lines for the release order. You can create the releases in any currency, and the total values are updated in the currency of the contract.

You can define how the system responds when this value is exceeded. You can assign an order to a contract, either at header level or item level, but the contract values will only be updated if you assign it at the item level. Figure 6.10 displays the information flow of how the data or values are updated in the contract.

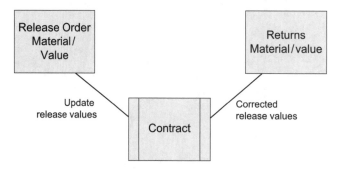

Figure 6.10 Contract-Flow of Information

You can bill the value contract directly or you can bill each release order. To bill a release order, you can use standard order OR. Billing can either be order or delivery related. The order type for billing contracts is WA. A billing plan allows you to bill the contract for several dates and quantities at one time. The transaction to create contract can be found under SAP Easy Access, by following this path: **Logistics • Sales and Distribution • Sales • Contract • Create**.

To create a release order, go to the contract change and within the sales document go to the menu to create the subsequent order. The configuration for item category needs to be defined for value contract. The menu path for this configuration step within Display IMG is: **Sales and Distribution • Sales • Sales Documents • Contracts • Value Contract • Define Item Categories For Value Contract And Contract Rel**.

Figure 6.11 displays the item category **WKN**, SAP standard supplied. As you can see the **Completion rule** is set to **E**, which stands for **Item is completed after full target value is referenced**. If you scroll down the screen (not seen in Figure 6.11), you will see the section **Value Contract**, where you will find

the **Contract Release** setting. You can set the **Contract Release** to warning or error, if the target value is exceeded.

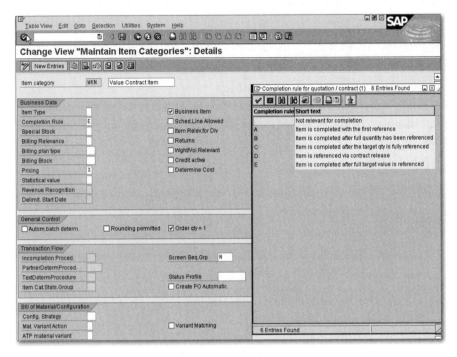

Figure 6.11 Completion Rules for Item Category

There are two types of value contracts in the standard SAP system, as seen below:

▶ **WK1**

General value contract, which allows you to refer different materials and services, according to the selection options.

▶ **WK2**

Material-related value contract, used when the contract contains one material.

The following are some key distinguishing points for value contracts, which need to be considered in processing these documents:

▶ In Customizing, you can distinguish between the sales document type for value contract WK1 and WK2 in the screen group for document header and item.

- You can maintain the value-contract material in the item category group. The value contract material acts as a technical vehicle in the contract item for determining important data, such as account assignments, taxes, or statistical updates.

- Document type WK1 is assigned to item cateogry WKN, and WK2 is assigned to WKC. Based on what you enter the item, the system chooses between two usage indicators: VCTR and VCIT.

- In copy control you can decide at item level if the value contract material should be copied to the release (WKC) or not (WKN).

- The standard pricing procedure WK0001 with condition type WK00 is used for agreed target value.

Companies' profitability is determined by the difference in cost and the final price charged to the customer. The internal cost is determined by the cost involved in either manufacturing them internally or procuring them externally. Let's now discuss the costing and profitability interface.

6.4   Interface with Profitability Analysis (CO-PA)

A profitability report identifies the profit for a certain market segment during a certain time period. Data such as sales quantity, revenue, shipment, and packing costs, discounts, and other sales deductions are transferred from SAP SD. This means that SD sends data to profitability analysis. After deducting various costs, the analysis calculates different profits, such as the contribution margin.

Every company needs to analyze its profits. For an extensive analysis, you need to describe and evaluate business transactions from a market-oriented viewpoint. Profitability analysis allows you to implement different profitability analyses because it examines the profitability of individual partial markets or market segments. You can define the market segments to match your requirements. They are identified by characteristics such as customer, product, division, sales organization, distribution channel, and so on. The system determines important sales figures for each segment and uses them to calculate the profits. The evaluations and analyses may form the basis for any future decisions in various areas in the company.

6.4.1 Evaluation and Reporting

Controlling uses special organizational units for its evaluations. The first level is the operating concern. This represents the marketing side of the company and describes the sales market in a uniform manner within an operating concern. The operating concern can be subdivided into different partial markets. An operating concern includes one or more controlling areas. The controlling area is a cost-oriented organizational element used to represent a closed system for cost accounting purposes.

The controlling area includes one or more company codes. When transferring data from SD to CO, the system finds the relevant operating concern by following the following assignment sequence:

- **Sales Organization**
  This represents the organizational structure that is reponsible for selling goods and services.

- **Company Code**
  This represents the smallest organization unit of Financials Accounting for which a complete self-contained set of accounts can be drawn up for purposes of external reporting.

- **Controlling Area**
  This represents an organization unit within a company, used to represent a closed system for cost accounting purposes.

- **Operating Concern**
  This represents part of the organization for which the sales market is structured in uniform form..

Table 6.4 shows you the different aspects of these organizational elements for reporting.

Organizational Unit	Reporting
Operating concern	Market oriented
Controlling areas	Costing oriented
Company codes	Balance sheet oriented
Sales organizations	Sales oriented

Table 6.4 CO-PA Reporting With Organization Elements

Evaluations are carried out by comparing costs and revenues and take place within an operating at the level of profitability segments. A profit is calcu-

lated for each profitability segment. Profitability segments are partial markets or market segments in the operating concern that are uniquely identified with classifying characteristics.

6.4.2 Profitability Analysis Procedures

There are two procedures for profitability analysis, as seen below:

▸ Costing based

▸ Account based

Both procedures can be used in parallel. However, before drill-down reporting you must select either a costing based or an account based procedure. With cost-based analysis, data is transferred when it is created immediately with current data and transfer value and quantity fields. With account-based profitability analysis, data is transferred when it is posted to FI, it corresponds to finance, and transfer is done at account level.

Figure 6.12 displays the data transfer with these two different procedures. In costing-based profitability, data is transferred to CO-PA as soon as an order is entered. The system generates a line item with a profitability analysis document for each sales order item. In the same way, the billing data is also transferred online. The system generates a line for each billing item. In account-based profitability analysis, data is transferred to CO-PA when it is posted to FI from Sales and Distribution.

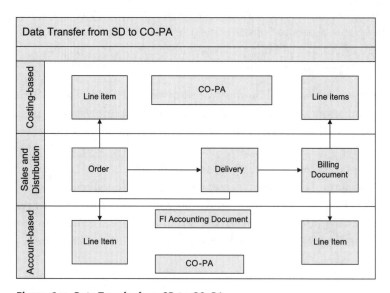

Figure 6.12 Data Transfer from SD to CO-PA

This means that when the FI documents are generated for goods issue and in billing, the system creates line items in CO-PA and transfers the data to the accounting valuation base. Data is not transferred when a sales order is entered because nothing is posted to FI at that stage.

CO-PA calculates the profit for a certain profitability segment by transferring data from SD. In costing-based profitability analysis, the key figures are the quantity and value fields such as price, quantity, discount, and weight. This data comes from SD documents. In account-based profitability segments, the evaluation takes place in account groupings. The data is taken from the relevant accounting documents in FI.

An important part of the billing document is its interface with FI. This allows documents to be created automatically in FI and CO when you create billing documents. In FI, the business transactions are created, saved, processed, and posted at company code level. Because a unique assignment is made between sales organization and company code, the company code is automatically determined when you enter the relevant sales organization in the sales order. The business area represents an organizational unit for which you can carry out internal reporting.

6.5   Summary

The term billing document refers to the information from the previous sales transaction in invoicing to the customer. There are documents used for statistical purpose and others for posting into the account. In this chapter we looked at some of the special billing documents, meant for specific purposes and already predefined in the system.

Account determination is based on the procedure maintained in the system. Account determination helps determine the right account into which to post the financial values. The payment processes are then posted to acknowledge the receipt of payment. The financial system integrates well with the supply chain management processes through Financials Supply Chain Management. It optimizes the supply-chain management processes. We looked at two of these functions: Credit Management and Electronic Bill Presentation and Payment. The costing information is passed on from the SD document to the CO-PA. The COPA provides the profitability analysis on the sales transactions.

Finance closes the transaction that started with the sales order. There are other processes embedded within SD to enhance the process. Quality Management is one of these. Service Management, another function derived from SD, helps you manage the service processes within your company. Chapter 7 will highlight the influence of QM and SM on SD Processes.

Customer service, a process within Service Management (SM) involves selling and providing services and associated products. Customer returns and repair are derived from the combination of customer service and sales order process. Quality Management (QM) is embedded within the entire process flow of sales and production to delivery and service. Quality Management involves quality inspection, certificate within the sales order and delivery process. Workflow is used as a notification and approval tool within the QM and SM functions.

7 Influence of SM and QM in SD Processes

Companies would like to implement quality management within the sales and distribution processes. SAP Quality Management (QM) supports every aspect, from sales and production to delivery and service. Examples include sales order, purchasing, production, inspection, storage, shipping, complaints, and returns.

Let's take the example of a make-to-order product; here the customer requirement and characteristics are specified in the sales order. You can use these characteristics to inspect the part in production. While shipping the product to the customer, you can include the certificate that the product complies with the customer specifications. With make-to-stock production, products are manufactured and inspected according to your own specifications and standards. You can use batch determination to meet customer specific requirements in the sales order or delivery, and when you ship the part you could generate a certificate stating that the product meets the customer specifications.

SAP's customer complaint and returns functions have integrated quality-management processes. You can represent a complaint in a quality notification. Workflow will help you process the complaint, as we will explain later in this chapter. When goods are returned, inspections can be performed during the receipt, and then you take follow-up action.

Customer services can be considered as an extension of SAP Sales and Distribution (SD). Customer service supports the execution of services, such as help desk, with recording, processing, and forwarding of incoming customer requests. The other processes are assembly of technical objects on site at the customer, dispatching the spare parts to the customer, and repair of the customer devices by field service technicians on site at the customer. The process continues with repair of customer devices in the service center, with regular inspection and preventive maintenance of customer devices in the service center or the customer site, and regular inspection and preventive maintenance of customer devices in the service center or at the customer site. The service could be agreed to in a contract or provided without contractual cover.

Service Management is processed through service order and notification. We will cover this in detail in Section 7.1

7.1   Service Management

Customers are service recipients. They might own technical assets and equipment. These technical assets and equipment need service. The service provider concludes with the customer, in which particular services are agreed. If the customer requires a service, they report the requirement or enter a request. The service provider might issue a quotation for extensive work. The request for service is initiated by the customer by sending a purchase order.

The service provider plans the work and resources required (personnel, material, utilities). If necessary, work is requested from the vendors or required materials ordered from the vendor. After the work is completed, the service provider issues an invoice. The process is completed when the customer makes a payment. Figure 7.1 displays the organizational elements for a service order processing.

In Figure 7.1, note that **Group** corresponds to the client. As part of the consolidation, **Group** is divided into companies. The **Company Code** is assigned to **Company** and the **Controlling Area**. The **Controlling Area** is the highest-level organizational unit in cost accounting and comprises one or more company codes. In Profitability Analysis (CO-PA), the operating concern is the highest-level organizational unit. Work centers represent people or groups of people assigned to a plant and cost center. People can be assigned to organizational management and to work centers. Cost centers, work centers, peo-

ple, and organizational units are master data. All other organizational elements are maintained in Customizing.

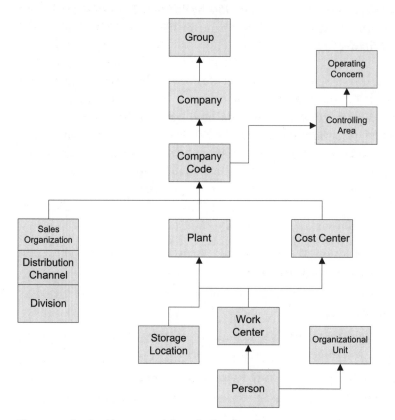

Figure 7.1 Service Management Organization Structure

Work centers are maintained through the menu path: **Logistics • Customer Service • Service Processing • Environment • Work centers • Work Center • Create/change or display**. The definition and assignment of plants, planning plants, storage location, sales area, company code, etc. are maintained in Customizing under Enterprise Structure. The planning plant is a plant where you create service orders. Organization units are created under Organizational Management in the Human Resource application component.

Material Master for Service Applications

Material master records are used for different purposes in service. Service material or service products are used to describe services provided for the customer. These service products can be entered in the items of a sales order

or a contract, and in the header data for service order. Materials can be fixed, configured, or configurable. An individual description of the service features for configurable materials is made possible by characteristics valuation in the order. For configured materials these characteristics values are connected to the material master.

Technical Objects

When managing technical objects, material numbers can be enhanced with serial numbers to track individual units. Material numbers are used to represent types of customer equipment. Alternatively, material records can be used in bills of material items to structure the technical objects more accurately as assemblies and spare parts. In service processing, materials are used to describe the components that are sent to customer. There are four categories of technical objects, as seen below:

▶ Functional locations are elements in a technical structure and represent areas of a system at which objects can be installed.

▶ Pieces of equipment are individual objects that are to be regarded as autonomous units.

▶ Serial numbers are materials which can be considered as individual items through the assignment of a serial number.

▶ Assemblies are used to structure functional locations and pieces of equipment in more detail.

7.1.1   Documents in Customer Services

Table 7.1 displays different document types and the characteristics they represent.

Process	Entry of customer inquiry	Planning tool	Cost collector	Relevant for billing	Relevant for delivery
Service Notification	Yes	—	—	—	—
Service Order	—	Yes	Yes	Yes	—
Customer Repair Order	—	—	Yes	Yes	Yes
Sales Order	—	—	Optional	Yes	Yes

Table 7.1 Service Document Type

The customer repairs order is a special form of sales order and is used for returns and repairs processing. You can generate service orders from the customer repairs order to plan repair work. The sales order contains an agreement with the customer regarding the delivery of certain goods or the performance of certain work. Figure 7.2 displays the information captured in a typical notification structure.

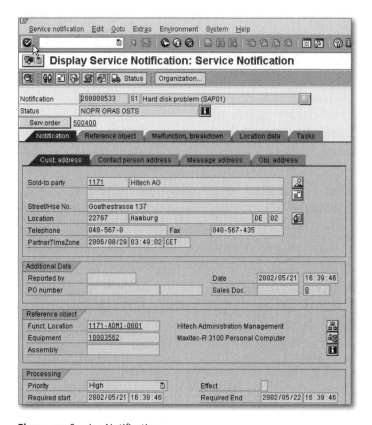

Figure 7.2 Service Notification

The notification header is where you maintain data for customer and contact person, such as partner information, employee responsible, and technical reference objects such as functional location, equipment, serial number, and assembly.

In Figure 7.2, the **Notification** tab and the **Cust.address** sub-folder have been shown as selected. The first section displays the customer address, **Sold-to party** and the address. The **Reference object** area displays the equipment details; e.g., the location or identification number. The description of the

problem is entered in the short text, next to the **Notification** number at the top **Hard disk problem (SAP01)**. The execution data contains the notification priority, deadline, and details of the department responsible for processing the notification. This information can be seen within the Processing section in the lower part of Figure 7.2.

The notification items (not shown in the figure) are used to give an exact description of the problem that has occurred by selecting codes to specify the object parts, damage, and cause of damage. Task describes the activities that must be performed to solve the customer's problem. The task status indicates whether the tasks are outstanding, released, or already complete. Activities likewise can be assigned directly to the notification header or to item.

7.1.2 Notification Types

Notification is a key object in the service processing and is configured in the Implementation Guide (IMG). Notifications in the system are represented by notification types. When you create a notification type, you initially use the origin indicator to assign it to the notification category Service, Plant Maintenance, or Quality Management. You can define default values for a catalog profile for catalog selection for each notification type. This catalog profile will only appear in the notification if you have not maintained a catalog profile in the notification object.

You can configure the screen templates for the notification type so as to structure the interface for the notification type individually. You can assign the following three order types to the notification types:

▶ Default service order type for notification without contract

▶ Default service order type for notification with contract

▶ Sales document type for sales orders created from the notification

If automatic contract determination is activated when you create a service notification, then, when you enter the reference object, the system checks if valid service contracts are available for the customer or reference object in the notification. The settings for the credit limit check contain the type of check and the assignment of order type to a credit group Order.

To enter partner information in the notification, you must assign a partner determination procedure to the notification type. You can also use standard functions from workflow to define partner functions for notification and task processor. If individual user statuses are assigned in addition to the system status, then you must assign notification type to a user status profile.

Let's now go over some of the key configuration steps required for setting up the notification:

1. **Define Notification Type**
   You can do this either by reviewing the existing one or by creating a new one by copying with reference to the standard one. Make necessary changes per your business requirements. The IMG path for notification types is: **Plant Maintenance and Customer Service • Maintenance and Service Processing • Maintenance and Service Notifications • Notification Creation • Notification Types • Define Notification Types**.

2. **Maintain Screen Templates for Notification Type**
   These screens appear as you try to create notifications or enter data for notification creation using notification type. For maintaining screen templates, this is the configuration: **Plant Maintenance and Customer Service • Maintenance and Service Processing • Maintenance and Service Notifications • Notification Creation • Notification Types • Set Screen Templates for Notification Types**.

3. **Maintain Long Text and Field Selections**
   Texts are used for updating the issue or the problem for which service is required. To configure long text control, use the following configuration: **Plant Maintenance and Customer Service • Maintenance and Service Processing • Maintenance and Service Notifications • Notification Creation • Notification Types • Define Long Text Control for Notification Types**. To configure field selection, while you are in the Notification Types sub-tree, go to **Set Field Selection for Notifications**.

4. **Define and Assign Order Type**
   The defined notification type needs to be assigned to an order type, as these notification types are converted into regular order for process it through the supply chain. For assigning order types follow this path: **Plant Maintenance and Customer Service • Maintenance and Service Processing • Maintenance and Service Notifications • Notification Creation • Notification Types • Assign Notification Types to Order Types**. For defining order types and special parameters, follow this path: **Plant Maintenance and Customer Service • Maintenance and Service Processing • Maintenance and Service Notifications • Notification Creation • Notification Types • Define Order Types and Special Notification Parameters**.

5. **Define Action Boxes**
   Actions are required to trigger tasks and activities from notification type. To configure action boxes, follow this menu path: **Plant Maintenance and Customer Service• Maintenance and Service Processing • Mainte-**

nance and Service Notifications • Notification Processing • Additional Functions • Define Action Box.

6. **Define Print Notification**

   You need to configure this if you want to enable printing of forms. For printing notifications, go to Plant Maintenance and Customer Service and follow this path: **Maintenance and Service Processing • Maintenance and Service Notifications • Notification Processing • Notification Print Control.** Then define **Shop Papers**, **Forms** and **Output Programs**.

7. **Define Partner Determination**

   As with any sales document type, you need to define partner determination. For configuring Partner determination and assignments go to Plant Maintenance and Customer Service and follow this path: **Maintenance and Service Processing • Maintenance and Service Notifications • Notification Creation • Partners • Define Partner Determination Procedure and Partner Function.**

8. **Object Information**

   This contains master record fields for equipment or functional location, and information about tasks already performed. By defining and assigning this, you can display the information about equipment in the notification or order processing. For configuring Object information, go to Plant Maintenance and Customer Service and follow this path: **Maintenance and Service Processing • Maintenance and Service Notifications • Notification Processing • Object Information • Assign Object Information Keys to Notification Types.** While creating the notification, object information will appear for capturing details about the equipment or functional location.

9. **Catalog Profile**

   The catalog captures the qualitative information for processing a notification type. For example, if the technician is performing a service, he or she can pick from the catalog the list of services to be performed to solve the problem. Menu path: For Creating Catalog Profile. go to Plant Maintenance and Customer Service and follow this path: **Maintenance and Service Processing • Maintenance and Service Notifications • Notification Creation • Notification content • Define Catalog Profile.**

10. **Response Time**

    Here you define how you would like to respond to a notification, in terms of priority and how much time to devote to resolve this problem. For defining response time, follow the menu path:. **Plant Maintenance**

and **Customer Service · Maintenance and Service Processing · Maintenance and Service Notifications · Notification Processing · Response Time Monitoring · Define Response Monitoring**.

You can get an overview of all necessary configuration needed for notification type by going to Display IMG and then following this path: **Plant Maintenance and Customer Service · Maintenance and Service Processing · Maintenance and Service Notifications · Overview of Notification Type**. Now you have defined and configured the notification steps.

To test your newly configured notification type, use the menu path: **Logistics · Customer Service · Service Processing · Notification · Create (General)**.

For creating catalog while in SAP Easy Access, or the screen you see, as you logon, follow this path: **Logistics· Customer Service· Service Processing· Environment· Catalog · Code Groups· Individual Maintenance**. Here is the menu path for maintaining the solution database: **Logistics · Customer Service · Solution Database · Create**. There are four possible options:

▶ Create

▶ Display

▶ Change Symptoms

▶ Solution

7.1.3 Catalogs

In catalogs, code groups are combined according to content. Depending on the notification type, you can access catalogs for object parts, damage and causes of damage, tasks, activities, and coding in the notification. In code groups, codes are combined according to related contents. Codes are used to describe a particular type of damage, an activity, and so on. Table 7.2 provides the structure of a catalog along with an associated business example.

Structure of catalog	Example
Catalog	Defect
Code Group	Mechanical or Electrical
Code	01 — Corrosion 02 — Broken arm 03 — Internal damage

Table 7.2 Catalog Structure

Here is the sequence for setting up catalogs:

1. Maintain catalog types and check them.

2. Define code groups for each catalog type. Codes with related to contents are grouped together into code groups.

3. Create catalog profile. In the catalog profile, one, several, or all of the code groups are assigned for each catalog type.

4. Assign the catalog types to each notification type for the following pre-defined areas:

   ▸ Coding

   ▸ Problems

   ▸ Causes, Tasks

   ▸ Activities

   ▸ Object parts

7.1.4 Solution Database

The system can propose the tasks to be performed when you enter or process a notification. These are referred to as solutions. Each system is assigned to a symptom type. The symptom type is used to define which catalogs are used to describe the symptoms, object parts, and causes, of problems and symptoms. Each symptom type can be subdivided into symptom categories for more exact classification. The object type defines which business objects (e.g., material, equipment, etc) can be assigned to symptom. Each solution is assigned to a solution type. Each solution type can be further subdivided into solution categories.

Notifications are converted into service order for processing. Section 7.2 will detail service-order processing.

7.2 Processing Service Orders

You can create a service order directly, by entering the order type and planning plant. You can also create a service order from notification. If several notifications are combined in an order, these will appear in the object list for the order. To create a service notification with a service order, you can go to the menu path: **Logistics • Customer Service • Service Processing • Notification • Create (Special) • Problem Notification.** Confirming a service order is

under the menu path: **Logistics • Customer Service • Service Processing • Confirmation • Entry • Overall Completion Confirmation**.

You can automatically generate a service order for planning, executing, and confirming services sold in this sales order from a sales order item. The material entered as sales order item also must be recorded in the service product master data. Figure 7.3 displays the process flow in service-order processing.

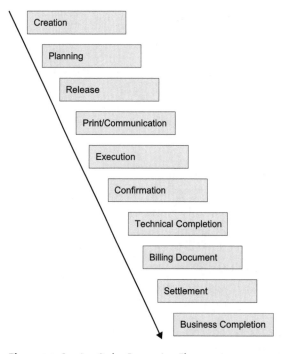

Figure 7.3 Service Order Processing Flow

The process step shown in Figure 7.3 represents all the steps involved in service-order processing. You can skip certain steps, like printing and confirmation, or perform certain steps simultaneously, e.g., you can perform execution and confirmation in one step. You can also automate certain steps such as billing, settlement, and conclusion.

7.2.1 Order Components

Order components have three different item categories as seen below:

▸ **Stock Items**
Material to be withdrawn from a warehouse for the order. Reservations are created.

▸ **Non-stock Items**

Material to be obtained specifically for the order. You do not have to enter a material number. Purchase requisitions are created.

▸ **Text Items**

User-defined text is entered. Text items are used for materials without material master records or for comments.

Stock material goes through the process flow of component assignment with the sequence of availability check, material reservation, order release with automatic availability check, printing, and goods issue.

Non-stock material process flow goes through the sequence of component assignment, purchase requisition, purchase order, order release, goods receipt, and invoice receipt.

7.2.2 Advance Shipment

Advance shipment sends the information of a shipment coming to the interested party. As a vendor yourself, you might send a note to your customer or you might expect the same from your vendors. The customer consignment enables you to optimize the process of advance shipment. A sales order of sales document type consignment fill-up (CF) is created from the service order. This makes it possible to bill the spare parts after the consumption posting. Deliveries of the materials required are generated based on this sales order. The materials are posted to customer consignment stock.

The customer consignment stock is reduced as a result of the consignment withdrawal. The goods movement is assigned to the service order. In resource-related billing of the service order, the customer is charged for the materials withdrawn from the consignment stock. Materials that are not required can be posted back from the customer consignment stock into your own stock using a sales order of sales document type consignment pick-up (CP) or manual goods movement.

Resource-related billing is processed using the transaction under the menu path: **Logistics • Customer Service • Service Processing • Completion • Billing Request • Process Individually**.

7.2.3 Customer Consignment

In consignment processing, goods are delivered to the customer but remain the property of the company until they are actually used. An invoice is not

created until the customer withdraws the goods from the consignment stock. The customer has the right to return consignment goods up to that point. You can use the special stock partner function if the consignment stocks are managed at a central point rather then by the sold-to party. Figure 7.4 illustrates the process flow for customer consignment.

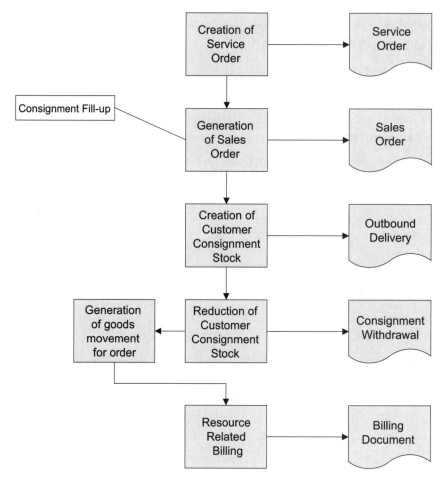

Figure 7.4 Customer Consignment Flow

Consignment Fill-Up and Issue

The process of consignment fill-up is accomplished by the order type CF, which is delivered in the standard SAP system. The goods issues are set up as a special CF order type, which is already defined in SAP stock at the customer's location. However, the goods remain in the valuated stocks of the delivery plant. Consignment issue is processed with order type, CI. When

goods are issued, both the customer's special stock and the stock in the delivery plant are reduced. This transaction is relevant for billing. Consignment fill-up flows follows these process steps:

- Outbound delivery
- Goods issue
- Customer special stock. consignment issue flows
- Outbound delivery
- Goods issue
- Billing document.

Consignment Pick and Return

Consignment pick and return work together, with return following the pick-up. If the customer returns the goods, you can represent this with order type CP. This transaction credits the special customer stock during the goods issue. Like consignment fill-up, this transaction is not relevant for billing. If you want to reverse a consignment issue, you can process this with document type consignment return (CR). The goods issue again sets up the special stock at the customer's location. A credit memo is generated based on the consignment return.

7.2.4 Paging and Mobile

During notification and order processing, you can send short messages to one or more partners using a pager. These short messages can also be predefined standard texts. You can also send messages using the Internet or SAP Office.

The partner function that you specify on the partner data screen must be assigned to one of the following partner types using the partner determination procedure. The following data must be also defined for the partners, as seen below:

- **Contact Person/Customer**
  The communication type PAG must be entered in the address for this partner under **Further communication**.
- **System User**
  The communication type PAG must be entered in the address for this partner under **Further communication**.

▶ **Personnel Number**
The personnel number must contain info type 105 (communication) and be assigned to a system user name. The communication type PAG must be entered in the user master record under **Further communication**.

▶ **Address or User Master Record**
You must also define in each address or user master record this subtype of the pager service available to the partner, and define one service as a standard service.

▶ **Partner Function**
You must define partner function for paging in Customizing for relevant notification or order type.

To send pager messages, you must define subtypes for the pager services in Customizing with Basis Components. When defining subtypes, check the availability of the information that the paging providers certified for the SAP system. The standard text table for notification is VIQMEL and for order is CAUFVD. The standard text needs to be assigned to notification type or order type in Customizing. Standard text can be created under the menu path: **Tools · Form printout · SAPscript · Standard Text**. Figure 7.5 shows the architecture and technology behind the paging.

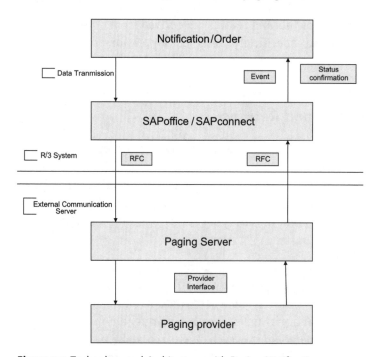

Figure 7.5 Technology and Architecture with Paging Notification

Field personnel might use the mobile device for performing their tasks or entering updates into the system with service-order processing. A mobile device could be a handheld device, used for getting specific information on the service to be performed and acknowledgement back. The process works as follows:

1. The processor enters the personnel number of the technician in the service order operation, and then releases the order.

2. The next time a technician calls up the order list, the data is transferred to the mobile device. The technician can see the operation detail screen by clicking on the hyperlink.

3. The technician confirms the time required and material consumed on the mobile device, then performs technical completion confirmation.

The prerequisite is that the user master record must be linked to the personnel master record for the technician who is logging on to the Internet server. To do this, enter the user (info type 0105 and communication type 0001) in the personnel master record. If you also want to represent the technician as a customer, you have to link the customer and personnel master records for the corresponding company code.

Notification and service-order processing are the two key processes of Service Management. Complaints and returns are derived from notification and service-order processing, specifically designed for customer returns and repair.

7.3 Complaints and Returns

Repair processing is initiated with a customer's request to repair a defective serviceable item by creating a service notification. A customer repair order is created from the notification. You can also create a customer repair order to start with. Figure 7.6 displays the flow of the repair process. The part or item to be repaired is received into the customer special stock for the repair order when a goods receipt is posted.

Technicians perform technical checks. During this process, the technician decides which operations are necessary to fulfill the customer's requirements. The results of the technical checks are confirmed in order. If the technical check indicates that a part is not worth repairing, the material can be scrapped, and a credit memo and/or exchange parts can be delivered to the customer. If the item is worth repairing, the system generates a service order

describing the technical execution of repairs. Once the repair has been completed, you return the item to the customer. The cost of the repair or the previously agreed fixed price is then billed to the customer. Repair processing is initiated by a customer repair order through the menu path: **Logistics • Customer Service • Service Processing • Order • Customer Repair • Create**.

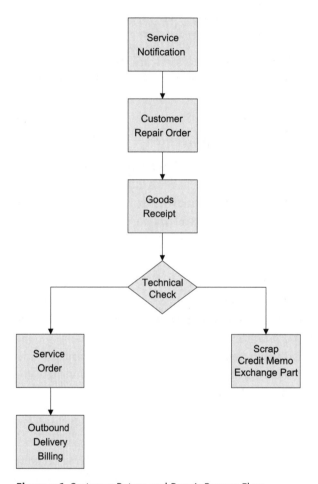

Figure 7.6 Customer Return and Repair Process Flow

An item is created in a customer repair order for each serviceable item category or material number (repair request item). The system typically generates a return item as a sub-item of this. Depending on the results of the technical check on the customer part received upon goods receipt, the system generates one or more sub-items. These represent extended an business process: repair, delivery of exchange parts, scraping, or creation of a credit memo. The system automatically generates a service order from the sub-item

for the repair that is used for planning, execution, and confirmation of the repair work.

A service product table is maintained through the following path: **Logistics • Customer Service • Service Processing • Environment • Sales and Distribution • Service Products**.

Once the repair work is complete, the repaired part is returned to the customer. The return is initiated by using a delivery document. If you perform resource-related billing, billing-relevant sub-items are created in the customer in the customer repair order, which the system copies to the billing items during billing.

7.3.1 Business Processes and Scenarios

Customer return and repair is a business process with very specific business functions. Let's see how this is met by the service notification and order function. You can use the service notification as Return Material Authorization, and the system will copy it to the external purchase-order number when you create a repair order from service notification. A service product can be used to describe the work to be performed and be used for pricing when a fixed price is being calculated.

You can use the serial number to uniquely identify a part in the repair process. Depending on the setting in the material master, you can make the serial number mandatory for goods movement. You can use loan-equipment processing where the loaned equipment is shipped to customer for use while the part is being repaired. You can use inspection lots in Quality Management (QM) during a technical check.

Order Types

Depending on the setting in the order type, you can enter a serviceable item in the item and the service product. SAP standard system delivered-order type RA allows you to use only serviceable item, and type RAS allows you to enter both the serviceable item and the service part.

The serviceable item is the category of the device(s) to be repaired (e.g., laptop). The service product represents the service material that describes the service for the customer; examples are upgrading or repairing a laptop for a fixed price. You can use a fixed price for the work. Alternatively, you can determine a task list using the service product from which the system copies the operations and components of the automatically generated service order.

The system uses the corresponding condition records in material determination to link the service products with the relevant serviceable items. If you also use the functions for lending serviceable items, you can use material determination to determine material numbers for the items that can be sent as loan equipment.

Statuses in Repair Order

The status in the repair order specifies the progress of the repairs processing. The status controls which activities can be executed at particular stages of repair processing. For example, you can only return serviceable materials to the customer if the repair-request item has the status Repaired. This is controlled by the copy requirements. Figure 7.7 displays the different repair statuses that can be assigned, based on the stages involved.

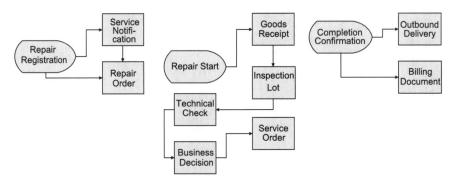

Figure 7.7 Repair Status Based on Repair Stages

7.3.2 Customizing Settings

Let's go over some of the configuration setting that are specific to return and repair; i.e., Customizing settings that are specific to the repair process. As mentioned, there are two order types for repair processing in the standard setting, which are:

▶ **Repair Order (RA)**
Repair process, where the service is performed only after a technical check is performed or the service product is defined later or not at all.

▶ **Repair Service with Service Product (RAS)**
Here, the customer might request a define service and the service product is the principal material in the sales document item.

The above order types are distinguished by identification, which defines where the sales document type should be used with or without a service product. These are identified by a single character and its associated description, as seen below:

- **F**

  Repair order without service product
- **G**

  Repair order with service product

The billing type used as default for billing customer repair orders (standard billing type FR).

Item Category

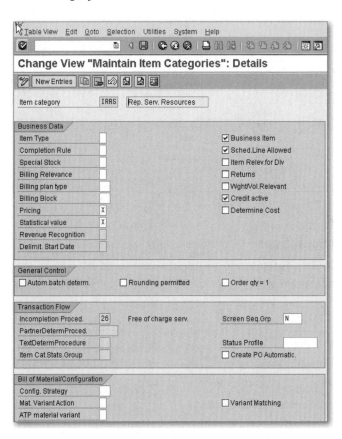

Figure 7.8 Item Category IRRS Definition

As you should know, item category controls the features of the sales document items. You can define the relevance for billing to control what item with quantity should be the basis in the billing document. The repair procedure assigned controls the process flow and the options for repair processing. The billing form defines whether billing should be resource related or flat rate. The DIP profile controls the resource-related billing. Item category IRRA is the principal item category for sales document type RA and IRRS is for RAS. Figure 7.8 displays the item-category definition in configuration for the item category IRRS.

Repair Procedure

The repair procedure contains rules, according to which lower-level items are created in the repair order. The procedure is divided into stages and operations. Stages represent individual steps within repair-processing, such as repair registration, repair start, and completion confirmation. Operations are the activities required to fulfill the repair request from the customer. Table 7.3 displays a typical repair procedure.

Time	Description	Operation	Description	Repair Indicator	Mandatory	Default
101	Repair Registration	101	Returns	—	—	Yes
101	Repair Registration	104	Sends item	—	—	—
102	Repair start	102	Repair	01	—	Yes
102	Repair Start	103	O/bd delivery	02	Yes	—
102	Repair Start	106	Exch Part	—	—	—
102	Repair Start	107	Scrap	03	Yes	—
102	Repair Start	108	Credit memo	—	Yes	—
103	Comp. Conf.	103	O/bd delivery	04	—	Yes
103	Comp. Conf.	105	Picks up Item	—	—	—
103	Comp. Conf.	107	Scrap	03	Yes	—
103	Comp. Conf.	108	Credit Memo	—	Yes	—

Table 7.3 Repair with Serviceable Item/Exchange

The repair procedure can be build through the following menu path: **Sales and Distribution • Sales • Sales Documents • Customer Service • Returns and Repairs Processing • Define Repair Procedure**.

Billing

With repair, you can either bill the customer for a fixed amount based on the set of prices you have for different repairs or based on the actual cost incurred in the repair, using the resource-related billing process. When a service order is complete, the technician records information about the costs incurred and whether the resource related billing is chosen. The system then creates separate and dynamic items. A dynamic item is system-proposed for billing. The debit memo is created based on this dynamic item.

In the standard system, the pricing procedure PREP01 has been defined for pricing in the repair order. It contains the condition type PRRP to define fixed price for service products and/or serviceable materials.

Service Management was more of an extension of SD that uses the sales process for processing its functions. Quality Management (QM) is a process that is embedded and has processes unique to itself QM exits out of the sales process and enters once the process is complete. In essence, Service Management complements the sales processes, and QM enhances the SD processes.

7.4 Quality Processes in SD

When a sales process is triggered, you might want to introduce a quality-management process to inspect a part being shipped out, or to provide a certificate of the inspection carried out. These processes are performed out of the sales function and they return the results to continue with the sales process. Companies might create certificates under agreements with their customers. These certificates will confirm the customer requirements. Quality certification has two phases for managing the process, which are:

▸ Planning

▸ Processing

Certificate planning allows you to structure the certificate in terms of layout/design, product specific contents, and customer-specific contents and characteristics. With control data, you can specific the lot sizes, inspection results, etc. Automatic generation can be enabled by output determination

within the appropriate process, shipping and the recipient. You can also create the certificate manually based on your batch or inspection. Certificate processing involves output generation by printout specific to process, batch, or inspection lot, and archiving of the certificates for future retrieval.

7.4.1 Certification Planning

The information that needs to captured and printed in the certificate needs to be chosen ahead of time. Certificate planning starts with defining the layout of the form to be printed. You structure the content of the certificate using variables. Then you maintain the profile with the control data, in terms of original characteristics, sequence, and how the form will be used. There might be many profile tied to one form. You also assign the certificate specific to material or group of material or to a ship-to party.

As you define the data related to individual characteristics in the certificate profile, it gets copied into the certificate. Data is pulled into the certificate based on the certificate profile. During the delivery-note creation based on the ship-to party and material/batch information, output determination generates the certificate.

The certificate profile defines what information goes into the certificate, the origin of the data, and how it is displayed. You can view the certificate profile for material using the menu path: **Logistics • Quality Management • Quality Certificates • Outgoing • Certificate Profile**. The Display Certificate Profile configuration is maintained under Display IMG using the following path: **Quality Management • Quality Certificates • Certificate Profile**.

The output determination for certificate configuration is within the menu path: **Quality Certificates • Output Determination**.

Certificate profiles can be based on standard certificate types, the ones available in the system are: certificate of analysis, works test certificate, and source inspection certificate. The system also supplies a standard form: QM_QCERT_01. You can build your own profile and form based on these.

Figure 7.9 displays the certificate profile with the header data. Inspection lot information is maintained under **Restriction for inspection lot selection**. The specification can come from an inspection or can relate to the batch. If it relates to a batch, this information can originate in batch determination in SD, from the allowed values for the material, or from the allowed values in the classification.

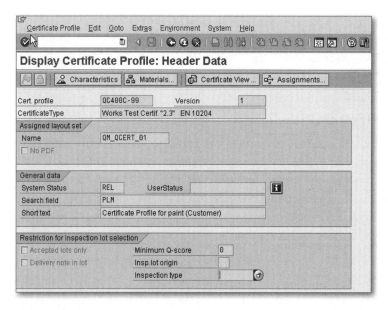

Figure 7.9 Certificate Profile-Header Data

Figure 7.10 displays the characteristics in detail. You can define the **Result Origin** within **Data origin** for characteristics information (**Batch classification**). Similarly, you can define in **Insp. Spec origin** the origin for inspection characteristics (**Batch specification**).

In the certificate profile, you can also define how the information will be presented in the certificate. Within the output control of Characteristics Details, you define when you would like to generate the output, for batch or inspection, etc. A certificate is created only when all the required data isfound. Certificate characteristics can be created in three ways:

▶ From manual entry in the overview screen.

▶ Copy from the inspection plan, routing, master recipe, etc.

▶ Entry of sort number and category, allowing creation using the characteristic selection and detail screens. Here you enter the master inspection characteristics and the link with the class characteritics, using material specifications.

You can also specify in the certificate profile that stock transfers be taken into account. Versions are maintained for certificate profile. As mentioned earlier, certificates are assigned at different levels: Material/Ship-to, Material, or Material Group. This helps characterize the certificate as general or special. You can designate it specific to customer or group it for a material that has

similar inspection characteristics. The certificate profile assignment is time dependent, as a validity period. If you want to assign certificate profiles, they must be in release status.

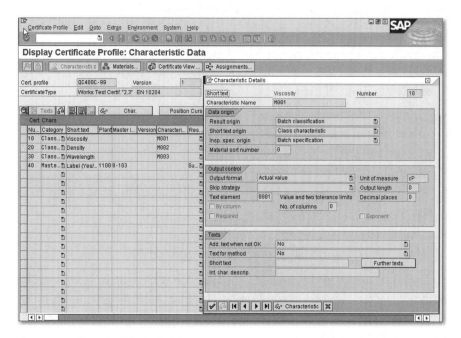

Figure 7.10 Characteristics in Detail

7.4.2 Certificate Processing

The recipient defines who will receive the certificate, the time the certificate needs to be created, and the language used. By defining the timing, you can define that the documents are send via email as soon as the post goods issue happens. In Customizing, you can define how to assign the recipient data for objects, such as customer, customer/sales, etc. This is the menu path to create receipt information within SAP Easy Access: **Logistics • Quality Management • Quality Certificates • Outgoing • Certificate Receipt • Create**. Then you can specify the output type.

As mentioned earlier, certificates are generated as part of output types. Some of the standard output types delivered in SAP systems are: LD00-delivery Note, LQCA-quality inspection certificate for ship-to-party, and LQCB-quality inspection certificate for sold-to party.

With Customizing, you can define which partner function to send the certification to. To generate the certificate use the transaction within the menu

path of SAP Easy Access: **Logistics · Quality Management · Quality Certificates · Outbox · Certificate Creation · For Batch**. Then select a recipient, customer number. The following conditions for the output procedure are delivered with the standard system for Customizing certificates.

▶ **Condition 12**
This checks whether all items have been picked for delivery and prevents a certificate for a batch split item; i.e., it allows you to create the certificate on the higher-level item.

▶ **Condition 13**
This is for the sold-to party. It prevents issuance of a certificate if ship-to party and sold-to party are identical.

▶ **Condition 15**
This only allows the certificate to be printed after the goods have been issued.

▶ **Condition 16**
This is for the sold-to party, and is similar to condition 13.

You need to maintain the procedure and assign it to an item category. The output determination uses condition techniques such as pricing. You can define the output medium in the output condition record and also the time when the output needs to be generated.

Using EDI, you can electronically send and receive quality certificates. The quality certificate is created as a PDF file and packed in an intermediate document (IDoc). During electronic certificate receipt, a certificate record is updated from the incoming IDoc, and the quality certificate is stored in the optical archive. From release 4.6C on, the quality certificate can be electronically transferred with the formatted data.

7.4.3 Batch Determination

If you specify class characteristics in the certificate profile, the data is taken from batch classification when certificates are created. The characteristics system enables you to classify objects such as batches and group them into classes. If batches are classified, the characteristics always refer to the relevant material master.

When a sales order is created, the system can search for a suitable batch. If the search is successful, the batch number is passed on to delivery and warehouse management. If is it not successful at the sales order level, it is attempted at

the delivery stage and passed on to the warehouse management. If the batch is not determined until the delivery stage, a batch split can take place.

Batch information in the delivery can be found in the **Picking Overview** screen. To have the batch determination in sales process, you must create a strategy record. The record contains fields such as customer and material for the appropriate transaction. In the batch-determination process, the classifications of the batch records are compared with that of the strategy record. The search is successful if the matching records are found. If the search is not successful, you must change your search entries and start the batch-determination process again.

7.4.4 QM in Delivery

When a delivery is created, QM automatically generates an inspection lot for the delivery items relevant for inspection. For this, the material needs to be activated for QM inspection in the material master record. Figure 7.11 on the next page displays the QM view of the material master with the inspection setup details.

Before the goods issue, the usage decision must be made, and this decision or information will allow the system to complete the post-goods issue delivery. The usage indicator can be set in the header or the item for the sales order. It describes whether this is a regular supply to the customer, or whether the goods are intended for a specific purpose. The following are some of the configuration steps that need to be defined:

▶ One inspection lot origin must be entered for each delivery type.

▶ You can define your own task list usage for each inspection type.

▶ One or more inspection types are assigned to each inspection lot origin.

▶ Different inspection types can be controlled using the usage indicator for the sales order (delievery category).

Inspection types are entered in the material master. The quality information records relevant to SD are maintained under the SAP Easy Access menu path: **Quality Management · Quality Planning · Logistic Master Data · Quality Info Record: SD**.

The inspection results are recorded within the menu path: **Logistics · Quality Management · Quality Inspection · Inspection Result · Results Recording**.

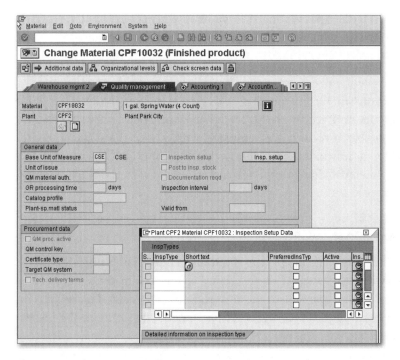

Figure 7.11 Inspection Setup Data

You might accept or reject the part and record the reasons in the usage decision. Usage decisions are updated through the menu path: **Logistics • Quality Management • Quality Inspection • Inspection Lot • Usage Decision • Record**. You can also use the menu path: **Logistics • Quality Management • Quality Inspection • Worklist • Inspection Lot Completion • Inspection Lots Without Usage Decision**.

We have described some key processes and concepts involved in quality management. The quality management process depends on the personnel who inspect or review the part and provide the approval for use. This process of notification and approval can best be managed through workflow. In the next section, we will see how this works.

7.5   Workflow

Workflow is built on the concept that someone responsible for a pending action needs to be notified, and once the task is performed he or she either can send the flow to next responsible person for further action or make a decision to approve or reject the request. In other words, workflow is a notification pro-

cess, where someone can request the task or approval needed and the person responsible gets this through the system with details necessary for action. Once acted on, the task or approval flows through the process to the next step.

Let's take a simple and often-used example with purchase requisition. The requestor who wants to procure the part sends a request to his or her manager. The manager reviews it and provides the decision, in terms of approval or rejection. If rejected, the process stops there, and the requestor is notified. If accepted, it is translated into a purchase order to procure the part or the item requested. Workflow Management consists of three major task areas as seen below:

▶ **Process Definition**
Process definition involves defining the correct sequence of the information to be delivered.

▶ **Organization Modeling**
Organization modeling calls for delivering this information to the acccurate responsible people.

▶ **Application Encapsulation**
Application encapsulation involves delivering with necessary or right information. It also provides the end-user support to help people responsible to complete their work at the right time. It provides process control in providing the information in correct sequence and time. Finally, it provides process evaluation in terms of reporting and analysis of who did what and when.

7.5.1 Workflow Architecture

There are three distinct layers in workflow definition or design. Figure 7.12 on the next page displays the pictorial representation of the workflow architecture. The top layer consists of the **Organization**, where you define the people, positions they hold, and the organizational unit they belong to. It also contains the role and task definition. The layer under that is **Process**, where you define the workflow definition and steps. The last layer is the definition of **Business Objects** with **Attributes**, **Events**, **Methods**, and **Objects**.

Let's understand the **Business objects** layer in detail. The Business Object Repository provides a process model and standard interface for workflow runtime system. Object types consist of the following:

▶ Interfaces
▶ Key Fields

- Attibutes
  - Virtual
  - Field references
  - Object references
- Methods
  - Synchronous
  - Asynchronous
  - ABAP code, transaction, function module, or report
- Events

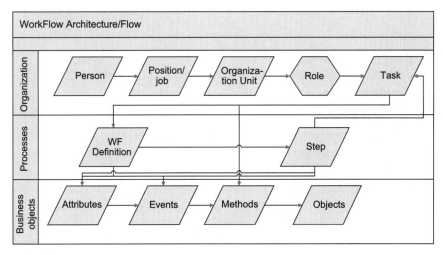

Figure 7.12 Workflow Architecture

The basic object properties are:

- Data encapsulation definition represents the abstraction for the modeler. The runtime represents a standard interface for calling application functionality.
- Inheritance represents object properties such as attributes, methods, and events that are passed to subtypes. Properties inherited can be redefined in the subtype.
- Polymorphism depends on the object type, since the object manager always selects the relevant implementation for the property requested.

When we implement an interface, we look for an assurance of a particular behavior. To create or change object type you can use the menu path within

SAP Easy Access: **Tools • SAP Business Workflow • Development • Definition tools • Business Object Builder**.

For establishing a linkage between event execution and change document, follow this path: **Tools • SAP Business Workflow • Development • Definition tools • Events • Event creation • Change documents • Linkage**.

7.5.2 Workflow Design

Workflow design involves coming up with a workflow template, which refers to workflow definition. Workflow definition consists of a sequence of steps you perform to accomplish a task. The workflow design or template involves the following:

- Reference to workflow definition
- Definition of triggering events
- Interface definition (import and export parameters as elements of the workflow container)
- Initial value assignment
- Agent assignment for starting from the workflow development environment.
- Tasks, usually started via the step definition. Tasks can be started via the Workflow entry in the System menu from the application transaction, if an appropriate link is provided by the application.
- Roles used to restrict or define more closely the number of recipients according to business considerations. The definition of a role contains:
  - The specification of the rules for role resolution (function module)
  - The specification of the runtime-dependent role parameters required for role resolution.

For role creation, you can use the SAP Easy Access and follow the menu path: **Tools • SAP Business Workflow • Development • Definition tools • Standard roles • Create**. For the function module navigate to this path: **Tools • ABAP Workbench • Development • Function Builder**. For organizational structure use the path: **Tools • SAP Business Workflow • Development • Definition tools • Organizational Management • Organization plan • Display**.

Events must be defined in the Business Object Builder for the relevant object type. Not all defined events must be triggered, but all triggered events must be defined. Implicit triggering via change documents does not require any

ABAP coding. Customizing activities for the triggering applications are necessary instead.

Figure 7.13 displays the workflow definition and runtime system overview. The workflow manager reads the workflow definition and the step definition and creates one work item per step using the work item manager. The work item manager manages the work item and triggers the application via object manager. The workflow manager controls execution of the workflow definition. The workflow item manager controls the processing of individual steps in a workflow definition.

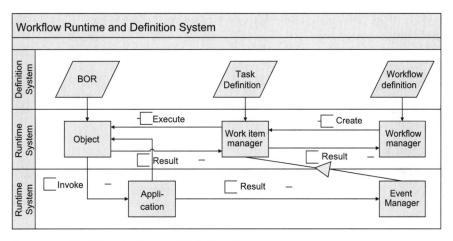

Figure 7.13 Workflow Runtime and Definition System

7.6 Summary

Service Management and Quality Management are well integrated within SAP SD. Quality-management processes are embedded within the sales process. The quality process helps facilitate the quality product being shipped to the product and records all the complaints and actions taken.

Service Management extends to the sales process and complements the sales process by providing enhanced functionality specific to service. Service Management uses sales processes for many of its supply-chain executions or order management. Service Management involves functionality specific to the service-order processing, where the process is focused on the field services and uses sales process where needed. Customer return and repair are derived out of the service management, and specifically designed for the repair process.

Quality Management enhances the sales process, as we saw. QM processes exit from and enter into the sales process, once they are complete. The input from quality inspection is used to further process the sales functions. Workflow helps in managing the notification and approval process. Workflow is applied to many functions within SAP system, but used extensively in QM. Workflow automates quality notification and further action based on the decision taken by the person responsible.

Chapters 1 through 7 covered the functional aspects of Sales and Distribution. Your knowledge is not complete, however, without knowing the technical aspects of any implementation. We will next devote our attention to reports, user interface and development tools in Chapter 8.

The sources of SD information reside in the master data and in the transaction documents. ABAP queries and SD lists and reports are used within the ERP system to directly extract this data. Information systems within ERP are stored as information structures (info structures), where these data are extracted for standard analyses and flexible reporting. The SAP Business Information Warehouse (BW) provides reporting capabilities company wide and cross-system. There are various tools within SAP to customize and personalize your application before you decide to modify or enhance the system.

8 Reports, Analysis, User Interface and Development Tools for SD

SAP provides list functions to create work lists in sales, delivery, picking, and billing. If standard reports do not fulfill your requirements, you can use ABAP queries to extract information from the database into a report. The system provides lists to support the entire sales-order management cycle. You can generate quick views and query with no or little programming or technical knowledge. An online list displays such information as sales delivery or billing documents for a customer, a material, or a combination of both. Work lists allow you to select certain tasks in sales and distribution and to process them afterwards. You select the tasks according to your area of responsibility and to various selection criteria (such as date, organizational element, or customer).

The Sales Information System (SIS) is part of SAP Sales and Distribution (SD). With SIS, you can compress data from sales documents to obtain information to help you make strategic business decisions. SIS contains standard analysis as well as flexible analysis to help you evaluate statistical data. The Logistics Information Library (LIL) allows you to integrate standard and flexible analyses as well as your own reports. You can structure and enhance the information library as you need.

Online transaction processing (OLTP) refers to the type of data processing typically done in an R/3 system. The reporting requirements in this type of

system vary greatly from those in an online analytical processing (OLAP) environment. SAP BW is an OLAP system, providing users with data in a form that makes reporting possible across different systems and different applications.

The SAP system offers you a wide range of information and analysis tools for sales and distribution. Some of the functions used by the business users for evaluations are listing and evaluation, work lists, functional analyses, and information on individual sales documents. Now let us examine some of these tools, which can be applied to SD reporting.

8.1 Quick Views, Query, Lists, and Reports

There might be a need for an ad hoc report within the area for which a particular business person might be responsible. For example, to list all the customers falling in some region or list the customers whose credit limits have been exceeded. The QuickViewer is a tool for developing ad hoc reports and is available with the 4.6A release. The following are the general steps are involved in preparing a QuickViewer and SAP Query:

▶ Defining database

▶ Structuring lists and selection screens

▶ Executing lists and selection screeens

Reports are available within different functions or areas for such tasks as displaying open orders. You can display information for a particular sales document that you are working on. You can get a document flow for a particular document. If you display an order, you can see the preceding and subsequent document.

8.1.1 QuickViewer and Query

With QuickViewer, you can choose the data source that accesses information from a table link to several tables (also called InfoSets), database views, and logical databases. You can view these directly using transactions to view tables, view directly, and create a SAP Query. You can start the QuickViewer by using the transaction code, SQVI. This transaction also provides you with the overview of this transaction and documentation on how to use this for list display or viewing the data. Figure 8.1 displays the screen shot with the information that needs to be maintained for creating a QuickViewer.

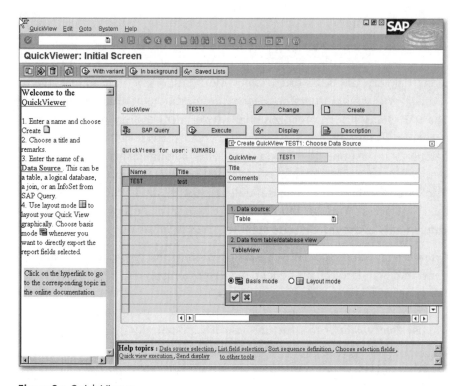

Figure 8.1 Quick Viewer

You can join tables when you define the query. The join needs to be defined, and, once defined, it becomes the source of data. A screen automatically appears so that you can define the join before you can define the selection screen and list. This join is defined graphically. A join condition between two tables is filled when both of the joined fields have the same contents. You can only use tables once for each join. However, you can enter an alias name for a table. You can only include transparent tables in a join, and not pool or cluster tables.

The output of the quick view can be transferred to an external tool such as MS Excel or MS Word, or you could save is as a local file. The outputs within an SAP system are:

▸ SAP List Viewer

▸ Table with functions for sorting or displaying in SAP List Viewer

▸ List output, a form of output especially suited for hierarchy lists

8.1.2 SAP Query

There might be a need for query to find in-transit orders for a particular customer. This information is stored in multiple tables, which could be shipment, delivery, and sales order tables. With SAP query, you will be able to come up with a quick query on these tables to pull the information you need. The SAP Query has an organizational environment that enables you to give user-specific authorizations. Users can create and start only when they belong to at least one user group. A user can belong to several user groups. In turn, user groups have InfoSets (called functional areas prior to 4.6C). The InfoSet determines the database tables or the fields of those tables that a query can access. You can allocate an InfoSet to several user groups. The individual fields in the InfoSets are split into field groups.

Queries reside in the query area and are of two kinds: global (client independent) and standard (client-dependent). You can generate SAP Query using the same principal as QuickViewer. SAP Query takes you through a sequence of screen fields for selections, assignments, and retrieving information. You can use Query Painter to structure basic lists graphically.

You can use transaction SQ01 or use SAP Query on the initial screen of the QuickViewer. QuickViewer can also be accessed through the SAP Easy Access menu item by following the path: **System • Services • QuickViewer**.

When creating a query, you have to choose an InfoSet for it. These are called InfoSet Queries. InfoSets can be based on logical databases. A logical database is an ABAP program that reads predefined data from the database and makes it available to other programs.

When you use the global query area, you are asked to specify development class the first time you save a query object. Assigning a development class is a prerequisite for saving your query object in order to more it from one system to another, for instance, from development to quality control. The development classes are created with the transaction SE80, and they need to be in the customer name space, which starts with **Y** or **Z**.

When you execute a query, a generated ABAP program runs in the background. The InfoSet serves as a template for this program. The person who creates the InfoSet should have a basic knowledge of ABAP; he or she can be a technical analyst belonging to the project or your team. Figure 8.2 displays an example of a created query. There are three different lists available with SAP Query, as given below:

▶ **Basic List**

This is typical example and can be a list of orders that are due in a particular time period. These are presented in rows, one record followed by another, in a list.

▶ **Statistics**

Here you might want to list the information with some values, such as the price along with the other details. For example, you might like to see how much of an overall discount you have so far given to a customer for a particular product or a period. This information could be presented along with the transaction or as part of total revenue.

▶ **Ranked List**

This is the list of order while presenting. You might want to sort it based on some rank, or you might want to look at all the orders pending shipment, with high delivery priority.

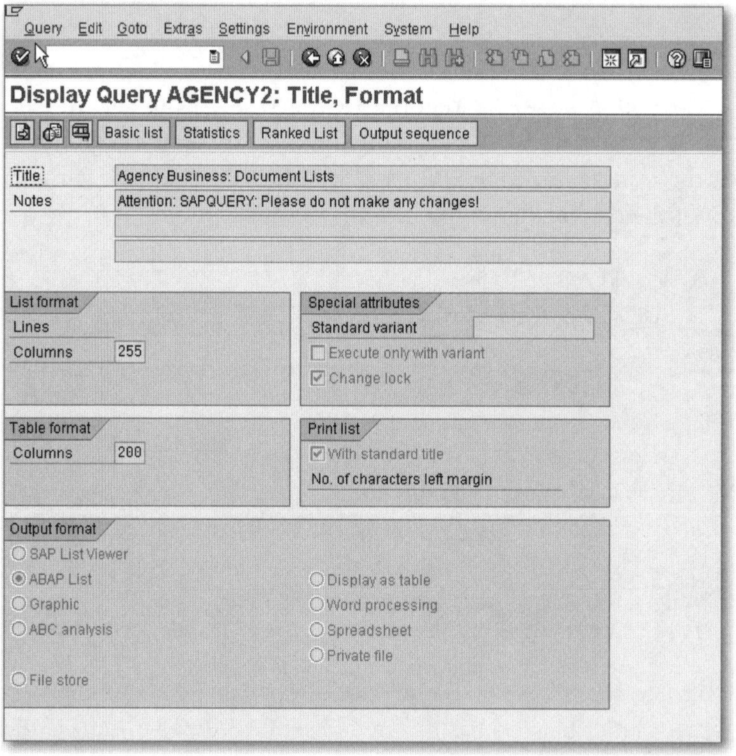

Figure 8.2 Query Display

Once these queries are run, the output can be displayed in the following different formats:

▶ **SAP List Viewer**
This appears in the screen as a list. Standard SAP allows you to navigate within the list, sorting, filtering, and so forth. When you double-click on the list items, they will provide you with further details for the particular record.

▶ **Graphics**
You can convert the data retrieved into a graphical form, like the pie chart or bar chart.

▶ **ABC Analysis**
You could do a ABC analysis on the data extracted. For example, with open sales order, you could classify orders into categories A,B and C, based on the value of the order.

8.1.3 Lists and Report

You could also develop an ABAP report to extract data from the system. These reports are written in ABAP program. You can run ABAP programs or reports using the transaction code SA38 and by using the selection variants for restriction of the data being pulled into the output report.

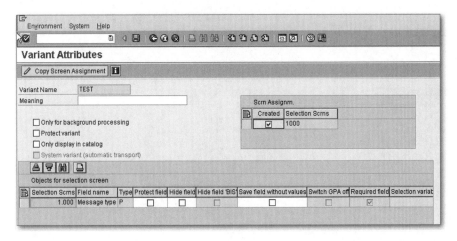

Figure 8.3 Variants

While in SE38, you need to key in the program, select an appropriate subobject—let's say a **Variant**—and than click on display or change. If you already have a variant, you can select it from a drop-down menu or enter a

name and click on **Created**, as seen in Figure 8.3. Note the **Variant Name**, seen as **TEST** in Figure 8.3. This will take you through the program selection screens for maintaining the variant. The attribute screen you can save after deciding on the different fields available. Figure 8.3 displays the selection variant for a program variant. Once you have created the variant or made necessary changes to the existing variant selection, you can execute the program with the variant option

SD documents have associated statuses. These provide important information about the state the document or the process is in. These are captured in the sales documents at header and item levels, and with the lists and report you could view them at one glance. Let's look at a few examples of status by document type and item category, below:

▶ **Quotation/Contract**
Reference status

▶ **Returns**
Delivered/billed status

▶ **Credit Memo/Debit Memo**
Blocked for billing, rejected, billed

▶ **Sales Order (Standard Item)**
Confirmed, delivered, billed status

▶ **Sales Order (Invidivual Purchase Order)**
Ordered, order confirmed, goods receipt posted, delivered status

▶ **Sales Order (Third-Party Item)**
Ordered, order confirmed, goods receipt posted, delivered

▶ **Free-of Charge Item**
Delivery status

Another example of an individual document information is the making of changes in the document that has been captured. While you are in the display or change, you can navigate to the menu path: **Environment • Changes**. This helps you display all the changes been made after the initial creation and save. Lists might fall under the following two categories:

Online Lists
These lists can display sales, delivery, or billing documents for customers, materials, or a combination of both. Other online lists display documents with a status that requires processing.

The document flow is another online list function. It displays the history of related documents. Document flow tracks the progress of a sale order in order to respond to customer inquiries. It shows all documents associated with the sales order. You can select a document to display it and then return to the document flow. You can also display the status of the entire document and of each line item.

Work Lists

These lists allow you to select certain tasks in sales and distribution and process them afterwards. You select the tasks according to your area of responsibility and to various selection criteria (e.g., date, organizational elements, or customers). Enter the information you want to use to restrict the options, on the selection screen. The system then displays a list of the relevant documents.

You can edit the list further by, using filter, sort, and sum-up functions. By adding or deleting additional fields (columns) you can display document lists using the date and some additional selection criteria. For example, you can display lists of inquiries or quotations that are to be processed by a specified time, display a list of sales orders that still have to be delivered, or display lists of incomplete sales and distribution documents in which important information for the subsequent process steps is missing.

The Delivery Due List and Billing Due List are examples of work lists. The system provides tools that you can use to process different work lists. In the first step, you use specific criteria (for instance, date, responsible organizational units, and so on) to select from all documents that need to be processed. By doing this, you can organize the work to meet your business requirements. In the second step, the system processes this work list. Tasks from various reference documents can be grouped together appropriately. Multiple tasks from a previous document can be split into several documents.

Lists and work lists can be found by following the menu path: **Logistics • Sales and Distribution • Sales • Information System**. Figure 8.4 shows you a screen that displays the different list and reports available in the system.

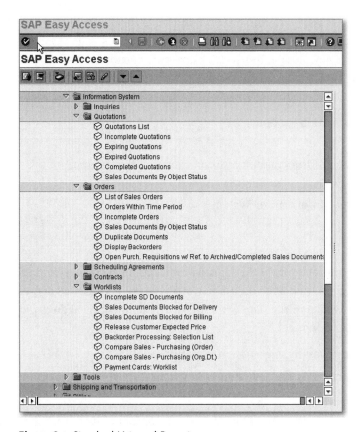

Figure 8.4 Standard Lists and Reports

8.2   Sales Information System

The Sales Information System (SIS) allows you to analyze data from different corporate perspectives. Decision makers can carry out multi-level analyses on data specific to one application or a variety of applications. The Logistics Information System (LIS) is used to review and analyze key figures throughout the entire logistics area in the system. In the area of LIS, a series of application-specific information systems are available which have a standardized interface and similar basic functionality. The following information systems are available in Logistics:

▶ **SIS**
Sales Information System

▶ **PURCHIS**
Purchasing Information System

▶ **INVCO**
Inventory Controlling

▶ **TIS**
Transportation Information System

▶ **SFIS**
Shop Floor Information System

▶ **QMIS**
Quality Management Information System

▶ **PMIS**
Plant Maintenance Information System

8.2.1 Analysis

When you use the transactions in the logistics applications, LIS-relevant data is updated. You can also update from other systems in the LIS. The LIS aggregates and stores this data in the data warehouse. The data can be aggregated with regard to the following:

▶ Quantitative reduction by aggregation at period level

▶ Qualitative reduction by the selection of key figures

To analyze the aggregate data, you can use various SIS tools. Aggregation improves response times and the quality of the resulting reports. The integrated application components online transactions are processed within the OLTP, the aggregated information are kept in form of data warehouse and the analytical processing is called OLAP.

SIS is based on Info structures. These are special statistical tables that contain data from processes carried out by the different applications. This data is constantly collected and updated by the system. Info structures comprise three basic types of information, as seen below:

▶ **Characterisitcs**
Criteria that you specify to collect data on a certain subject.

▶ **Period Unit**
A criterion used in information strcutures. You can update data for a particular period (a day, week, month, or a posting period, for example).

▶ **Key Figures**
Metrics for services rendered. They provide key corporate information regarding a particular characteristics. In SD, for example, incoming orders, sales, and returns are of key importance.

The standard system contains a variety of info structures for SD (e.g., S001 to S006). You can use the standard analyses to evaluate data without having to make additional settings in Customizing. The standard system also contains information for internal use. These include info structures for credit management, rebate processing, sales support, or contact processing. You can also create your own info structures in Customizing in the name range S501 to S999.

The analysis is based on the info structures. You need to select the required data scope, depending on the characteristics and period of the information structure. This data is first displayed in a basic list, from which you can drill down to different characteristics. All analysis is archived. A variety of tools are available that allow you to analyze the selected data further and the present your results. These can include cumulative curves, ABC analyses, time series, correlations, top-n evaluations, and other comparison options. These data can be displayed graphically. The evaluations results can also be printed, downloaded as files to your local system, or sent to one or more employee via your system's office system.

Flexible analyses in LIS allow you to determine which data in which format are combined to create an individual report. You need to define the format and content of your required list. Let's take the example of one analysis to see how this is done:

1. While in SAP Easy Access or the screen as you logon, follow the path: **Logistics • Sales and Distribution • Sales Information System • Standard analyses • Customer**.
2. After running this report, save your selected data in selection version by using the icon **SelectVers**.
3. Double click on **Selection versions KUNNR**, to bring up the **Customer Analysis – Selection version CUST1:Basic List** screen.
4. To carry out the analyses, choose **Settings**, then **Characteristics** to display Key and description.
5. To reach the next level of the drilldown, place cursor on a characteristic in the left-hand column and choose **Detail**.
6. Choose **Extras**, then **Display** standard drilldown to compare the sequence recorded above with the standard drilldown for this analysis.
7. Keep cursor selected on key figures.
8. Choose **Extra**, then All **Key Figures**.

9. Double click to see the Key Figure details

10. Choose **Edit**, then **ABC analysis**.

11. Choose **Total Invoiced sales (%)** for carrying out ABC analyses.

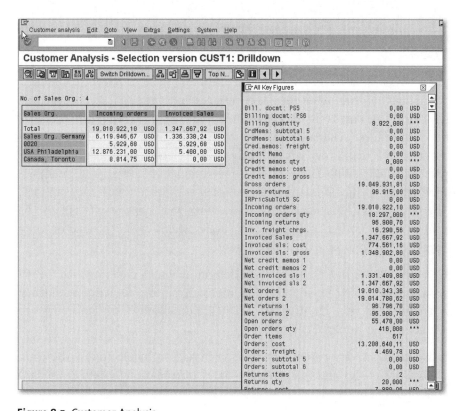

Figure 8.5 Customer Analysis

Figure 8.5 displays the screen output with standard analysis for the customer, seen as **Customer Analysis**. Standard analyses for Material, Sales Organization, Shipping point, Sales employee, Sales office, Variant configuration, and Sales support are delivered with the SAP system. You can also use selected versions based on the info structures.

8.2.2   Information Structures

Info structures form the data basis for the respective standard analysis. Some examples of info structures are: S001 (Customer), S002 (Sales Office), S003 (Sales Organization), S004 (Material), S005 (Shipping point), S006 (Sales employee). Let's highlight some of the key configuration steps in creating

your own info structure. The IMG menu path is: **Logistics General · Logistics Information System**.

Create the defined info structure while in Display IMG by following this menu path: **Logistics-General · Logistics Information System (LIS) · Logistic Data Warehouse · Data Basis · Information Structures · Maintain self-defined structures · Create**.

> **Note**
>
> You need to use the number standard from S501 through S999 for your own info structures, as the numbers from S001 through S501 are reserved for SAP standard info structures.

I recommend creating a new info structure with reference to an existing one and making necessary changes, as required. Let's say we take a reference of S004 in the copy from, as it might be closest to the information you are trying to build. On that basis, you can take the following steps:

1. Double-click on **Characteristics** and **Key Figures**.
2. The technical field information pops up.
3. The screen for creating Info structures, shown in Figure 8.6, is displayed.
4. Scroll down to select the field and field attributes.
5. Click on the **Continue** button.
6. Review the **Characteristics** and **Key Figures**.
7. For **Key Figures**, choose **Sum** or **Fix** as needed.
8. Save your changes.
9. Click on the generate icon(a red and white circle) to generate the structure.

Maintain the update group by following this path: **Logistics Data Warehouse · Updating · Updating Definition · General Definition Using Update Groups · Maintain Update Groups**

Maintain updates rules using this path: **Updating Defintion · Specific definition using Update Rules · Maintain Update Rules · Display.** Then do the following:

1. Assign statistical groups by using these configuration steps: **Updating · Updating Control · Setting Sales · Statistics Groups**
2. For header and item level, you need to assign update groups within Updating by doing this configuration: **Updating Control · Settings · Sales · Update Group**

3. Activate the SIS update by following these configuration steps: **Logistics Data Warehouse · Updating · Updating Control · Activate Update**

4. Choose your **Activity** as **Sales and Distribution**

Execute the info structure by going to SAP Easy Access or the Sap screen you see, as you log on, by following this path: **Logistics · Sales and Distribution · Sales Information System · Standard Analysis · Self defined analysis**.

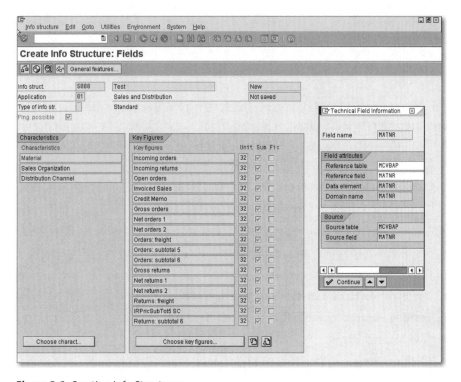

Figure 8.6 Creating Info Structures

Within flexible analysis, there are reports for evaluation. You can also create your own evaluation structures (with ZF prefix). Figure 8.7 displays the flexible analysis of structure **S001 (Customer)**.

So far we have looked at reporting and analysis within the ERP system. We looked at the different tools available to report against the master data and the transaction data from one system. There might be a need for reporting from multiple systems and for analysis on the historical data. In the next section, we will look how SAP BW helps you meet your reporting requirements.

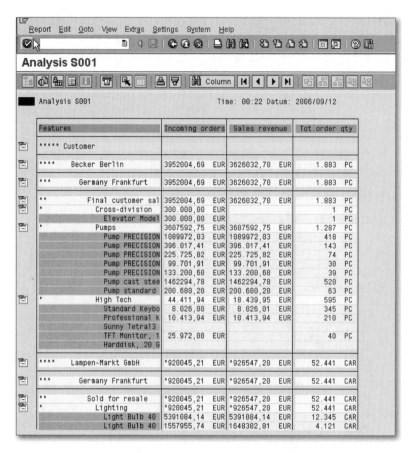

Figure 8.7 Customer Info Structure-Analysis

8.3 SAP BW and Reporting Requirements

Companies run reports on volume and historical data. These data can be freed from the transaction system and fed into a reporting system. Also, companies might have multiple systems and might like to use one common reporting system to pull data from all the systems connected to it. The SAP Business Information Warehouse (BW)—also known as the Business Intelligence Warehouse (BI)—allows you to analyze data from operational SAP R/3 applications or any other business application.

You can also extract and analyze data from external sources such as databases, online services, and the Internet. Figure 8.8 shows you how SAP BW interfaces with other systems. The system (data storage, loading and reporting), which is pre-configured by Business Content for core areas and pro-

cesses, allows you to examine relationship in every area of your company. BW was designed to meet the above-mentioned requirements. These are been accomplished in concept and design by the following architecture:

▶ Data-warehousing system with optimized data structure for reporting and analysis

▶ Separate systems

▶ OLAP engine and tools

▶ Comprehensive data-warehousing architecture base

▶ Automated data warehouse management

▶ Pre-configured using SAP global business know-how

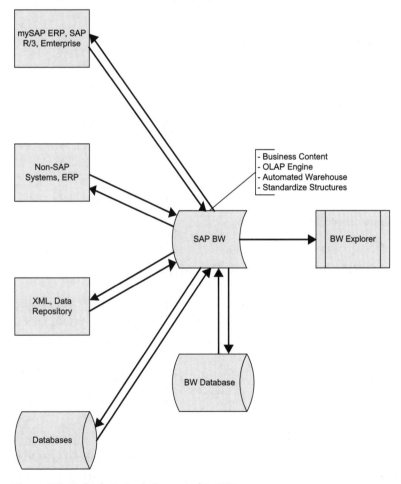

Figure 8.8 Multiple Systems Connected to BW

Note

Look at the difference between ABAP reports from R/3 and the BW analyses. ABAP reports are completely up-to-date (in real time) and give a detailed view of individual documents that meet the selection criteria. The BW analyses also provide information for meeting predefined selection criteria. The focus here, however, is on providing an overview of a certain trend or information about aggregated figures. The data for a BW query is extracted from the online transaction processing system (ERP) to BW system and then published in HTML format in the portal. It is therefore not real-time data, though it can be updated at very regular intervals.

With BW, SAP introduced some concepts and terminology. Understanding this terminology and related objects will help you make best use of BW and will also aid in communication within your team.

8.3.1   InfoObject

Business analysis-objects (customers, sales volume) are called InfoObjects in SAP BW. These are further divided into characteristics and key figures. Characteristics are further divided into units, time characteristics, and technical characteristics (e.g., IDs). Key figures are all data fields that are used to store values or quantities; e.g., volumes, costs, etc. Characteristics describe the affiliation of key figures. For example, costs belong to a cost center, wherein the cost center is a characteristic.

8.3.2   InfoCube

The central data containers that form the basis for reports and analyses in SAP BW are called InfoCubes. They contain key figures (sales volumes, costs, orders, etc) and a link to the characteristics (master data such as cost centers, customer, and materials). Each individual InfoCube should contain a self-contained dataset, since queries refer primarily to one InfoCube.

An InfoCube consists of several database tables that are linked according to the star schema. These include a fact table that contains the InfoCube key figures, as well as several surrounding dimension tables that store the links to the characteristics. Keep the following in mind:

▶ Each InfoCube has one fact table and a maximum of 16 dimension tables.

▶ Each fact table can contain a maximum of 233 key figures.

▶ A dimension can contain up to 288 freely available key figures.

InfoCubes are stored in structures in the SAP BW system. If you want to store an InfoCube, you can create a new folder or use an existing one. These folders are called InfoAreas in SAP BW.

8.3.3 InfoProviders

InfoProvider is the super-ordinate term for an object that you can use to create reports in Business Explorer (BEx). InfoProviders are objects or views that are relevant to reporting. InfoProviders include various database meta objects that deliver data for query definitions. The type of data procurement performed depends on the InfoProvider used. InfoProviders deliver data that can be analyzed using a query.

8.3.4 Types of Data Stores

There are two types of data stores, physical and logical views. Physical stores contain:

▶ InfoCubes

▶ ODS Objects

▶ InfoObjects

Logical views of physical data stores include:

▶ InfoSets

▶ RemoteCubes

▶ Virtual InfoCubes

▶ MultiProviders

An Operational Data Store (ODS), stores data at the basic level (document level). It is normally used to resolve and consolidate datasets. These datasets are often from various data sources and/or source systems.

8.3.5 BW Architecture

SAP BW enables the analysis of data from operative SAP applications as well as from all other business applications and external data sources such as databases, online services, and the Internet.

Administrative Workbench (AWB) is a workplace for SAP BW administrators. AWB functions are used to configure, control, and administer SAP BW. AWB functions allow you to control, monitor, and maintain all data procure-

ment processes. Figure 8.9 displays the architectural view of SAP BW. With BW, you can perform OLAP for staging information from large amounts of operative and historical data. OLAP technology permits multi-dimensional analyses according to various business perspectives.

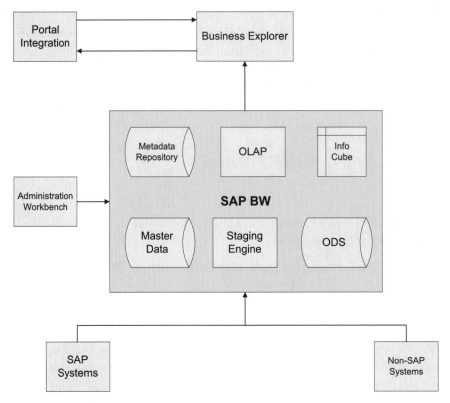

Figure 8.9 BW Landscape

The BW server, preconfigured by Business Content for core areas and processes, allows you to examine the relationships in every area within your company. Business Content provides targeted information to companies, divided into roles. Business Content also includes other preconfigured objects, such as InfoCubes, queries, key figures, and characteristics.

The Business Explorer (BEx) component provides users with flexible reporting and analysis tools. BEx allows a wide spectrum of users to access information in SAP BW; e.g.,the Enterprise Portal iViews and Mobile devices.

Web Application Design allows you to implement generic OLAP navigation in Web applications and in Business Intelligence cockpits. Simple user interface elements can be realized using standard markup language (HTML).

Some standard BEx functions are: Portal Integration, Query, Reporting and Analysis, Web Application Design, Formatted Reporting, and Mobile Intelligence.

8.3.6 Business Content

Business Content contains all the objects that enable you to structure your reporting quickly, from data extraction from SAP source systems, to roles that supply employees in a company with information they need to complete their work. These information models include the following:

▸ Roles

▸ Queries and workbooks

▸ InfoProviders that the reports are based on

▸ InfoObjects that provide the characteristics and key figures used in your reports

▸ Update rules and extractors for SAP R/3, mySAP R/3, mySAP.com business applications, and other selected applications

Objects are grouped together into roles for optimal use. A role corresponds to a specific function in company; e.g., a sales manager. A role is linked to particular tasks, areas of responsibility, and the information requirements that result from them.

BW releases delivers cross-company applications such as analytical applications in form of business packages. The areas of analytical applications include Sales Analysis, Campaign Management, Market Exploration, Procurement Analysis, Production Analysis, Inventory Analysis, Customer Credit Management, and packages for E-Analytics.

The metadata repository can be found in the Administrative Workbench (AWB) of the BW system. It contains definitions of all active objects delivered in business content, as well as their links to other objects and information available in Business Content, and to identifying objects that fully or partially meet your requirements. Note that you can obtain SAP Demo Sales and Distribution: Overview (0D_SD_C03) InfoCube and Query. The steps below show you how to do this:

1. Log on to the SAP BW system.

2. Follow this menu path to get to the Administrative Workbench: **Modeling • Administrative Workbench: Modeling. Open Metadata Repository.**

3. Review the InfoCube **SAP Demo Sales and Distribution: Overview** (0D_SD_C03) in the **Business Content** object.

4. Review the list of characteristics and key figures for this InfoCube.

5. Use the network data flow to obtain an overview of the queries structured on this InfoCube.

6. Find the **Complete Overview Sales and Distribution** query (technical name 0D_SD_C03_Q0021).

7. Display the information on the query—0D_SD_C03_Q0021.

8. Determine if this query is assigned to a role, and if so, which one.

9. Branch out to the activated objects of the metadata repository.

10. Check to determine if the Complete Overview Sales and Distribution Query is actively available in the system.

Having understood Business Content, let's see how information is used for Sales Analytics.

8.3.7 Sales Analytics

Sales Analytics uses business intelligence information and presents it to the new user groups such as sales managers or credit managers in the form of consumer patterns or by using the dashboard technology. ERP is all about improving the ability for an organization to read market and business drivers and react quickly to change.

Historically speaking, ERP was a means to improve business transaction flow and this still remains. Today, however, it is enhanced through enterprise analytics. MySAP ERP decomposes analytics as an isolated capability and embedding analytical tools and dashboard within the actual business process. This increases the visibility for every employee and role, using predictive analysis to guide business decision, leverages real-time actual data of business to form strategy, and spending more time breaking down performance measures than in constructing models. This is an attempt to embed into the process the analytical capabilities that help address questions that come up during the process.

SAP analytics for ERP is the new definition of both the strategic and operational analytical tools delivered in mySAP ERP. Within Enterprise Sales and Distribution there are two available roles, as described below:

► **Customer Service Manager**

The customer service manager is able to evaluate detailed information about each individual customer, whereas the sales manager receives information for analyzing sales at a more global level.

For Customer Service Manager with Quotation Processing, you have workbooks: quotation success rates by customer, customer quotation general information, and tracking for quotation by customer. Within order processing, there are tasks for incoming orders; e.g., order, delivery, sales volume, and values, and for faultless sales order processing, including quantity and value of returns, proportion of credit memos to sales volume, etc.

Similarly, you have tasks within deliveries for delivery delays and processing times and weights and volumes. Finally, there are volume/costs and deliveries analysis and comparison tasks. These include channel analysis and weekly/monthly deliveries. Every task corresponds to a cluster from one or more workbooks, which contain several queries that yield the relevant information.

► **Sales Manager**

The sales manager is responsible for sales within the sales area and for tasks similar to the customer service manager's for quotation information and tracking incoming orders, faultless sales order processing, product, delivery delays and processing times, analyses and comparisons. This role includes administrative and management functions; e.g., cost center and controlling for cost center..

Lists, reports, and views provide information on the master and transaction data. This information might be used for operational purpose to help with day-to-day work or analysis of historical data to help in planning. SAP has come up with different features to enhance the user productivity using different tools. Section 8.4 will focus on some of those user productivity features.

8.4 User Productivity

With mySAP ERP, attempts were made to develop individual user interface and Enterprise Portal roles, such as the sales representative. The sales representative is a role with SAP Internet Sales in ERP. SAP Internet Sales is a new business-to-business user interface. There are two applications with Internet Sales, which are:

▶ Catalog and Order Management

▶ Web Shop Management

Figure 8.10 displays the architecture of SAP Internet Sales in mySAP ERP. The system landscape in this figure represents the minimal system landscape for SAP Internet Sales in mySAP ERP, as well as an optional MS SQL Database. The catalog of SAP ERP is cached in the main memory of the J2EE engine and all pricing is retrieved from the back end.

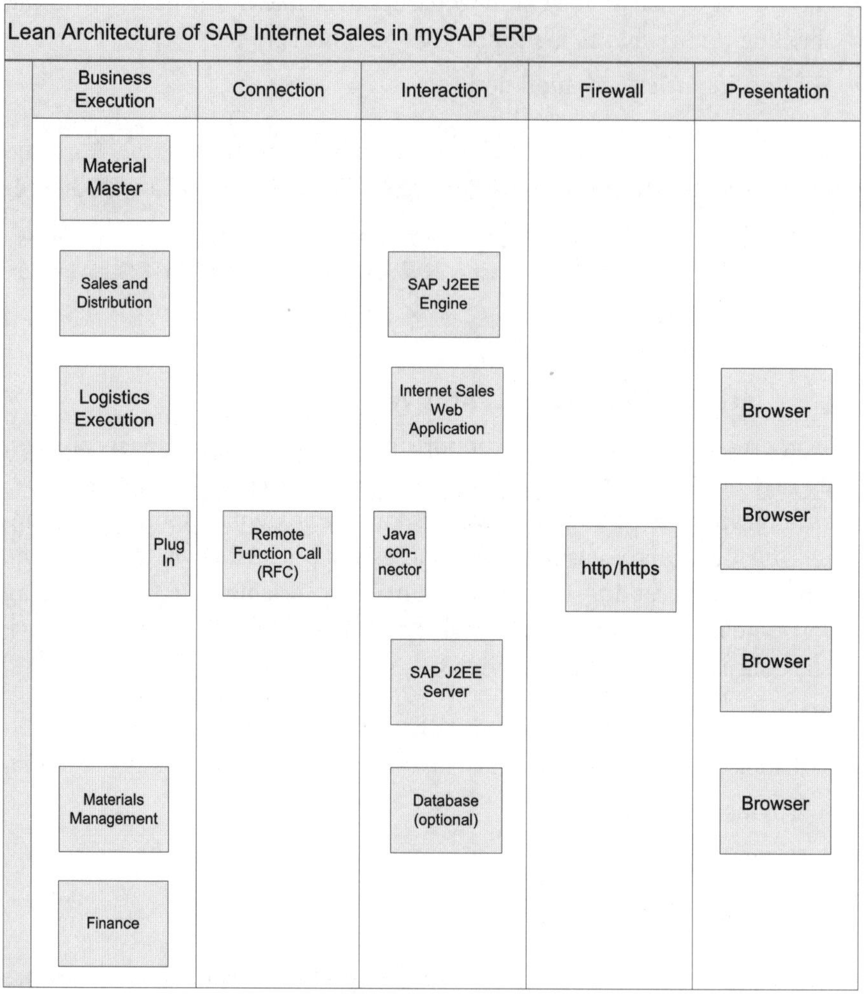

Lean Architecture of SAP Internet Sales in mySAP ERP				
Business Execution	Connection	Interaction	Firewall	Presentation
Material Master				
Sales and Distribution		SAP J2EE Engine		
Logistics Execution		Internet Sales Web Application		Browser
				Browser
Plug In	Remote Function Call (RFC)	Java connector	http/https	
		SAP J2EE Server		Browser
Materials Management		Database (optional)		Browser
Finance				

Figure 8.10 SAP Internet Sales Architecture

A MS SQL Database is needed for the storage of shopping baskets. A plug-in is required for SAP R/3 and mySAP ERP comes with this plug-in. Some features and functionality available with SAP Internet Sales are given below:

▶ Order change and display of billing documents switch on/off the Web Shop Management

▶ Order search with status

▶ IPC integration for pricing or configuration

▶ Have a list of master data ship-to parties available in the basket (without the plug-in, the sold-to is proposed as possible ship-to)

▶ Support inquiries and quotation

▶ Support scenarios of catalog and order management for Internet users

Note
For a complete list, refer to the OSS note 671893. OSS note 622049 also provides information on supported R/3 releases, as well as information on the R/3 back-end system.

8.4.1 Internet Sales Representative Role

Sales representatives assist and support the sales team in all aspects of sales. They may do this by maintaining and updating customer master data, corresponding with prospects and customers, preparing quotations and sales contracts, taking orders, ensuring the successful processing of these orders, receiving and accepting inquiries, maintaining pricing data, or preparing reports and analyses for the sales manager. The Internet Sales Representative Portal consists of the following views:

▶ Sales Overview
  ▶ Quick view
  ▶ To dos and workload
▶ Customer care
  ▶ Customers
  ▶ Contacts
  ▶ Customer agreements
▶ Sales Data
  ▶ Prices and Conditions
  ▶ Products

- ► Sales Support
  - ▹ Overview
  - ▹ Inquiries
  - ▹ Quotations
  - ▹ Sales Order
  - ▹ Sales Contracts
  - ▹ Scheduling Agreements
  - ▹ Billing Documents
- ► Order Fulfillment
  - ▹ Delivery List
  - ▹ Delivery
  - ▹ Backorders
  - ▹ Availability overview
  - ▹ Shipments
- ► Analysis

The sales support queries are based out of mySAP ERP reports. Let's take a quick look at some examples:

- ► **ERPSLS_INCDOC**
  Used for incomplete documents

- ► **ERPSLS_BILLBLOCKDOC**
  Used for list of orders blocked for billing

- ► **ERPSLS_DLVBLOCKDOC**
  Used for list of orders blocked for delivery

- ► **ERPSLS_EXPDOC**
  Used for expiring documents

- ► **ERPSLS_COMPDOC**
  Used for complete documents

The analyses are collected in one workset for the Internet Sales Representative. This is called *analytical content*. In standard delivery for the Internet Sales Representative, I have chosen to include analyses that I think he or she needs to order to support or provide information to the Sales Manager.

The Internet Sales Representative (or user) can modify the analyses that are delivered here. Of course you can decide to display completely different

analyses in the portal, depending on the queries that you have created in the BW system. The analysis workset pages consist of the following:

- ▶ Sales Support Analysis
  - ▶ Quotation Tracking
  - ▶ Incoming Orders
- ▶ Order Fulfillment Analysis
  - ▶ Delivery Delays in Last 6 Months
  - ▶ Delivery Delays by Month
  - ▶ Backorder Processing.

Analyses are taken from BW queries, which are displayed in the worksets in the iViews format. Templates are created for relevant queries. The templates are converted into iViews, which are then added to the relevant pages and worksets in the portal for each role. Let's consider an example. The Sales Pipeline (Query 0CSALMC02_Q002) has a sales manager template taken from a view of the query (0TPL_0CSALMC02_Q002_V003), created as a Java iView (*com.sap.pct.crm.slsAnalyt.spa.SalesPipe*).

There are several steps in mySAP ERP for configuring the portal interface. We are using the example of Internet Sales here. You need to go to IMG path in mySAP ERP and follow the path: **Sales and Distribution • Portal • Overview**. Then do the following:

1. Maintain **Portal Targets**

2. Maintain **Task Areas**

Figure 8.11 displays the configuration screen shot of the step of maintaining portal targets. This selection controls the portal target navigation from the workload application. A portal target definition depends on the portal role you are going to use; e.g., SA for the Sales Assistance or PA for Purchasing Assistant (these are not seen in Figure 8.11).

Furthermore, the system defines the backend report that is triggered using this portal target, the **Report Name** and the **Location Path**. In this figure, we are defining a query on a blocked billing document. Therefore, you should first get an idea of the different fields:

- ▶ **Target ID**
  Blocked billing document
- ▶ **Description**
  SD document blocked for billing

▶ **Report Name**
Name of the report being called or that is being run

▶ **Location Path**
Portal content path to the target iView

▶ **Location Path**
Extended path (dynamic iView parameters)

▶ **Mode**
Windows/navigation mode

▶ **Counter OFF**
Mark to disable execution of report

▶ **Static Parameters**
PA purchasing agent role specific

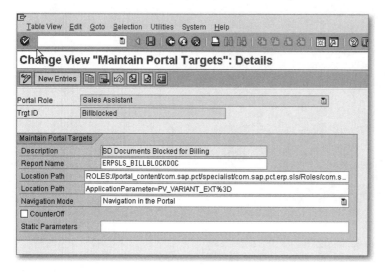

Figure 8.11 Maintaining Portal Target

Within Maintain Task Area you define the following, as seen in Figure 8.12:

▶ **Role**
SA for Internet Sales Representative

▶ **Workset ID**
Standard or to-do

▶ **Username**
mySAP ERP user ID for the portal user

► **Language**
Common logon language of this user

► **Layout**
Select the layout on the BSP (TextView, Trays or Group Box)

► **Lock**
Mark to block front-end user presonalization.

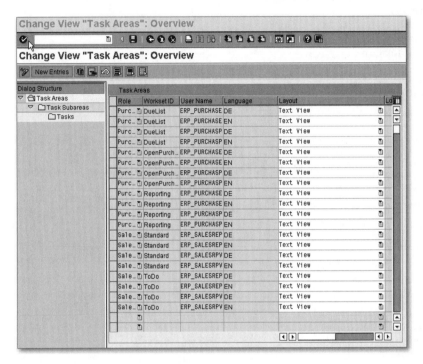

Figure 8.12 Maintain Task Area for Portal

Figure 8.12 displays the configuration screen shot of the Task Areas set up.

To define a sub-area task, make the following settings:

► **Subset ID**
Enter a description; this will be visible for the sub-area on the BSP

► **Sequence**
Sequence of task areas

► **Alignment**
Alignment of tasks within the sub-tasks

► **Closed**
Works only with the *tray* layout

To define a single task, you need to have the following settings in the system:

▶ **Link ID**
Enter a description

▶ **Target ID**
Report name for your query

▶ **Selection Variant Combination**
selection variant prepared for this report

▶ **Trgt ID**
Role (portal) targets

▶ **Report Name**
Filled automatically after **Target ID** selection is made

▶ **Variant**
Corresponding selection variant for Report Name field

▶ **Spec. Variant**
Only for Role PA Purchasing Agent

▶ **Counter**
Number of documents

▶ **Date**
Last selection (Report/Variant)

▶ **Time**
Same as date

▶ **Counter OFF**
No selection possible, is determined through **Trgt. ID**

8.4.2   Enterprise Portal

A portal enables personalized access to appropriate information, which could be transactional or analytical, and Web content from various sources for a specific purpose. Let's say a sales manager would like to know the performance of his sales representatives based on their sales targets and whether or not they closed any critical accounts. The information is often scattered in various formats in various filing systems, such as a file server, Web servers, or the database. The task of the portal is to provide this information specifically to the user at a single source. The relevant information and applications are consolidated for the users by content editors and portal administrators.

The portal server creates the HTML from various sources. Content metadata and user data are stored in the persistence layer. Other components of the Enterprise Portal enable single-sign on (SSO) based on the Lightweight Directory Access Protocol (LDAP) for user management and session management for locking and unlocking data. The unification server and the unifiers provide information from the various back-end systems on how to relate one set of data to another (drag and relate functionality). The processing and supplying of unstructured information takes place through the Knowledge Management component of the portal. Portal content consists primarily of iViews.

Each iView brings to the portal desktop specified data from an information resource such as a relationship database, ERP system, CRM system, enterprise application, collaboration tool, e-mail exchange system, intranet or the World Wide Web. iViews return up-to-the minute information each time they are launched. iViews are generally displayed through portal pages. You can import predefined pages or create your own pages. The page definition includes a list of associated iViews and layout specifications. Worksets bundle related pages, iViews, and roles.

User access to content is determined by role definitions, such as a sales manager, sales representative, field specialist, and so forth. A portal role is a collection of task-oriented content. While portal content is developed to enable access to information relevant to the organization in which the portal is deployed, role defines the subset of content available to each functional role within the organization. Users are assigned to the role or roles that provide content relevant to them. A user has access to the content that has been assigned to all of his or her roles. The role definition determines the navigation structure within portal. The navigation structure consists of the top-level navigation bar and the detail navigation tree. Business packages are groups of related worksets. They are available from iViewStudio (*www.iview studio.com*).

Any implementation consists of development and enhancements. I will try to address some technical aspect of an implementation. However, you should be aware that SAP provides configuration tools to define your business processes based on standard business practices. There might be instances where these might not be met by the standard configuration, and you would like to make additional modifications and enhancements. Now I will address some development aspects of an implementation.

8.5 Modifications and Enhancements—Concepts and Application

With Customizing, you can set up specific business processes and functions based on the Implementation Guide. The need for this change has been already identified and implementation procedure has been developed within the SAP system. You can personalize the SAP screens by making changes to the global display attributes for particular fields, which might involve setting up default values, hiding fields, or creating user-specific menu sequences. These are accomplished by the tools found in Implementation Guide, through the Display IMG.

Modification signifies changes to the SAP repository objects made at the customer site. If SAP delivers a changed version of the object, the customer's system must be adjusted to reflect these changes, otherwise these programs might have errors in them, and problem might arise when they are used. Enhancement involves creating repository object for individual customers, which indicate the objects that already exist in the SAP repository. Customer development involves creation of repository objects unique to individual customers in a specific namespace reserved for new customer objects. These are accomplished with the tools available within the ABAP Workbench, e.g., ABAP Dictionary, BAPI Explorer, or Business Object Browser.

8.5.1 Concepts

An object is in its original version in only one system. So when SAP delivers any ABAP code or program change to its system in terms of notes, service packs or upgrades, these are in the original version in the SAP system and are called copies in the customer systems. The same concept applies to your pipeline. When you develop a program in a development system, it is original there, and when it is transported to other systems such as the quality system or production system, and it is called the copy. You can only move to other systems once you have assigned it to a change request with a correction type Development/Correction.

Changes to the original are called corrections, and when you change a copy, these are recorded in the task type called Repair. These changes called modifications. When changes are applied to your own copies, you must correct the original immediately to keep it in synch. With SAP-supplied objects you would be able to modify SAP supplied objects, but you should only modify

the SAP standard if it is absolutely necessary for optimizing workflow in your company.

With upgrades or applying support packs, your system might be impacted or have conflicts with the object being modified. This might happen because you changed the object that SAP's import transport affects. Your changes will be lost unless you perform a modification adjustment to the objects. As standard practice, you want to apply the modifications in your development system and transport the adjustment to other systems.

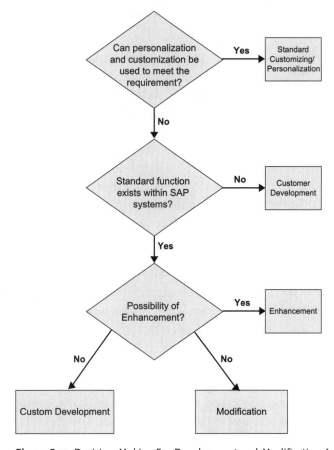

Figure 8.13 Decision-Making For Development and Modification Approach

Let's look at the flow shown in Figure 8.13. You need to first look at the requirements being met by the standard Customization or the applications and functions available within SAP. You might want to personalize it for specific user based on the role or job function. If any particular requirement or function is not met within the SAP standard system, you might want to check

whether any of the SAP's Complementary Software Product solutions can meet the requirement within the SAP Service Marketplace.

You can also try enhancing a function to meet the requirement by filling the gap using user exits. User exits help customer enhance functions by adding their own code into the space provided. After all these attempts you might want to use the option of either applying the modification to the SAP standard or use the SAP program as a standard template and perform your own customer development.

8.5.2 Personalization

Personalization might help to adjust the application without the use of ABAP Workbench or changes to the programs. You can create variants to the transaction with the most frequently used parameters, and you can SET/GET parameters or table-control settings valid throughout the entire system. You can also personalize your menus by providing a role-based menu, favorites, or shortcuts to the desktops. These can be done very easily using the menu options available with the SAP Easy Access Favorites. For creating Favorites and for variants within the transaction, you save the selection parameters and the application will walk you through the creation of variants.

Transaction and screen variants can be created using the transaction code SHD0. Figure 8.14 displays the screen. You need to type in the transaction code and the variant name you want to save the parameters into. There are also folders for **Standard Variants** and **Screen Variants**.

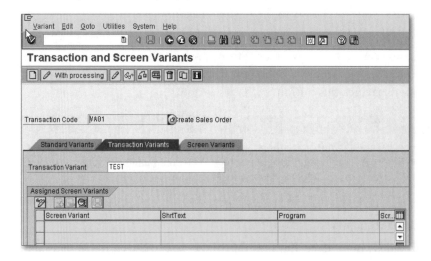

Figure 8.14 Transaction and Screen Variant

8.5.3 Modifications and Enhancements

Any changes made to the SAP standard object are modifications. During an update, these modifications need to be reviewed and analyzed for future use. For instance, if the new updates are applied over your existing code or you keep using the old SAP standard program with your code, this could affect the functionality. Therefore, you should test for any errors. You can use the Modification Assistance available with the ABAP Workbench to help you with this.

Enhancement can be applied in the following different levels:

▶ Function module exits with ABAP programming

▶ Menu exits within the Graphical User Interface (GUI)

▶ Field exits by providing a customer code that indicates a specific field on the screen

▶ Table enhancements within the ABAP dictionary tables and structures

The enhancement is always used to call an object in the customer namespace, which might involve one or more of the following techniques:

▶ **Customer Exits**
A special exit function module is called by the SAP system.

▶ **Business Transactions Events**
The SAP application program calls a function module in the customer namespace.

▶ **Business Add-ins**
The application—known as a BAdI—calls a method of class or an instance of a class, and the class is in the customer namespace.

Menu enhancements permit you to add additional menu entries to SAP standard menu. You can use customer exits or BAdIs. When the function code is implemented, you can change the text of the menu entry, provided the SAP developer specifies this option.

> **Note**
>
> Screen exits are a type of customer exit. They allow you to display additional objects in an SAP application program screen. You can implement screen exits by creating sub-screens, possibly with flow logic.

Table Enhancements

SAP provides you with techniques that allow you to attach fields to a table without needing to modify the table itself. Append structures may be only

assigned to one table. During activation, the system searches for the entire active append structure for that table and attach them to the table. An append structure allows you to attach fields to a table without actually having to modify the table itself.

Another option is the customer include. The customer include allows you to use the same structure in multiple tables. Some of the tables and structures delivered with the SAP R/3 Enterprise standard system contain special include statements and Customizing includes. These are often inserted in the standard tables that need to have customer-specific fields added to them.

Text Enhancements

Possible text enhancements include customer keywords and customer documentation of data elements. Text enhancements differ from other enhancements, in that they take effect globally in all related SAP applications after activation (global enhancements). All screen fields that use the keyword text of data elements can be renamed. A short text in a data element will appear in the **F1** help of the screen field. Keywords need to be restored after a release upgrade.

You have the option to create your own data element documentation independent of the SAP documentation. Please note that this is not recommended as you lose the SAP documentation reference.

Application Enhancements

Application enhancements are pre-planned by your SAP system and normally consist of several components. The developer creates SAP enhancements from the function module exits, menu exits, and screen exits. To manage this function you can use the transaction code SMOD. Customers are given a catalog which contains an overview of the existing SAP R/3 Enterprise enhancements. They can then combine the SAP enhancements they want into an enhancement project using the transaction code CMOD.

User Exits

User exits are a type of system enhancement originally developed for the SD module. The original purpose of the user exits was to allow the user to avoid modification adjustment. A user exit is considered a modification because technically the objects in the SAP namespace are being modified. The SAP developer creates a special include in a module pool. These includes contain

one or more subroutines that satisfy the naming convention and user exit. The calls for these subroutines have already been implemented in the program. After delivering them, SAP never alters the includes within the SAP programs created in this way. If new user exits are delivered in new releases, they are placed in a new include program.

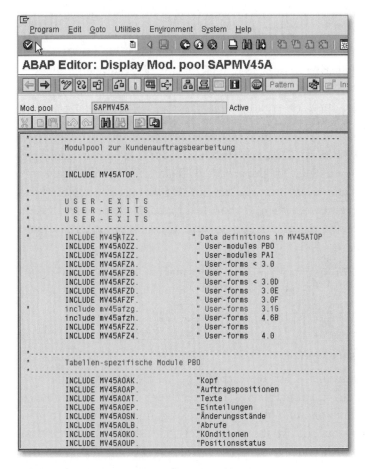

Figure 8.15 Sales Order Program Includes User Exits

User exits are actually empty subroutines that the SAP developer provides for you, where you can fill in your source code. For example with program **SAPM45A**, the include is **M45AFZB** (see Figure 8.15). You can find a list of user exits and associate documentation in the SAP Reference Implementation Guide. Figure 8.15 displays the program **SAPMV45A** with the user exists listed. If you double click on one of the includes listed under the heading **USER-EXITS**, it will bring up that user's exit codes.

Business Transaction Event

There might be a specific requirement met by an external system with input fed back to SAP. For example, you might interface with another system for getting tax data. This external system might consist of content related to tax and will feed this information based on the request from the SAP system. Business Transaction Events (BTE) are predefined interfaces that help you interface with external system for gathering information and continuing with the process. BTE has one of the following types of interfaces:

▶ **Publish and Subscribe**
This informs the external software that certain events have taken place in an SAP standard application and provides them with the data produced.

▶ **Process Interfaces**
These intervene in the standard process and return data to the SAP application.

With publish and subscribe, interfaces can start one or more additional operations when a particular event is triggered. They don't influence the standard SAP R/3 Enterprise program in any way. Multiple operations do not interfere with each other, and add-on components can only import data. With process interface, when an event is triggered, a process in the standard program can be replaced only by one external process. Data is exchanged both ways. BTEs are being introduced in the Financial Accounting module.

Business Add-Ins

As opposed to customer exits, Business Add-Ins (BAdIs), take into account the changes to the software-delivery process. A Business Add-In contains the components of an enhancement, program enhancements: In the BAdI, the interfaces for program enhancements are defined in the form of interface methods, menu enhancements. These menu entries are available in the GUI definition and are made visible when the BAdI is implemented. Several components are created when you define a BAdI, of which two important ones are listed below:

▶ Interface

▶ Generated class that implements the interface

To implement BAdI's, use the transaction SE19 or go through this menu path: **Tools ABAP Workbench · Utilities · Business Add-Ins · Implementations**. Figure 8.16 displays a BAdI, and lists some of the methods being used, under the **Method** column.

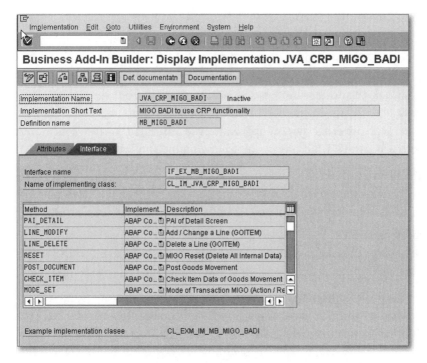

Figure 8.16 Confiiguration Option for System Modification

All the system modifications related to SD are found within the Display IMG. You can follow this menu path: **Sales and Distribution • System Modifications**. Let's review some of the configuration settings available:

▶ **Creating New Fields (Using Condition Techniques)**
These modification can be applied to the communication structure, condition tables, and access sequence. The communication structures KOMK (header fields) and KOMP (item fields), for example, contain all fields that are used to acess condition tables in the area of pricing.

▶ **Create New Fields (Without Consistion Techniques)**
The changes can be applied to places where condition technique is not used, for example, copying customer master and material master fields in Sales Document, and new fields for billing interfaces.

▶ **Routines**
These are short sub-programs that carry out various checks during document processing.

▶ **Users Exits**
All the user exits within the SD area are listed here.

▶ **Business Transaction Events**

This helps you connect components, such as function modules you developed or a product from an external software provider, to a standard R/3 system.

▶ **Business Add-Ins**

This lists system emhancements you can accomplish within SD using BAdIs. The ability to update planning values for sales order is delivered with SAP standard, which allows you to define conditions for updating planning values (program RMCSS008) in profitability analysis and in accounting.

Modifications

The manual changes made to the SAP sources and the changes made to the ABAP Dictionary objects must be registered by the designated developer. Exceptions to this registration are match codes, databases indexes, buffer settings, customer objects, patches, and objects, the changes of which are based on automatic generation, such as occur in Customizing. After an object is registered, the related key is stored locally and is automatically copied for later changes, regardless of which registered developer is making the changes. The registration helps quick error resolutions by the SAP support and avoids unintended modifications.

During modification adjustment, the old and new versions of ABAP Repository objects are compared using the transactions, SPDD and SPAU as seen below:

▶ **SPDD**

For domains, data element and tables. Use the menu path: **SAP Menu • Tools • ABAP Workbench• Utilities • Maintenance • Upgrade Utilities • Dictionary Compare**.

▶ **SPAU**

For ABAP programs, interfaces, screens, search help, views, and lock objects. The menu path is: **SAP Menu • ABAP Workbench • Utilities • Maintenance • Upgrade Utilities • Program Compare**.

During modification adjustments, you should use two different change requests to implements the changes made. One is for SPDD adjustments, and the other is for SPAU adjustments. Transaction SE95 provides modification assistance for objects.

Modification is useful because your live repository objects do not lose connections to the SAP standard. Conversely, copying is useful in that no modification adjustment will be needed for your live repository objects during subsequent upgrades. You will want to choose copying over modification, if there are many changes to the SAP programs and your requirement would not be met by future SAP releases.

SAP Note Assistant

The SAP Note Assistant automatically imports the note corrections (new programs; changes to existing programs) into the system using the Modification Assistance. Dependencies between this and other notes are recognized automatically, and if they have not been implemented SAP Note Assistant instructs you to import these notes into your system. Using SAP Note Assistant, you can download existing SAP Notes from the SAP Service Marketplace.

The Note Browser includes an overview of all the notes you have implemented in your system. The Modification Browser provides you an overview of all the objects that have been corrected by the note applications. You can use the transaction code SNOTE for help with note administration. Figure 8.17 displays the SNOTE transaction with the connection to note retrieval for displaying the SAP Note.

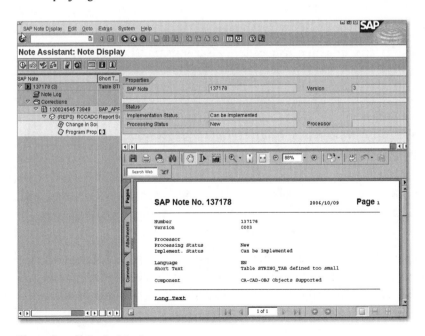

Figure 8.17 Note Assistant

8.6   Summary

There are several quick and useful ways to extract data or information from the system without the need for any programming or technical development work. For operational reporting and to help with the day-to-day operation, standard reports are available within the system. There are also info structures for analysis.

Business Intelligence helps for enterprise wide reporting, where you might get data from multiple systems and SAP ERP could be one feed to the BW system. You can use configuration and personalization tools to build the application to suit your needs. There are other delivered enhancement tools to help you meet the gaps within the application.

The other key technical aspects of an implementation involve the data transfer from a legacy system, and communicating with external system and interfaces. We will conclude our book in Chapter 9 by describing the interfaces and communication between different SAP and non-SAP systems.

SAP provides different technologies and methods for transferring data to and from the ERP system. There might be a need for one-time conversion or ongoing data transfer or a way to provide notification through print or any other electronic media. You might also need to establish communication between systems for regular data transfer. Sales and Distribution (SD) processes are enhanced and extended with SAP's Customer Relationship Management System, primarily the customer-facing processes; e.g., marketing, campaign management, and lead management. Global Trade System interfaces with the SAP ERP for trade solution, and closely interfaces with SD for export solutions.

9 Data Transfer, Outputs, Communication, and Interfaces with Other SAP Systems

On occasion, companies need to transfer data from other SAP systems, other SAP modules or even non-SAP systems. The system imports and converts the data from a sequential input file that was created from the data of your lagacy or other SAP system (feeder system). Output determination helps determinate the output specific to your business transaction. Like pricing, output determination uses the standard tools available within SAP, e.g., condition techniques and output contol.

Communication between SAP and non-SAP involves various technologies, and methodologies. Communication and data interfaces differ. Communication interfaces are channel-to communications, whereas, data interfaces are used for read and write access to the SAP data. Interfaces with other SAP systems can be triggered from within an SAP function module. For instance Global Trade Services can be triggered through SAP SD sales orders, deliveries and MM purchase order. In the case of mySAP CRM, the function is triggered from CRM to the SD system. Let us now take a deeper look into data transfer, outputs, communication and interfaces with other SAP systems.

9.1   Data Transfer

When companies convert from legacy systems to SAP ERP, there might be large datasets, and these might call for a systematic or automated way to transfer these data in volume and in background. You might want to transfer data from external systems to the SAP system or from the SAP system to the external systems on an ongoing basis. To ensure data integrity (system checks), you need to follow procedures for importing the data into the SAP system. SAP provides many ways to transfer data out and in with checks. The two main tools available in SAP to transfer from another SAP system or non-SAP system into SAP are given below:

▶ Data Transfer Workbench (DX-WB)

▶ Legacy System Migration Workbench (LSMW)

These two tools, both discussed in this chapter, provide a central access and make it simpler for the programs developed with the application to do the actual transfer. LSMW allows you to format and map the data. DX-WB helps you import or load the data, which is converted into SAP format. DX-WB provides a framework and allows you to schedule the tasks. Apart from the formatting, the most important step is mapping of data. This involves mapping of the data to SAP structure and specifying any conversion.

SAP transactions support the conversion process by helping identify the fields and performing the relevant checks. You need to check for transfer logic, if these transactions provide it, before using them. Business Object Repository (BOR) is the central repository of SAP business object types, SAP interface types, and their definitions and methods. The data-transfer objects in the DX-WB orient themselves by the business object numbers and names in the BOR.

The key techniques available in data transfer are batch input; call transaction, direct input (online), BAPI, and IDOC. Batch input uses the application transaction in background by creating the relevant data and data are imported into the system as per the session scheduled. With call transactions, the data are entered online in real time into the application, unlike batch input.

With direct input, the data integrity is checked by the program used for updating the tables within the SAP system. Intermediate document (IDoc) is another standard format for data transfer between systems. SAP uses an Application Linking and Enabling (ALE) model to enable exchange of data between systems, where data are converted into IDoc format and passed to

ALE inbound processing. An IDoc is created in the database for each record, and a function module is associated with this IDoc, which checks the data before updating the application table.

Using Electronic Data Interface (EDI), documents like sales orders can be exchanged by different partners, such as sold-to parties and ship-to parties. An open interface permits incoming and outgoing EDI messages with the SAP system. Incoming EDI messages can be inquiries, sales orders, order modifications by customer, and shipping notifications. They are converted by the appropriate EDI format (example, ANSIX12 or EDIFACT) into the intermediate document (IDoc) and archived.

Business Application Programming Interfaces (BAPIs) are standardized programming interface that provides access to business process and data within SAP system. Like online transaction, they make the integrity check. You can also use a transaction recorder to record the sequence of transactions, including all screens that run, and execute this as a program using a batch input or call transaction. Given below are some examples of a BAPI used with SAP SD:

▶ **BAPI_SALESDOCU_CREATEFROMDATA**
Creating a Sales and Distribution Document

▶ **BAPI_SALESORDER_CHANGE**
Sales order: Change Sales Order

▶ **BAPI_SALESORDER_CONFIRMDELVRY**
Sales Order: Confirmation of Delivery; Document Flow Update

▶ **BAPI_SALESORDER_CREATEFROMDAT1**
Sales order: Create Sales Order

▶ **BAPI_SALESORDER_CREATEFROMDAT2**
Sales order: Create Sales Order

▶ **BAPI_SALESORDER_GETLIST**
Sales order: List of all Orders for Customer

▶ **BAPI_SALESORDER_GETSTATUS**
Sales Order: Display Status

▶ **BAPI_SALESORDER_SIMULATE**
Sales Order: Simulate Sales Order

9.1.1 Techniques in Detail

Batch-input programs provide structured work areas for data to be transferred in the form of an internal table (BDC table) and provide them in the

body of the batch-input session. A batch-input session consists of header part (session header, as described by the ABAP Dictionary structure APQD) with general data. The session body contains all application-specific transaction data. The batch input session is a three-step process: opening the batch input session, inserting data for transaction, and closing the batch input session.

Table 9.1 shows you the structure of a BDCDATA, where each screen that is processed during the transaction flow must be identified in the form of a record.

PROGRAM	Screen No/DYNPRO	Start of Screen/ DYNBEGIN	Field Name	Field Value
SAPMV45A	101	X	VBAK-VKORG	OR

Table 9.1 BDCDATA Structure

The batch inputs are processed through sessions in background either through the Batch Input Monitor (BI Monitor) manually or automatically using the program RSDBCSUB. Batch Input Monitor can be accessed through SAP Easy Access or the SAP Screen as you log on, by following this menu path: **Services • Batch Input • Sessions**. You also can use transaction code SM35.

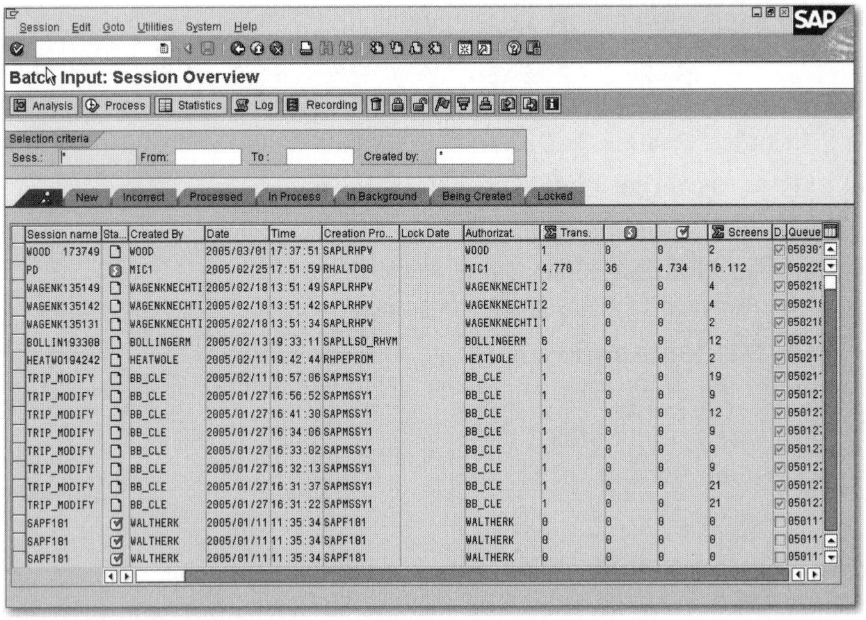

Figure 9.1 Batch Input Session

Figure 9.1 displays the BI Monitor transaction. You can review the sessions you have created and select them for processing through this BI Monitor transaction. The system will ask you to respond to the processing mode and additional functions before you can save the processing.

Table 9.2 provides the list of BI functions and OK codes, which can be applied to while recording your sessions or writing a program for batch input. When you create a program for data upload—let's say, converting your legacy sales order into SAP ERP—you might want to record the sequence of transaction with the SAP ERP sales-order create-and-save function. These OK codes will be in use while you are creating the BDC program and then use the input file to update the data.

You can export and import the session contents at operating system level while you are in the BI Monitor by following the menu path: **Utilities • Export/Import Session**.

BDC OK Code	Function	Details
/n	Next Transaction	Terminate current batch input transaction and flag as incorrect
/bdel	Delete Transaction	Delete the current batch input transaction in session
/bend	Cancel	Terminate batch input processing and flag session as incorrect
/bda	Process in Foreground	Switch display mode from display errors only to process in foreground.
/bde	Display Errors Only	Switch display mode from process in foreground to display errors only
/bdx	Expert Mode	When you exit BI, processing errors are suppressed
/bbeg	Restart Transaction	Back to start of transaction

Table 9.2 BDC OK Codes

9.1.2 Data Transfer Workbench

A workbench is a platform or a group of utility programs available within the SAP system. The Data Transfer Workbench (DX-WB) provides a range of standard programs for loading data into your SAP system and they are registered as task type LOA.

The typical steps involved include the selection of object type from the application, selection of supporting program type, and selection of data-transfer program or method.

DX-WB can be accessed via this menu path: **Tools • Data Transfer Workbench**. This tool allows you to copy data between application server and the presentation server. The tool also allows you to split based on your defined criteria and merge later. You need to define a mapping plan from the target structure to the source structure with the following commands:

▶ **M**
Move

▶ **F**
Fixed value

▶ **V**
Variable

▶ **M + C**
Move and conversion

DX-WB is a project-management tool that enables you to create projects, sub-projects, process flows, and tasks. Data-transfer methods can be used in the DX-WB only if they have been registered first. When you use the program to upload data, it utilizes three steps:

▶ Opening the dataset, process by reading the dataset

▶ Transfer of dataset

▶ Close the dataset

This utility could be used for uploading master data; e.g., customer master, or material master.

9.1.3 Legacy System Migration Workbench

This utility was provided by SAP to help with legacy data conversion. It provides you different tools to define your upload data from a legacy system. Legacy System Migration Workbench (LSMW) has a recording function, enabling you to generate data migration object from an entry transaction or a change transaction. It uses the comma-separated values with a three-step process of importing the file into LSMW format, conversion of data for formatting and assigning it to appropriate structure, and then calling SAP standard transfer programs, BAPIs, or IDocs to transfer the data.

As with DX-WB, you need to provide a mapping plan. This can be accessed through the transaction code LSMW. You could use this to upload data either directly into the table within SAP or through transaction codes such as sales order creation (VA01), or by converting delivery notes from your legacy system. You can use the standard functions to upload the data directly into the SAP system with no programming or with little programming; e.g., validating the data before upload, or performing a conversion before upload.

9.1.4 Direct Input

An alternative to the batch input is the direct method. This method is preferred over other methods when transferring large datasets. Unlike batch input, no sessions are created, as the data is updated directly. The data is entered directly into database tables by calling function modules that carry out the necessary checks. If an error occurs during data transfer, direct input has a restart mechanism. Program RBMVSHOW or transactions BMV0 (direct input monitor) are provided to manage and start direct input programs. Some examples of direct input programs available in the SAP system are:

▶ Sales Document (RVINVB10)

▶ Material Master (RMDATIND)

▶ FI document (RFBIBL00)

9.1.5 Intermediate Documents

Intermediate Documents (IDocs) are based on a message-oriented data structure, where data is extracted from the application and transferred into the IDoc formats, also called application documents. The IDoc communicates between these application documents, in the language spoken by both applications. Data can be stored before the application document is created. This is important, for instance, when incorrect data is transferred. In this case, the application document is only created when the data is corrected. Each IDoc in the SAP database consists of a control record, data record, and status record. The data record includes the application data in their segments and describes the hierarchy in which these segments are organized in the IDoc. There are standard IDocs within SD for order acknowledgement or sending a bill to your customer. These can be used as part of your EDI process.

9.1.6 Business Application Programming Interfaces

Business Application Programming Interfaces (BAPIs) are a standard set of programs supplied and maintained by SAP for different business objects or processes, like sales order create or change. External data in the IDoc format is required for calling BAPIs from the DX-WB. Mapping tools, such as the LSMW, therefore must be used to convert the external data to the IDoc format. BAPIs can also be called by external clients as methods of objects that are instantiated in the client itself. BAPIs can be invoked for data transfer as part of BOR. This can be accessed through SAP Easy Access by following this path: **Tools • ABAP Workbench • Development • Business Object Builder**. BAPIs can be access through this path: **Tools • Business Framework • BAPI Explorer**.

9.2 Output Control

Data transfer is used for uploading data into the SAP system. There is no need to send data out of your system in different formats for communicating with external partners and internally as well. In the subsections that follow, we will go over the output processing.

9.2.1 Output Determination: Applications

Output is a means of communication for exchanging information between partners and systems. You can set requirements to determine whether an output should be created, who will receive it, and which transmission medium should be used. The output determination components offer output functions for sales, shipping, transportation, and billing to help you manage sales transactions with your customers and within your company. The information that influences output determination is stored as master data, in the form of condition records. Some examples of output types in SD are given below:

- Order confirmation BA00/BA01 (EDI)
- Delivery note (LD00)
- Invoice (RD00)
- Invoice cash sale (RD03)
- Sales activity (KO00)
- MAIL credit processing (KRML)

▶ Scheduling agreement (LP00)

▶ Quotation confirmation (AN00)

The outputs are different for header and item level. The different transmission media available are: printouts or inclusion in printed documents, telex, email, external transmission, SAPoffice, and EDI. Processing the output is controlled by a processing program, which itself consists of programs with the relevant layout sets assigned to individual output type and transmission medium.

The program, when called or invoked searches for a communication strategy, which represents the sequence of communication types. The system will search for the central address management for the communication types; e.g., in the sequence of e-mail, fax, and than print out. This information is mentioned in the additional data of the output condition record. Figure 9.2 displays the SAP screen of output maintenances.

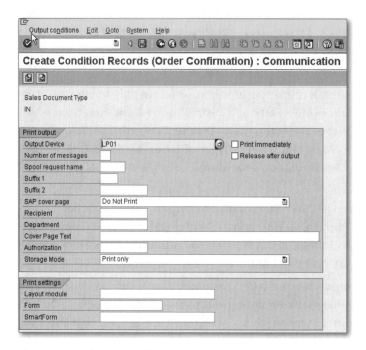

Figure 9.2 Condition Record

The output issues are controlled by the data maintained in the output record. The standard program RSNAST00 set to run at regular intervals based on the time maintained in the condition record. The time of execution is identified by numbers, as seen next:

▶ **1**
Output is selected when the program is run next time

▶ **2**
At the time specified by the user

▶ **3**
Process the output online or batch

▶ **4**
Issued when document is posted

9.2.2   Output Determination: Condition Techniques

Output is determined using condition techniques such as pricing or text determination. A condition record for an output type contains the requirements for that output type. If these are met, then the system proposes that particular output type. You can run the analysis against the output determination while you are in the sales document create, change or display screen by following this path: **Extras · Output · Header (or Item) · Process · Goto · Determination analysis**. Following are the configuration steps in setting up output determination:

▶ To assign output determination procedures, follow this menu path: **Display SAP Reference IMG · Sales and Distribution · Basic Functions · Output Control · Output Determination · Output Determiation Using Condition Technique · Maintain Output Determination for Sales Documents · Assign Output Determination Procedure**.

▶ To maintain output conditions and access sequence, follow this path: **Display SAP Reference IMG · Sales and Distribution · Basic Functions · Output Control · Output Determination · Output Determiation Using Condition Technique · Maintain Output Determination for Sales Documents · Maintain Output Types and Maintain Access Sequence**.

▶ To maintain output determination for outbound deliveries: **Display SAP Reference IMG · Logistics Execution · Shipping · Basic Principles · Output Control · Output Determination · Maintain Output Determination for Outbound Deliveries**.

▶ To define print parameters follow this path: **Display SAP Reference IMG · Logistics Execution · Shipping · Basic Principles · Output Control · Output Determination · Define shipping printing parameters**.

Figure 9.3 displays a typical output determination procedure.

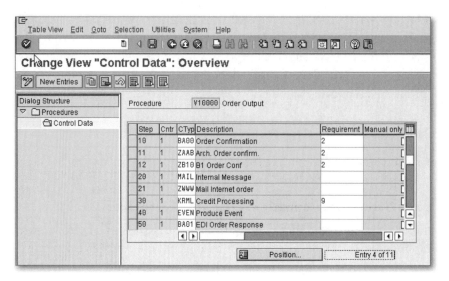

Figure 9.3 Output Determination Procedure

When you have communication or interfaces with multiple systems, there might be a need to trigger a process or function from one system to another. Let's say you have an interface with mySAP ERP and Global Trade Services (GTS), and when a sales order is created, it is configured to call GTS. There are function modules or remote function calls invoked in the SAP ERP system, which calls the GTS system for performing trade checks. Following the checks, it returns the results back to the originating system with an OK-to-process or a not-OK-to-process the sales order. Let's discuss the remote function call in the next section.

9.3   Communication

Remote function call (RFC) is based on the Common Programming Interface—Communication (CPI-C), which allows programs to communicate with each other. It consists of so called CPI-C calls that a program uses to set up a connection to another program, to transmit, or to receive data, and then disconnect the connection again. Figure 9.4 displays the communication and data interface between any remote system and SAP system.

Communication interface and data interfaces are different. In addition to the file I/O, the communication interfaces are the gate to external communication, whereas the data interfaces are used for read and write access to the R/3 database. In the example of SAP ERP and GTS with sales order, there might

not be any update back into the SAP sales order, but there might be other processes with the interface that might need to update SAP ERP based on the result from the GTS system. Such processes might be sending customer master records from SAP ERP to GTS, where the mySAP ERP system keeps track of all successful updates to the GTS system.

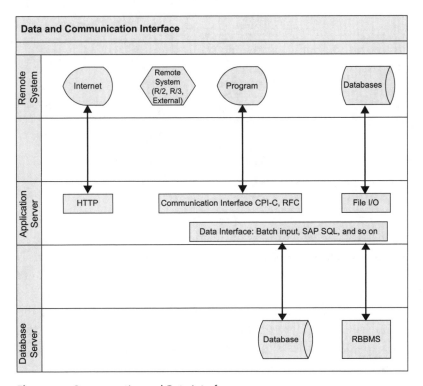

Figure 9.4 Communcation and Data Interface

9.3.1 Synchronous and Asynchronous RFCs

You can call an RFC within a SAP system; in which case it runs the same work process as the calling program. You need to maintain an RFC destination for the RFC to call. Transaction code SM59 is used to maintain RFC destination, which specifies an ABAP program when calling a remote function module in the RFC side of the information table, RFCDES. RFCs can be synchronous or asynchronous.

Synchronous processing is stalled in the calling program until the called remote function is processed and its output is returned. Processing in the calling program continues after the call. Asynchronous mode is meant for parallel processing, where the called remote function is started and process-

ing continues immediately afterwards in the calling program. Remote function is separate from the calling program, and the output of the function can be received later in the program.

With both synchronous and asynchronous RFCs, each call makes up a single logical unit of work (LUW) in a remote system. You can use transactional RFCs (tRFC) to bundle several remote functions into one LUW (with an automatic rollback mechanism in case of error). Use of tRFCs guarantees return confirmation of the remote processing status and ability to manage tRFC LUWs using transaction SM58. LUWs generated through tRFC are processed independent of each other. If you want to ensure LUWs are processed in the same order they were generated, you might want to use queued RFC (qRFC) as an extension of tRFC. You can manage the RFC queues using transaction SMQ1.

9.3.2 Configuration Set-Up

RFC destinations are maintained in the source system only. RFC destinations are maintained using the transaction code SM59. Figure 9.5 displays the SAP screen shot of typical connections. One destination is maintained for the corresponding type, depending on the remote system. In the figure you can see, in red (shaded section on the right-hand side) are the trusted system with error in opening up the RFC connections. Figure 9.5 displays the result of the transaction SMT2 run.

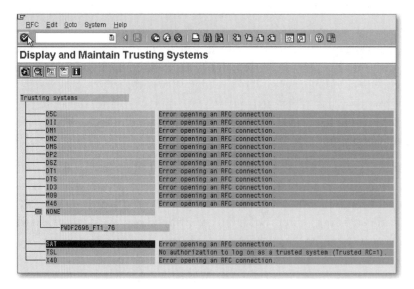

Figure 9.5 Display of Trusting System

If you want to connect to an R/3 you need a destination type 3. The name on the type 3 destination is case sensitive, and when you connect to one R/3 system, you set the Load distribution option to **No** (meaning not applicable). Then you need to specify the R/3 application server using the target host and system number parameters. If you do want to use load distribution when you log on, set the load distribution option to **Yes**.

In this case, you must specify the system ID, the message server, and the required logon group. This information can be found through the transactions SM51 (overview of R/3 servers) and SMLG (overview of logon groups) in the SAP R/3 target system. The message server can be displayed using the transaction code RZ11 or report RSPFPAR. In the destination system, you can specify the logon data of the user in the target system. This must be a user of the type dialog or CPICCPIC (this type is named *communication* in more recent releases). When the destination is used, the logon to the target system occurs automatically.

When you want to connect to the external RFC programs, you need a destination type **T**. There might be two different variations of the type **T**, which are given below:

▶ The external program is started when the actual communication is being established. In this case, you need to update the program names in the program path. You also need to specify the explicit host with the host name, where the program is located and the path of the location. You must also mention the front-end workstation where the external program is started or triggered.

▶ The second approach occurs when the destination variations let you access a program that has already started and has registered itself on a gateway. Here you specify the program ID—the identifier under which the external server program has registered on the SAP gateway—and the Gateway itself, where you specify the host and TCP/IP service of the gateway where the external program has registered.

With SAP R/3 release 4.7 and with SAP Web Application Server 6.20, you can check the authorization at the destination. You can declare a trust relationship between two SAP R/3 Systems so that you can perform certain RFC logons in the trusting system without requiring a password for released users. You need to grant the authorization object S_RFCACL to the user you want to release in the trusting system. You always declare the trust relation-

ship in the target system. You can use transaction SMT1 to define trust relationship. You can use the transaction SMT2 in the trusted system to display which trusting systems are declared for the local system.

When you want to call functions through the intranet, Internet or Web, you will use the WebRFC. WebRFC is the term used when you call special function modules in R/3 using the Internet Transaction Server (ITS). ITS connects the three-tiered client server architecture of R/3 with two tiered HTTP client/server architecture. From R/3 point of view, the ITS and HTTP servers from an intermediate layer between the application and presentation layers. From the Internet user's point of view, the ITS takes care of the interactive HTML pages.

9.3.3   RFC Utilities

SAP provides some transactions or utilities to manage and monitor RFCs. I'll describe some of the most popularly used transactions, below:

▶ Use transaction code ST22 in the remote system to analyze short dumps. Short dumps are programs that failed to execute or complete their jobs. With this transaction, you can analyze why a RFC failed to complete its designated job.

▶ Use transaction SMGW to display all running remote connections on the R/3 gateway. This transaction can give you a snapshot of all the remote connections between systems.

▶ Trace captures information on processing of the remote function call. It keeps tracks of all the activities or steps the remote function goes through from the initiation to complete as described below:

   ▶ ST05 for user-related: With this you can analyze the user involved in running the RFC, and if any issues encountered; e.g., the user didn't have sufficient authorization to execute the RFC and it failed.

   ▶ SM59 for destination-related: This transaction will capture information on the destination system, when the RFC makes a call to the other system.

   ▶ SMGW gateway-related: This will capture information on any issues with the communication gateway.

When you communicate between SAP systems, you might use the different functions modules to perform different functions within the target system.

Let's say, you have a website where customers can log on and request a product. This calls for a creating a sales order in your SAP SD system and—once it is complete—to send an acknowledgement to the customer, with the sales order number. SAP delivers BAPIs, which are designed to perform these functions: sales order create, get status, etc. Let's see use the application of BAPI.

9.4 Interfaces with Other Systems

SAP provides a Business Framework to allow the technical integration and exchange of business data among SAP components and between SAP and non-SAP components. Let's say you have a non-SAP system for customer relationship management (CRM) and would like to process the CRM order through the SAP SD system.

You might want to map to one of the sales order create a BAPI for transferring the CRM order into the mySAP ERP system. A major component of the Business Framework is Business Application Programming Interfaces (BAPIs). The integration can include both components within a local network and components that are connected with one another through the Internet. BAPIs allow integration at the business level, not at the technical level.

BAPIs are special, remote-enabled methods of a business object; they are implemented as RFC-enabled function modules. They are interfaces to SAP data. BAPI can be used for different applications, such as Internet application components, building R/3 components for communication between the business objects from different R/3 components (applications).

BAPIs can be accessed from external clients like methods. SAP guarantees for no incompatible changes with upgrades. They are used with the SAP system to access business data, and they make it easier to add functions to the SAP system.

9.4.1 Basic Parts of the Business Framework

The basic parts of the SAP R/3 Business Framework are discussed below:

▸ **Business Components**
Business components consist of business objects and provide autonomous business functions.

▸ **Business Objects**
The business object encapsulates the business data and functionality and

defines the functional scope and boundaries of Business Component. Communication technologies, for example, Distributed Component Object Model (DCOM) and RFC use the Business Framework to access BAPIs. Business object type is used to break the SAP R/3 system down into smaller, specific units. Business object types form the point of entry to the data and the functionality of the SAP R/3 System. The business object type Sales Order represents a customer's request to the company to supply a particular quantity of material at certain time or to perform service at a certain time. The business object type contains all the necessary information for a sales order: sold-to-party, sales organization, document date, net value, etc.

▶ **BAPI**

BAPIs are defined as Application Programming Interface (API) methods of SAP Business Object Types. API describes how one program can get another program to carry out a service. These object types are used within the Business Framework to enable object-based communication between components. Applications can use BAPIs to directly access the application layer of the R/3 System. As clients; applications can use business logic of the R/3 System. BAPIs provide the client with an object-oriented view of the application objects, without its needing to know the implementation details.

BAPIs can be used for different types of integrations. For connecting an SAP R/3 system to the Internet using the SAP Business Connector or Internet Application Components (IACs). BAPIs also allow the creation of true software components, which enable communication between SAP components. It allows the integrations with other SAP components, like CRM with ERP and GTS with ERP, as well as implementation of distributed R/3 scenarios with asynchronous connections using ALE. You can also use programs using as a front end to the R/3 System, developed with Visual Basic or Java, for example. Finally you can develop a workflow application that extends beyond system boundaries.

You can use the transaction code BAPI (BAPI Explorer) to display all business objects with BAPIs, grouped by application. This is a logical view of the BOR in which only those objects that have BAPIs are displayed. You can also use the transaction code SE84 to perform a generalized search for objects, such as function modules or dictionary structures, without having to first access the related development tool. SAP delivers libraries for BAPI calls for various development environments (Visual Basic, C ++, Java). These libraries include technical details of the communication, enabling

developers to call a BAPI from outside the system without having to worry about how BAPIs are actually implemented in the system.

The BAPI Explorer is divided into two areas: Hierarchy and Work Area. In the Work Area you can view the details and documentation of the development object selected in the hierarchy display. Figure 9.6 displays the BAPI Explorer transaction.

▶ **ALE**
Section 9.5 discusses this in detail.

▶ **Communication Services**
Section 9.5 covers this in detail as well.

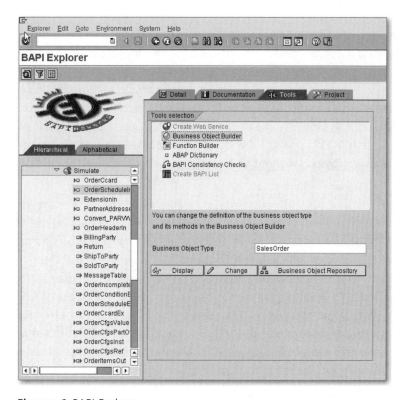

Figure 9.6 BAPI Explorer

9.4.2 Function Builder

Function builder is an important aspect of BAPI, which helps you create programs in modular form, implement, test, and document them with function groups. The Function Builder includes a Function Library that serves as the central storage for all function modules. You can access Function Builder

from the BAPI Explorer as well as accessing it directly with the menu path: **SAP standard menu Tools • ABAP Workbench • Development • Function Builder**. You can also use the transaction code SE37.

BAPIs that belong to the same SAP object type should be created in one function group. You should deviate from this practice only in exceptional cases. Similarly, BAPIs belonging to different SAP business object types must not be put into the same function group. Figure 9.7 displays the Function Builder transaction SE37 displaying the function module—**BAPI_QUOTATION_CREATEFROMDATA2** source code. The **Import** tab lists all the key values that will be passed to the BAPI by the calling program; e.g., the quotation number, if you would like to assign one external, header information, such as sold-to party and line information. The export tab lists the return values send back to the calling program; e.g., the document number, after the quotation is successfully created.

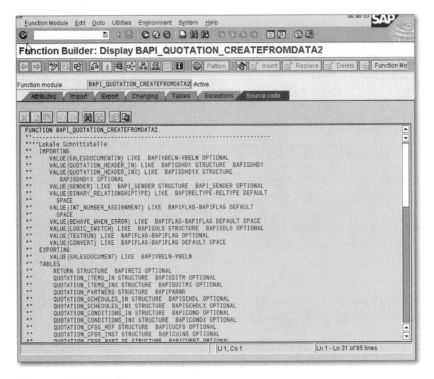

Figure 9.7 BAPI Display

The top command bar, the **Function module** documentation provides details on the BAPIs. There are four areas of the BAPI documents that you need to understand before implementing them. These are looked at next:

▶ **Business Object-type Documentation**
This provides a detailed documentation.

▶ **Method Documentation**
This describes the business fucntion of the BAPI, the method in detail.

▶ **BAPI Parameter Documentation**
Provides information on the individual parameters associated with the Function Module.

▶ **Data Element Documentation**
These documentations are done in the Data Dictionary for each field in the BAPI parameters.

9.4.3 Business Application

BAPI explorer provides documentation on the BAPI project implementation. This can be found under the project tab page with the BAPI Explorer. You need to describe the business scenario or business process, a series of individual business functions, separately from technical details. The following lists some of the high level you need to take before deciding on a BAPI:

▶ Determining whether application systems are to be integrated in the scenarios or if the frontends of the applications are to be connected

▶ Identifying the relevant components and the tasks they perform

▶ Determining information and process flow

Before the scenario can be converted and started with a concrete definition and implementation of the BAPI, it should be reviewed.

You can test the parameters in your function module in one test by entering the appropriate test values in the parameters to verify that the source code in the function module can run without errors. This also can ensure that error messages are tested as well. Figure 9.8 displays the test-function screen within the Function Builder. This can be executed by clicking on the Test/Execute icon (seen in Figure 9.7 as a wrench) in the command bar or by using **F8**.

Based on the mandatory fields required for the function module, you need to key them in within the Import parameters and Tables by selecting each section (header, items, schedule line, etc). The Return section should provide you with the return information after executing this function module. After entering the data, you can test this by clicking on the Execute icon or using the function key **F8**.

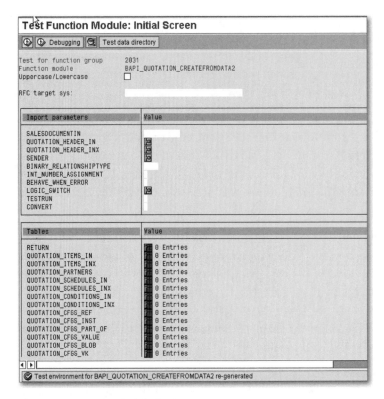

Figure 9.8 Function Module Testing

SAP provides a communication structure or model to interface with two SAP systems. These are called Application Linking and Enabling. This technology can also be used for communicating and interfacing with another sub-system, such as EDI or a non-SAP system. In the next section, we will go over the ALE and IDoc communications.

9.5   Access Shared Data

Companies might want to decentralize their business applications and at the same time ensure simultaneous data consistency. This might call for an access to shared data. Some reasons for distributed data or business application could include market globalization; independent business units; company -wide business process; data protection, industry, language and country versions; 24/7 availability; load distribution; communication with non-SAP systems and new dimension products, to mention a few.

In the decentralized warehouse, there might be one central warehouse system referenced by multiple ERP systems. Let's suppose that a sales order, once a delivery is created, might refer to the warehouse management system for performing warehouse functions and returning post-goods issue and creation of a billing document.

Application Linking and Enabling (ALE) was originally used to distribute business processes by forwarding the required data and triggering a workflow in the external system. ALE is independent of the communication layer and can implement business processes over the Internet. Using an IDoc or the IDoc interface, ALE enables business processes that go beyond company boundaries, e.g., business-to-business.

IDoc is a container for the data of a business object or technical R/3 object. Each IDoc has a message type, which indicates the type of business object or the business function of the data. Message types have processing rules in the receiving system. An IDoc contains the data in a segment hierarchy. The IDoc type describes the technical structure of the IDoc and they have versions. An IDoc has different characteristics: database tables, text, HTML file, XML datastream, RFC call parameters.

The message type specifies the semantic of application data. The message type is usually based on an EDIFACT message type. The syntax (structure information) of the data is described in the IDoc type.

9.5.1 ALE Applications

ALE supports data consistency and data availability in distributed business processes. ALE provides an infrastructure for coupling system loosely through asynchronous messaging using IDocs or coupling systems narrowly through synchronous BAPI calls. ALE also enables communications between different SAP systems, non-SAP systems. ALE business processes distribute master data and transactional data.

Master data transfer uses the asynchronous communication, where the data when created, changed, or deleted; the IDocs are created when a change pointer is processed. As master data calls for volume and data are stable for the long term, they are staged and then sent through this change-pointer program, job, or trigger. Figure 9.9 displays the ALE data flow between SAP R/3 systems.

ALE uses SAP R/3 Basis function for asynchronous communication using IDocs. The Basis functions carry out tasks of writing to the database, check syntax of IDoc type, and communicate low-level with output devices and R/3

port types. Partner profiles control the communication of asynchronous IDocs in outbound processing and inbound processing. Different partner types are used in IDoc outbound processing; e.g., logical system, customer vendor. The partner type for ALE communications is the logical system (LS). The partner profile with a partner-type logical system only exists for systems to which the current client sends messages or from which the current client receives messages.

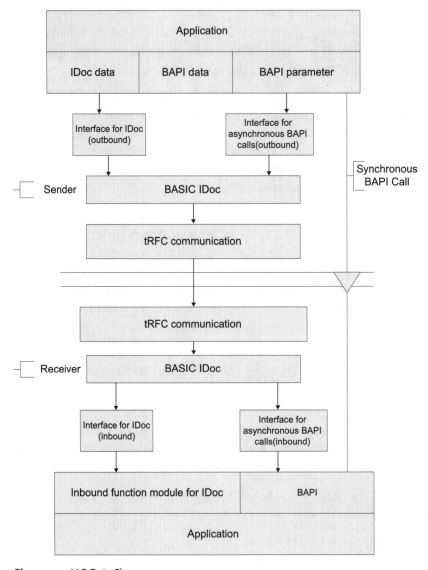

Figure 9.9 ALE Data Flow

ALE Configuration

The general configuration steps for ALE can be found by following this menu path: **Display IMG · SAP NetWeaver · SAP Web Application Server · IDoc Interface/Application Linking Enabling (ALE) · Basis Settings**.

Alternatively, you can use the transaction code SALE and get to the configuration item under IDoc Interface/Application Link Enabling (ALE). You need to configure the two steps needed within the LS: Define Logical Systems and Assign Logical Systems to Client. Messages in the ALE flow between logical systems. Logical systems are defined cross-client in R/3. Precisely one logical system is assigned to one client. When messages are posted, this logical system is transferred into application documents.

Local organizational units must be assigned to global organizational units in your systems to ensure that organizational units are standardized in the distributed environment. The settings for converting global organizational units can be found under the menu path: **IDoc Interface/Application Link Enabling · Modeling and Implementing Business Processes · Cross-Application Settings · Global Organizational Units**.

For enabling field contents and data conversion mapped from a sender field to receiver fields, follow this menu path: **IDoc Interface/Application Link Enabling · Modeling and Implementing Business Processes · Converting Data Between Sender and Receiver**. For example, a customer number in your system might not match the actual customer name (as they might be internal system generated number or your own created identifier). So you might want to maintain a conversion of these data fields:

▶ For maintaining distribution models, use this menu path: **IDoc Interface/Application Link Enabling · Modeling and Implementing Business Processes · Maintain Distribution Model and Distribute Views**.

▶ For defining partner profiles, use this menu path: **SAP Customizing IMG · SAP NetWeaver · SAP Web Application Server · IDoc Interface/Application Link Enabling (ALE) · Modeling and Implementing Business Processes · Partner Profiles**.

Partner Profile controls the processing of inbound and outbound IDocs. The important parameters are:

▶ Size of IDoc packets per RFC call

▶ Size of IDoc packets for processing

▶ Output and processing mode: collect or process immediately

Partner Profiles are client independent. An existing Partner Profile can be viewed, and you can create new ones using the transaction code WE20. Here it allows you to map the partner number (external number for communicating with the system or identifying the system), partner type, language, message type, etc. The settings for IDoc version change are made in Partner Profile maintenance in the field Segment release in IDoc type.

The Partner Type LS (Logical System) is supplied by default in the system. You can test the IDoc transfer by using the configuration step Generate Partner Profile under the Partner Profiles folder.

▶ For defining ports, use transaction code WE21. R/3 ports define the device interface and its technical parameters for IDoc outbound processing. The port type defines the output medium:

  ▶ Transactional RFC for ALE business processes

  ▶ File

  ▶ CPI-C connection to R/2

  ▶ Internet (email attachment)

  ▶ ABAP-PSS (programming interface/function module)

  ▶ XML (XML file format)

▶ The RFC destination contains the access settings for the target system of a Remote Function Call. Use the transaction code SM59. The different connection types for RFC destinations are given below:

  ▶ R/2 connections (entry type 2)

  ▶ R/3 connections used by ALE (entry type 3); you will have to specify the host name and communication service. As of release 3.0, you can choose to specify a load adjustment.

  ▶ Internet connections (entry type 1)

  ▶ Logical destinations (entry type L); type L uses information from the reference entry and adds its own informaiton to this. You can also enter a specific user name, password, logon language, or client.

  ▶ TCP/IP connections for Business Connector (type T); used for connections to external program with RFC libraries to receive RFCs. The activation type can be start or registration.

  ▶ Connections using ABAP drivers (type X) ; you should choose the host name and the device driver.

ALE Tool Box

The ALE tool box contains separate programs for monitoring, modeling, and error-handling, such as:

▶ ALE Audit

▶ Synchronization of customizing data

▶ Reduction of message type

▶ IDoc recovery following database crash

▶ Conversion of logical system names

Figure 9.10 displays the configuration options available with IDoc Interface/ALE:

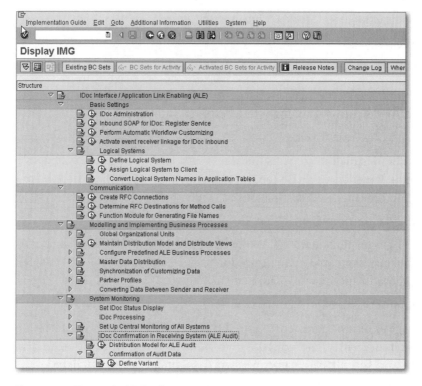

Figure 9.10 IDoc and ALE Configuration Settings

9.5.2 IDoc Applications

IDoc components consist of control record, data records, and status records in the database. Figure 9.11 displays the structure of a message type **MATMAS05**. You can see the hierarchy levels with the pop-up window dis-

playing the segment **E1MARAM**. The IDoc type of a message type determines which application data belongs to a message, in which order. The structure of the individual rows is determined by a segment type. The segments can be hierarchically dependent on each other.

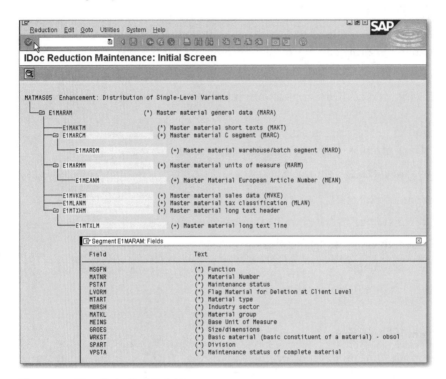

Figure 9.11 IDoc Reduction Maintenance

The IDoc types supplied by SAP are known as basis types. Basis types can be combined with customer-defined enhancements, according to strict rules. The segment type describes the row structure of a segment of the IDoc. For every segment field, the field name is stored along with the technical properties and semantic of the field. Note the following details on how the IDoc type is structured:

▶ **IDoc Type Attributes**
Information, such as the first release of the IDoc type.

▶ **Segment Attributes**
This indicates if segments must be included in the IDoc as mandatory or optional and also the number of segments of each type that are permitted.

▶ **Field Attributes**
The technical and semantic properties of a field.

IDocs use conditions for the following reasons:

▶ Filtering segments

▶ Dependencies of message types and BAPIs

▶ Distributing classified master data

Filtering can be defined in the distribution model to set conditions for the dispatch and processing of outbound messages. If the message type allows, the IDoc segments of message types can be filtered.

The task of the IDoc application interface is to process outbound and inbound IDocs based on message type. There is a close relationship between outbound processing and the distribution model. The application interfaces for IDocs provide special services for processing messages, namely:

▶ Data filtering

▶ Segment filtering

▶ Conversion of global organization units

▶ Data conversion in IDoc fields

▶ Version change

▶ Serialization using business objects

Outbound Processing

The application program determines with APIs of ALE whether the business object is to be distributed. The application program fills the data structure for the IDoc control record and the IDoc data record. The data is transferred to the function module MASTER_IDOC_DISTRIBUTE. For each potential receiver MASTER_IDOC_DISTRIBUTE creates a separate temporary IDoc, processes the IDoc data in IDoc services, and, if required, creates an IDoc for each receiver in the database. The IDocs are transferred in the communication layer. This forwards the IDocs to the partner systems.

You can check the current status of the IDocs by using the Status Monitor for ALE Messages. To display this, either call transaction BD87, or choose the following this path from the SAP Easy Access menu: **Tools • ALE • ALE Administration • Monitoring • Status Monitoring**.

Asynchronous BAPIs

Outbound processing for asynchronous BAPI calls is similar to IDoc processing. For the ALE user, the use of a BAPI is transparent and equivalent to clas-

sical message type. As an interim step ALE interface converts the BAPI parameters into an IDoc with the appropriate segments structure and message type.

IDoc Services

IDoc services tailor messages to the requirements of the receiving logical system. Business factors and the organizational structure play an important role in these requirements: data filtering, global organizational units, field conversion. The sequence of IDoc services in outbound processing is given below:

▶ Data filtering (IDOC_DATA_APPLY_FILTER_VALUES)

▶ Segment filtering (ALE_IDOC_SERVICES_APPLY_OUT)

▶ Conversion of global organizational units

▶ Data conversion

▶ Version change

Here is the sequence of IDoc services in inbound processing:

▶ Version change (ALE_IDOC_SERVICES_APPLY_IN)

▶ Segment filtering

▶ Data conversion

▶ Conversion of global organizational units

When IDoc segments are selected, the data filters check whether specified fields in IDoc segments contain predefined values. If the field does not contain the specified values, the associated segment is deleted. Another selection process is by classification, which means IDoc is only send, if the application object belongs to a class defined in Customizing. In ALE, Customizing you should set the classes that are to be included in the selection. Assign the classes to be used for distributing the master data to the message type and logical receiving system.

This can be found by following this path: **Display IMG · SAP NetWeaver · SAP Web Application Server · IDoc Interface/Application Link Enabling · Modeling and Implementing Business Processes · Master Data Distribution · Distribution Using Object Classes · Assign Classes to Receiving Logical System.**

Segment filters are set in ALE Customizing and can be found by navigating this path: **Modeling and Implementing Business Processes • Distribution of Master Data • Scope of Data for Distribution • Filter IDoc Segments**.

You reduce the message type to selectively send the data you want to send. This can be accomplished by copying the message type to reduced message type through the configuration step under the following menu path: **Display IMG • SAP NetWeaver • SAP Web Application Server • IDoc Interface/Application Link Enabling (ALE) • Modeling and Implementing Business Processes • Master Data Distribution • Scope of Data for Distribution • Message Reduction • Create Reduced Message Type**. When reducing a message type, a message is created in the customer namespace. The inbound function module of the IDoc basis type is assigned to the reduced message type.

You can maintain the data conversion rules with the configuration step by following this menu path: **IMG • SAP NetWeaver • SAP Web Application Server • IDoc Interface/Application Link Enabling (ALE) • Modeling and Implementing Business Processes • Converting Data Between Sender and Receiver**.

Change Pointer

SAP uses the concept of changes to the database to trigger any communication or data transfer. In other words, if there is any new data added to the object—e.g., customer master, or changes made to the existing data—the system will identify it and mark it for transfer. This process is called change pointers. ALE uses the shared master data tool (SMD Tool) for distributing master data changes. It is connected to the R/3 Engineering Change Management and logs master data changes relevant for distribution. The change pointer logs changes to the master data relevant for distribution. You must active the Write function for specific message types.

Change pointers can be manually processed or be in the background by calling the program RBDMIDOC. This allows you to restrict processing to a specified message type. Change pointers can also be processed for extended or reduced message type.

If a change pointer exists for the message type, program RBDMIDOC calls an application function module that creates an IDoc following the rules of master data replication and forwards it to the ALE application interface for IDocs. The change pointer must be activated. This is done after the reduced message type is created. Use transaction code BD61 to first activate the

change pointer generally. Once you have reduced the message type, you can use the transaction code BD50 to activate the message type.

When a master data record is created or changed, the application queries whether the change pointer mechanism and the change pointers for the application document are activated. To view the change documents, use the report RSSCD100 and to view the change pointers view the database table BDCPV. Table BDCPS provides you the change pointer status and in BDCP the change pointers are stored.

Administrative Tools

Finally, I would like to describe the tools available with the ALE, specific to the IDoc. Within the SAP Easy Access follow this menu path: **Tools · ALE**. This displays the tool options for ALE Administration, ALE Development, Distribution in Applications and Master Data Distribution.

Within Administration, there are settings for Monitoring, Runtime setting, and Services. ALE Development allows you to use development tools for IDoc and BAPI development for ALE application. Distribution in Application and Master Data Distribution provide function to distribute the data.

Having gone through the different communication and interface application, tool and techniques, let's see how it applies to interfacing mySAP ERP or SAP R/3 with the GTS system.

9.6   Interfacing with the GTS System

SAP Global Trade Services (SAP GTS) helps companies automate their trade processes while dealing with different business partners, managing high volumes of transactions within their supply chains, and extended enterprise-wide solutions while interfacing with different partners such as vendors, customers, freight forwarders, and customs authorities with constantly changing legal regulations. MySAP ERP or SAP R/3 and SAP R/3 Enterprise solution has a built-in Foreign Trade Solution, which was primarily an export solution tied closely to the SD module. Figure 9.12 is a simple pictorial representation of GTS landscape alongwith other systems.

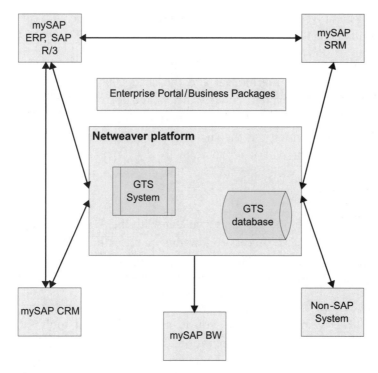

Figure 9.12 SAP GTS System Landscape

9.6.1   SAP Foreign Trade and GTS

SAP Foreign Trade, part of SAP SD system, has inherent limitations. For instance, each business unit might have its own ERP and Foreign Trade solution installed, and, unlike GTS, this is not a centralized solution. It becomes difficult to standardize the compliance process centrally, as the processes and data are spread across different ERP or SAP systems. Though it had the advantage of being very closely tied to SAP SD, the flip side is that any changes to the Foreign Trade solution calls for a change in the SD functions. Let's look at some of the major functionality missing from the Foreign Trade solution. These are listed below:

▶ Though R/3 Foreign Trade is primarily a export solution, much of the functionality within the export solutions is limited. For instance, the export determination only happens at the sales-order level, and also only value depreciation is available for licenses and not quantity.

▶ There is no import-control functionality for import licensing.

▶ The embargo functionality is not very flexible. You cannot define embargo by legs, so that you can specify which country is not allowed to ship the

product to specific countries, rather than stop all your branches from shipping to a particular country. A branch in the U.S., for instance, might not ship a product to Cuba, while you could ship to Cuba from a branch in Canada.

▶ There is no Sanctioned Party Screening or screening against the Denied Party List screening functionality, except that you can block a customer manually by updating a indicator in the customer master.

▶ You can't perform export check on some of the Materials Management (MM) document types, such as stock transport orders or plant-to-plant transfer with Foreign Trade.

▶ Data maintainance-wise, classications are maintained at plant level and within a country you might have many plants, which calls for a large volume of classification data.

▶ SAP Foreign Trade is tied to the ERP SD solution. GTS can be interfaced to more than just SAP ERP or SAP R/3, it can also used with other SAP products, like CRM, SRM, and non-SAP systems for trade solutions.

▶ There are standard XML standard upload available for contents with GTS; e.g., for Denied Party List content, Export Control Classification Number, Harmonized Tariff System, and License Determination.

▶ As GTS is powered by NetWeaver, you have the advantages of all the standard interfaces with the other SAP system, such as Business Intelligence, Enterprise Portal, mySAP ERP, etc.

▶ SAP Foreign Trade doesn't have any customs-management functionality, such as product classification, duty calculation, customs communications with authorities, or comprehensive trade document services.

▶ There is no risk-management functionality in SAP Foreign Trade. SAP GTS' Risk Management functions include Vendor declaration, Preferential Determination, and Customer Declaration, to name a few.

9.6.2 Plug-In

There is a set of programs or functions within mySAP ERP or SAP R/3 for plug-in and add-on called SLL-LEG. These allow you to communicate and set up the integration with the SAP GTS system. Within the SAP R/3 Enterprise and SAP ERP Central Component feeder systems, you have to install the PI_BASIS plug-in. The plug-in allows you to transfer master data (business partners, products, etc) and documents to SAP GTS system for performing the trade services.

The software component SLL-LEG is an add-on that contains the SAP Compliance Management, SAP Customs Management, and SAP Risk Management functions. SAP GTS has to be installed as a separate system, and the communication with the ERP has to be set up. As part of the ALE model, SAP ERP and GTS are identified as separate logical system for it to communicate with each other.

From SAP R/3 release 4.0 and higher, you can communicate from mySAP ERP ECC to GTS and from GTS to mySAP ERP ECC. With my mySAP CRM 4.0 and mySAP SRM 4.0, the plug-in to connect to SAP GTS system is built in or delivered standard With mySAP ERP Central Component, the SAP GTS functions are part of the PI_BASIS plug-in. The legal menu with different options for enabling GTS services and communication can be accessed using the transaction code /SAPSLL/MENU_LEGALR3.

Communication

The communication between ERP ECCN and GTS and from GTS to ERP uses RFC. Both ERP ECC and GTS systems are identified as logical systems within SAP system. With RFC, SAP invokes functions in other system or able to execute the programs in another system. The logical system and the RFC connections for communication from the ERP to GTS are set up within the transaction code /SAPSLL/MENU_LEGALR3. Once you execute the transaction, click on the folder **Basic Settings** and on **System Connection to SAP GTS**. Figure 9.13 displays the transaction.

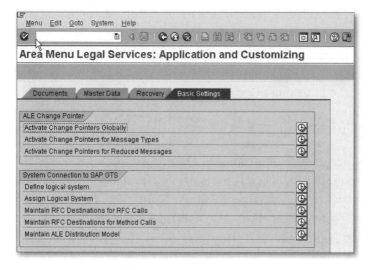

Figure 9.13 Area Menu: Legal Services

Data Transfer

Master data, for example customer or material, needs to be transferred to GTS so that when transactions are created they can be referred back for carrying trade functions or to invoke trade services. As part of master data, you would send all your business partners, product master records, and bill of material (BOM) if you want to carry out preferential determination. The initial transfer can be done using the transactions within /SAPSLL/MENU_ LEGALR3, under the **Master Data** tab and the section **Initial Transfer of Master Data to SAP GTS**.

Similarly, you can use transactions to do an initial transfer of documents: sales order, deliveries, etc. This can be found under the tab **Documents** and in the section **Initial Transfer of Documents to SAP GTS**. Any new documents or changes to the document are communicated when they are saved in the SAP ERP system. With regard to the master data after the initial transfer, the ongoing or regular transfer is done using the change pointers. This uses the message type specific to business object Customer Master Changes, new records use the reduced message type /SAPSLL/DEBMAS_SLL, product uses the reduced message type /SAPSLL/MATMAS_SLL, and the Vendor master uses /SAPSLL/CREMAS_SLL.

Based on these reduced message type-identified fields, the system recognizes the changes and uses this information to transfers them to GTS system. This is triggered through a running of a job using the program RBDMIDOC.

The **Recovery** tab as seen in Figure 9.13 consists of functions and transactions to recover the documents that could not be sent to GTS because the communication between the two systems broke down. If he GTS system was down and documents were created during that time, you can use the transaction to send them to GTS system. As far as the master data is concerned, the job schedule will keep attempting to send the data till it is successful.

9.6.3   Configuration

Configurations specific to GTS-plug in can be found under the menu path: **Display IMG • Sales and Distribution • Foreign Trade/Customs • SAP Global Trade Services – Plug-In with mySAP ERP ECC**. Figure 9.14 displays the screen shot of the list of configuration options. The first step in the configuration step is to configure or define the documents for transfer and indicate which services you would like to invoke. When you click on the configuration step **Configure Control Settings for Transfer**, it will display a folder for the application level and a sub-folder for document types.

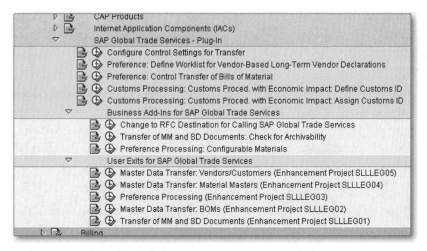

Figure 9.14 SAP Global Trade Service-Plug-In

Document types are put into different buckets called Application Level in the plug in. Following are the application levels listed in the system:

▶ **MM0A**
Receipt/Import: Purchase Document

▶ **SD0A**
Dispatch/Export: Sales Document

▶ **SD0B**
Dispatch/Export: Outbound Delivery Document

▶ **SD0C**
Dispatch/Export: Billing Document

Within the appropriate application level, you need to define the document type. For example, a sales order type OR will fall under the application level SD0A, and an outbound delivery will fall under SD0B. Similarly, a purchase order for import check will fall under MM0A, and billing document for export will fall under SD0C.

After defining the document type, you need to indicate which services you would like to call in GTS system; e.g., if you want to carry out export check for sales orders you want to invoke the SAP Compliance Management Services. Similarly, for any preferential declaration, you would turn on the SAP Risk Management Services, and for creating customs document or online submission to customer you would turn on the SAP Customs Management Services. Figure 9.15 displays the configuration setting.

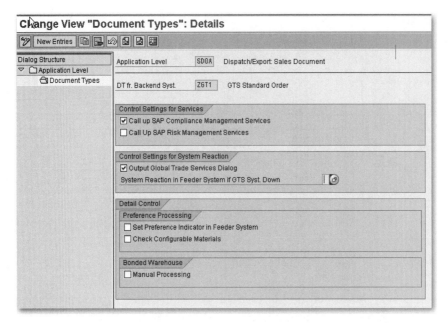

Figure 9.15 Document Type Transfer to GTS

GTS Configuration

Once you have the ERP ECC set up, you need to configure your GTS system to accept the data or communication coming from SAP ERP system. I would like to highlight some of the key configuration that needs to be done within GTS system to accomplish this. Let's take a look at these:

▶ You need to map the company code from SAP ERP to foreign trade organization (FTO) in GTS system. For that, you will to create the FTO as a organizational element in GTS system and map it to the company code of SAP ERP.

▶ Similarly, you will have to map plant in SAP ERP to legal unit in the GTS system.

▶ Document type and item category should be mapped for appropriate services, export, import for example.

▶ All the services in GTS are defined as Legal Regulations, and the countries would would like to perform the services for export or import should be activated for legal regulations. Legal regulations represent the law and regulations.

Figure 9.16 displays the organizational mapping between the ERP system and the GTS system.

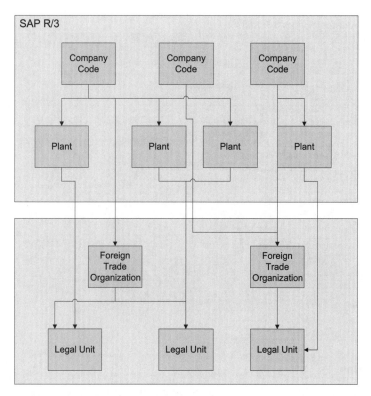

Figure 9.16 Organizational Structure Mapping

Influence of GTS on the ERP SD Transaction Processes

With GTS, for every transaction that you configure to send to GTS, the GTS system creates an equivalent document, called a customs document. This document performs the screening on these documents and the process for reviewing and releasing the document is done within the GTS system. As a function, this is centralized within the GTS system, and only minimal information is provides or available in the ERP system, stating that this document has been blocked for legal control.

GTS functions or trade checks interfaces closely with the SAP SD system for export checking. So when you create sales order, it will call GTS to perform an export check. With CRM, sales processes are triggered from the CRM system and processed through the SAP SD and Logistics Execution. We will look at another kind of interface, where the process is initiated from the other system into the mySAP ERP.

9.7 Sales Process with mySAP CRM

MySAP Customer Relationship Management (CRM) is a strategic business solution aimed at optimizing customer-facing activities for the greatest impact on business success. MySAP CRM supports marketing, sales/distribution, and service processes across all contact channels and supplies accurate analyses that can be used for decision-making. Customer related activities in marketing are Campaign Management, Customer Segmentation, Lead Management, E-Marketing, Trade Promotion Management (TPM) and Marketing Planning and Analytics. Similarly, the customer-related activities in SAP SD are Sales Order Management, Quotation and Contracts, Account and Contract Management, Opportunity and Pipeline Management, Task and Activity Management, Incentive and Commissions Management, Leasing, and Sales Planning and Analytics.

Enterprise Sales helps plan and forecast sales activities accurately, analyze the sales pipeline in a timely manner, manage tasks effectively, target cross- and up-selling opportunities, and promote collaboration in a team-selling environment. Telesales leverages the core capabilities of the mySAP CRM Interaction Center. It speeds customer interactions enabling real-time targeting, identification and transfer of qualified leads to an organization's enterprise sales force. Mobile Sales provides the ability to accurately plan and forecast sales, rapidly assess pipeline opportunity, effectively manage tasks, target cross-sell/up-sell opportunity, and enable collaboration within a sales team in real-time, through online and offline access from any mobile computing device.

E-selling empowers an organization's customers with personalized, convenient and consistent service, 24 hours a day, 365 days a year. Customers can access and research information and then purchase products or services anytime, anywhere. Figure 9.17 shows the Sales cycle and the closed loop CRM flow.

Customer related activities in Service are Service Request, Service Order and Contract Management, Compliance Management, Case Management, Installed Base Management Knowledge Management, Workflow and Escalation Management, Workforce Management, Professional Services, Service Planning and Analytics. Customer Service and Support enables customer service centers to manage and fulfil commitments to both partners and customers with efficient service planning and execution.

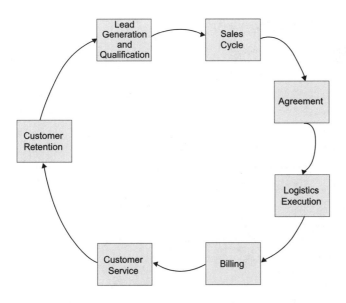

Figure 9.17 Sales Cycle with CRM

Service Operations Management centralizes service planning—tactically and strategically—through service administration, transactional support and operational/financial analytics. Mobile Service supports the Service Parts, and Service Order Management ensures that field staff is able to check inventory, locate materials, and place orders for specific components. E-Services leverages real time self-service potential of the Internet to help organizations lower costs and improve customer satisfaction around the clock. Figure 9.18 displays the solution overview and the business case that applies to mySAP CRM.

The key area of mySAP CRM Analytics is based on SAP BW, which allows you to collect all relevant information about your customers and use the resulting knowledge to make operative and strategic decisions. You might want to segment your customers, based on their geographical location, education background, or financial standing, and determine their buying habits for your product.

MySAP CRM supports your customer relations via all contact channels. The Interaction Center integrates all work processes and tasks in your Contact Center. The E-Commerce function within CRM offers a platform that allows your company to use the Internet as a possible sales and information channel for business customers and consumers. The Field Applications area allows you to use marketing, sales and service functions in an offline environment for the external sales and service force.

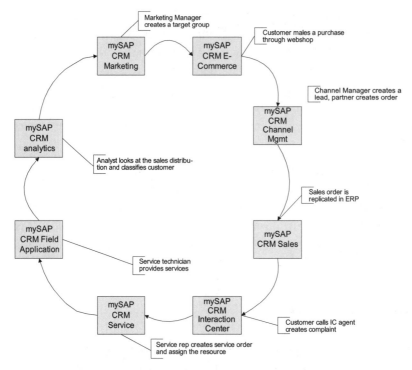

Figure 9.18 MySAP CRM Functionality Overview

9.7.1 MySAP CRM Architecture

MySAP CRM is the sum of all CRM functions and incorporates not only CRM components but also SAP BW, Enterprise Portal and Advanced Planner and Optimizer (SAP APO), and SAP R/3. MySAP CRM, which is part of the mySAP Business Suite, includes a central CRM server, which provides access to the system via different channels and connections to other systems. Here are some of the application components supported in mySAP CRM:

▶ **Interaction Center**
The integrated Interaction Center enables customers to use phone, fax or email to contact sales or service representatives.

▶ **Internet**
Internet users may configure and order products or services using the Internet components of mySAP CRM.

▶ **Mobile Clients/Handelds**
The mobile sales force or mobile service engineers can connect to SAP CRM system from their laptop computers or other mobile terminals to exchange the latest information with the central CRM server.

Data is exchanged between the CRM system and a connected OLTP R/3 (minimum release 3.1I) system primarily via CRM Middleware. A plug-in installed on the OLTP R/3 System acts as a counterpart to the R/3 adapter, supporting the communication of data between the two systems. The data exchange includes an initial transfer of Customizing, master data, and transactional data to the CRM systems, as well as delta data in both directions. Sales orders are entered in the Internet Sales application component, Interaction Center, Mobile Client or the CRM Server.

To confirm whether the requested items can be delivered on time, you need to carry out the Available-to-Promise (ATP) check. ATP triggers a call for the item requested and gets a response back in terms of the date; then the order can be delivered. This function is performed by SAP APO. The SAP BW is used as a data source for part of the mySAP CRM solution, but also contains data for consolidation and analysis.

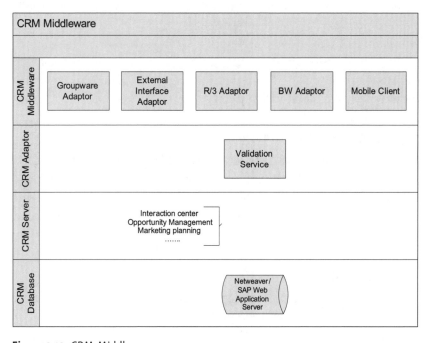

Figure 9.19 CRM Middleware

CRM Middleware is an integral part of the mySAP CRM Server and is the message hub. Figure 9.19 displays the CRM Server view. CRM Middleware is part of the my SAP CRM server, so it doesn't require any extra installation or server. The middleware layer supports the controlled data exchange with other systems-mobile clients, back-end systems, and data warehouses.

Especially for mobile clients, a replication mechanism ensures a consistent and up-to-date dataset on the distribution local databases. Software adapters are used to connect to external systems. These adapters assign data and convert it into various formats. The mySAP CRM application components also exchange data with the middleware layer via a CRM adapter. The mySAP CRM solution is built on the SAP Basis System, which provides a proven development platform, scalability, platform independence, and various other SAP R/3 tools. MySAP CRM solution is configured in the same way as SAP R/3.

9.7.2 Internet Sales and Customer Self-Service

The Internet Sales and Internet Customer Self-Service application components offer access to mySAP CRM solution for Internet users connecting to configure and purchase products from a published catalog, or request a particular service. Figure 9.20 displays the mySAP CRM 4.0 and Internet Applications. The Internet application components are available via a Web service. When customers place orders through this Web service, there is another component that complements the Internet sale and self-service applications with regard to pricing data. The Internet and Pricing Configurator (IPC) component provides configuration and pricing data for Web applications.

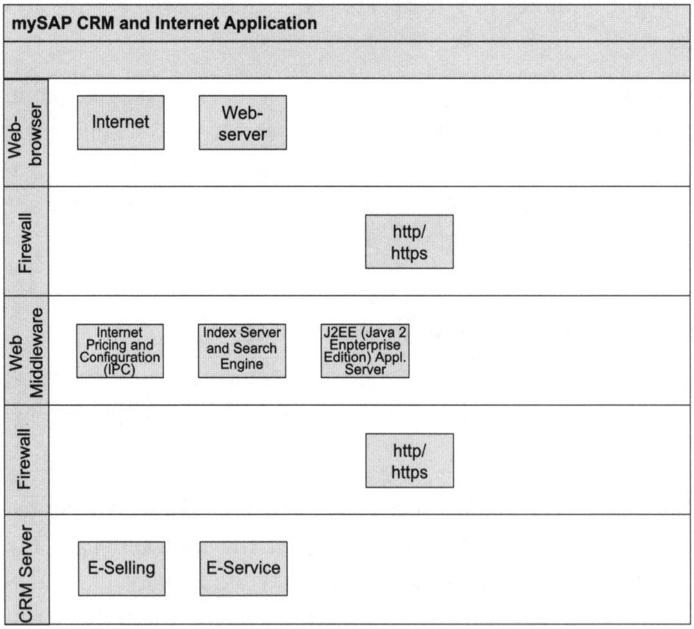

Figure 9.20 Internet Application with mySAP CRM

9.7.3 Interaction Center

The Interaction Center supports various communication channels, such as telephones, e-mail, and fax, and Internet applications such as call-me-back, co-browsing, and voice over Internet protocol (VoIP). For the Interaction Center WinClient, you can make telephone and e-mail connections using the SAP standard interfaces (APIs) SAPphone and SAPconnect. SAPphone forms an interface between the mySAP CRM application components and Computer Telephony Integration (CTI). CTI, in turn, creates the connection to telephone switching. CTI vendors can be certified through the SAP Complementary Software Program (CSP).

The SAPphone standard interface guarantees flexible scalability of the CTI components. The SAPconnect interface is used in combination with SAP workflow to support the complete e-mail cycle from and to business partners.

In the Interaction Center, WebClient multichannel options are consolidated through the Integrated Communication Interface. By leveraging new technology such as Extensible Markup Language (XML) and Simple Object Access Protocol (SOAP), mySAP CRM's open Integrated Communications Interface (ICI) supports the integration of mySAP CRM solutions with non-SAP communications products, such as universal queue, computer telephony, automatic call distribution, interactive voice response, e-mail management, and text chat systems.

With your traditional SAP SD system, the sales order can be acknowledged in the system by customers logging on to the Web (if you have a Web service) or representatives taking calls through telephones and keying the information into the system. CRM provides this enhanced interaction center for accepting these interaction through different modes of communication.

9.7.4 Integrating mySAP CRM with mySAP ERP

Integration is primarily for SD and for Logistics Execution processes. Sales orders with errors can be saved in the CRM system and are available for further processing.

Transfer to SAP R/3 is only possible when the processing of the sales transaction is complete. From the distribution status of the transaction in the mySAP CRM system, you can see whether the transaction is relevant for distribution and, if so, whether it was successfully distributed to SAP R/3. You

can check for successful delivery into SAP R/3 by viewing the status of the order in mySAP CRM.

After successful billing, the relevant billing status is set. This is, however, only supported if billing takes place via the Billing Engine CRM. For billing in SAP R/3, you cannot see the billing status in the CRM order. Figure 9.21 shows the sales-order scenarios with mySAP CRM and SAP R/3.

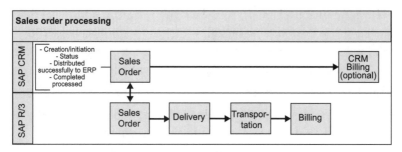

Figure 9.21 Sales- Order Processing with CRM and SAP SD

9.7.5 MySAP CRM Customization

As with mySAP ERP or SAP R/3, mySAP CRM has an Implementation Guide to help you configure the system using standard business processes. Let's say you would like to create a new business transaction for business opportunity you receive, which might be converted into a potential sales order. You researched the subject and found that the standard delivered ones don't support your business requirement, so you would like to create a customized one to meet this special need. Here's how you do it, just follow the steps below:

1. Create a new transaction type via the menu path: **SAP menu · Architecture and Technology · Configuration · Customizing· SAP Reference IMG · Customer Relationship Management · Transactions · Basic Settings · Define Transaction Types**.

2. Make specific settings for your new transaction type above.

3. Create a new item category via this menu path: **SAP Menu · Architecture and Technology · Configuration · Customizing, SAP Reference IMG · Customer Relationship Management · Transactions · Basic Settings · Define Item Category Determination**.

4. Maintain copy control for transaction type by following this menu path: **SAP Menu with CRM system · Architecture and Technology · Configuration · Customizing, SAP Reference IMG · Customer Relationship Management ·**

Transactions • Basic Settings • Copy Control For Business Transactions. Then do the following:

▷ Define Copying Control for Transaction Types

▷ Define Copying Control for Item Categories

5. To test the new transaction within the application, follow this menu path: **Sales rep role in People-Centric UI • Acquisition • Opportunties • Create**.

The sales representative user interface allows you to add an additional field to CRM objects using Customizing includes (CIs). A CI is a placeholder for a customer-definable data structure attached to a business object in the Data Dictionary. CIs allow the extension of the objects without modifications or upgrade problems.

While creating a sales order, you might want to bring in some additional customer master-related fields, such as, which industry segment they belong to, if you have classified them, what customer class they belong to; all of which might help process the order effectively. The additional fields can then be integrated into the People-Centric UI using the CRM Designer. CRM is a graphical tool for adapting or modifying the People-Centric UI of mySAP CRM to the user's needs in terms of look and feel.

If Customizing settings and parameters are not sufficient to realize your requirements, Business Add-Ins (BAdIs) can be used for further enhancements. By using Business Add-Ins customers can insert additional code without modifying the original objects. Follow this menu path: **SAP Menu • Architecture and Technology • ABAP Workbench • Utilities • Business Add-Ins • Definitions (SE18)**. You can also follow this path: **SAP Menu • Architecture and Technology • ABAP Workbench • Utilities • Business Add-Ins • Implementations (SE19)**.

> **Note**
>
> Marketing Attributes are special notes on a business partner that can help a salesman close a deal. The Business Partner Relationship setting allows you to select which possible relationship may be selected between business partners.

9.8 Summary

Different tools are available in SAP for transferring data into or converting your legacy data onto the SAP system. You can use these tools for ongoing data transfer as well. You could use the output determination to send notifi-

cation or acknowledgement to the outside enterprise. Output determination helps you send your data across to your partners. Remote Function Call can execute functions in another system.

We saw how a process that needs information from another system can use this RFC to execute the function in another system remotely. BAPI and ALE technologies allow you to connect and communicate with other systems. BAPIs are standard delivered program for performing a certain function. These are maintained by SAP for future releases and upgrade. ALE provides the model to connect two SAP or non-SAP systems. You can use IDocs to transfer data to and from between systems.

GTS is a xApp, which connects with your SAP system and non-SAP System. GTS provides global trade services, and it closely interfaces with the SAP SD system for export checking. CRM connects with your mySAP ERP for customer-facing processing. Sales processes initiated in CRM are processed through the SAP ERP system. This chapter should have given you a good idea of SAP SD's communication and interfaces with other SAP systems. It also had coverage of data transfer and outputs.

9.9 Book Conclusion

We are now at the end of this book. In these nine chapters I tried to give you a good idea about how SD works and how it can work for you. I wanted this book to give you a solid foundation about SD. Remember that the fundamentals of SD do not change. The processes are defined within the SAP system itself, though as one of the oldest modules it has matured over time. Explore SD as upgrades happen but you can always refer to this book for a deep and practical understanding of the fundamentals of effectively using SAP SD.

I have tried to address the key elements of SD in this book. I hope you now have an understanding about crucial issues and topics like a general overview of SD, master data, key techniques, SD's influence on MM, supply chain extension, key influence and interface with Financials and Controlling, the influence of SD on Service Management and Quality Management and report, analysis, user interface and development tools for SD. Armed with this SD-related knowledge, I hope you indeed find the coverage of SD in this book effective for your business needs. That is, after all, your goal.

Appendix

A   Glossary

ABAP   Advanced Business Application Programming, SAP's programming language.

ABAP Dictionary   Central repository for application and system objects and information.

ABAP Editor   ABAP program editor within the ABAP Workbench.

ABAP Object   ABAP's object-oriented programming component.

Acceptance   Inspection lot that satisfies quality standards or requirements.

Access   Fields used by the system to search a condition record.

Access Sequence   Represents the order in which the system searches for a particular condition record, as it moves from specific record to generic record.

Account   Refers to an object or placeholder to which values are assigned.

Account Assignment   Specifies the account to post to and from during a business transaction.

Account Determination   Automatic way to determine accounts for posting value to accounts.

Account Determination Procedure   Rules and sequence with account types that are valid for revenue account determination in sales documents.

Agreement   Contract with the customer defined in the system.

Append Structure   Structure assigned to a table, allowing the addition of customer fields to SAP tables.

ALE   Application Linking and Enabling: technology for setting up communication and functions between distributed applications.

Assortment   Function that allows the grouping of frequently ordered material and quantities.

Asynchronous Communication   The alternative to real-time communication; staged and batch transmission of data.

ATP Check   Functions to check if a product can be confirmed for a specific date.

Background Processing   Execution of a program in the background, based on schedule and trigger, and not online through user dialogue.

Back Order   Refers to an order-line item that could be confirmed due to non-availability of material.

BAPI   Business Application Programming Interface

BAPI Explorer   Repository or tool for developing and managing BAPI in integrated programming environments.

Batch   Material in inventory managed separately in subsets.

Billing   Sales and Distribution document that contains financial data for the accounting interface.

Billing DueLlist List consisting of items that need to be converted to a billing document.

Billing Plan Defines the schedule dates for billing creation.

Billing Type Defines the header data in the billing process.

Bill-to Party Defines the entity that will receive the invoice for goods or service.

Business Area Represents a separate area or organization to which financial values are allocated.

Business Partner Contact or relationship that exists for business interests.

Business Partner Role Responsibility and function a business partner has in a business transaction.

Business Partner Type Identification for business partner in categories such as customer, vendor, etc.

Business-to-Business Business process defining the selling of products and services through the Web; also referred to as B2B.

Business-to-Consumer Business process defining electronic interaction with consumers; also referred to as B2C.

Cancellation Document Document created for canceling billing document.

Cash Sales When customer pays for the goods or service received at the time of placing the order.

Catalog List of items with description, characteristic values; e.g., tasks, defects, etc.

Collective Invoice Billing document at end of period created out of several deliveries for a customer.

Communication Method Defines the how the information are send to a receipt.

Communication Interface Data exchange through programs based on standard protocol.

Company Code Smallest organization unit, based on commercial law, and based the way in which financial statements are reported.

Condition Record Data or values stored in the fields of a table for a task.

Condition Type Identification and business meaning of a condition.

Consignment Business agreement where vendor maintains the materials stock at customer site.

Contract Agreement between the vendor and the customer about a supply of goods and service, based on special condition, price, etc.

Controlling Information gathered on company activities to help management decisions.

Controlling Area Organizational unit within a company, meant for cost accounting.

Customer Business partner with whom transactions like the selling of goods and services are done.

Customer Exit SAP-delivered enhancement within the application.

Customer Master Information capture regarding the customer.

Customer Return Return of goods from the customer.

Customizing Implementation of SAP systems through the standard delivered settings based on the requirement.

Customizing Object Set of tables and views defined by the business entity they represent.

Customizing Request Change request to capture the client-specific table values for copying and transporting.

Customizing Setting Entries maintained in the Customizing table for the implementation.

Customizing Transaction Maintenance of Customizing table entries.

Delivery Inbound or outbound process of transferring goods, receiving, and sending.

Distribution Channel Channel through which goods or services reach customers.

Distributed Model Model that defines the information flow between logical systems.

Document Proof of business; used for processing it through the supply chain.

Document Flow Sequence of a document as it passes through the supply chain; e.g., from sales order to delivery to billing document.

Document Header Information that applies to the entire document.

EDI Electronic Data Exchange; electronic data exchange between business partners or data processing system.

End-to-end Scenario Chain of functions or business process that crosses functional areas and represents a complete business cycle or flow.

Enhancement Additional functionality for the SAP standard program, provided by SAP at the appropriate place.

Enterprise Portal User interface and platform to present enterprise application data and interaction with the services.

Export Sale and movement of goods crossing borders.

Function Builder Central repository and tool for managing function modules.

Function Group Group of function module that share the same program context at runtime.

Functional Area Organizational unit defined by accounting for capturing information such as expenses, purchasing, sales, etc.

Functional Location Organizational unit representing the place where the maintenance work is performed.

G/L Account General ledger account. Represented in chart of accounts, it captures the financial value of movement of goods and services within the company code.

General Ledger Values for transaction captured for financial reporting.

Go Live   When production system is started and is in use.

Goods in Transit   Goods that have shipped from the company but have not yet reached the customer.

Goods Issue   Reduction in stock due to the withdrawal or shipment of goods to customer.

Goods Movement   Physical or logical movement of material from stock or leading to consumption.

Goods Receipt   Movement of goods into the inventory management.

GUID   Global Unique Identifier; function module GUID_CREATE used to create unique identifiers.

Hierarchy   Structure with elements in different levels, arranged in succession and interdependent.

HTML   HyperText Markup Language; interface or language for creating HTML pages.

IDoc   Intermediate Document; document for capturing information for data exchange between partners and systems, using ALE model.

IDoc Interface   Format and methods for electronic data exchange between SAP and partner system.

IDoc Type   SAP format for transferring data with different business objects.

IMG   Implementation Guide; configuration and document for configuring the SAP system.

IMG Activity   Located within the IMG structure: the bottom-level node or step.

IMG Structure   IMG activities defined in the form of hierarchy.

Incoterm   Commonly used term in international trade.

Info Set   A single-level or multilevel key figure with a logical relationship.

InfoObject   Evaluation object in SAP

Inspection lot   Subset of inventory representing the quantity sent to quality check.

Inter-company Billing   When company codes belonging to the same enterprise, and one company sells to another and the selling company invoices for the goods or service.

Inventory Management   System component for management, tracking, recording, valuation, and planning function for materials used in the company.

Invoice   Billing document for getting paid for the goods and service to customer.

Invoice Correction Request   Billing document to correct quantity and price with the invoice.

Item Category   Characteristics that define the document item business process.

IView   View in the Enterprise Portal, where the information is retrieved from the source system and displayed, and users can act on it.

Join Condition   Condition to link two tables for data retrieval.

Key Figures   Represents values and quantities within BW reporting.

Logon In the graphical user interface, a function in SAP that allows users to log on to the system.

Logistics Information System Information system within logistics, helping to analyze the transaction, master and historical data for decision making.

Material Exclusion Way to restrict material sale to certain customers.

Material Master Information regarding the material used in the company, recorded for use in business transactions.

Method Call When one object calls another object through a method to perform specific function.

Movement Type Represents stock movement in Warehouse Management.

MRP Material Requirement Planning, a term used to represent requirements and planning of materials.

Net Price Price after taking out all the surcharges and discounts.

Net Value The value determined by taking away discounts or adding surcharges to the gross value.

Note Assistant Tool within SAP System that helps you manage and implement SAP Notes.

OLAP Online transaction processing: data organized in a multidimensional model for reporting.

Operating Concern Represents part of an organization where the sales market is structured for reporting of profitability analysis.

Organization Model Involves mapping of your company organization element into the logical enterprise structure.

Output Information transmission to external partner through different media; e.g., mail, print, EDI, or fax.

Packing Defines the procedure for packing the goods being shipped to the customer.

Partner Represents individual or group, an external entity with whom the business interest exists

Partner Function Represents the role and responsibility of a partner in a business transaction.

Partner Profile Definition for enabling electronic interchange of data.

Payer Partner role with responsibility for paying the bill.

Picking Defines the process for selecting the goods for shipment to the customer.

Pricing Defines the process of determining price with procedure and condition techniques.

Quality Management Defines the activity and process related to quality planning, inspection and control.

QuickView Tool for defining reports without any programming.

Receivables Payment to be received for the goods or service provided.

Reconciliation Account Represents G/L account where the subsidiary ledger— e.g., customer, vendor accounts— are updated for business transaction.

Reference Document Document from which the information is copied to another document.

Repair Modification of SAP standard objects.

Return Document in sales process, used for customer returns.

RFC Remote Function Call; function module to call another system for executing activities.

Route Defines the legs in delivery from starting point to end point.

Sales Area Represents the combination of sales organization, distribution channel and division.

Sales Document Document that captures information on the sale transaction with header information that applies to whole document and item information specific to the item.

Sales Document Type Helps define business process in sales, for inquiry (IN), Quotation (QT), etc.

Sales Order Contract document between supplier and customer on delivery of goods or service.

Schedule line Further split of line item based on the confirmed quality.

Schedule Line Category Allows you to control inventory management, MRP, and availability check at schedule-line level.

Serial Number Number given to a material, along with the regular material number, to uniquely identify the material in inventory.

Service Master Record Service maintained as material or product.

Sold-to Party Person or company, placing the order for goods or services.

Sub-Contract Purchase order Specified material provided to vendor to manufacture a final product, as per the requirement.

Supply Chain Sequence of operation from source of supply to the end customer.

Synchronous Method Method for getting a real-time response after the execution of the program.

Transfer Order Document to move material from source storage bin to destination storage bin.

Transport Placeholder to save the system component and move from one system to another.

Unit Price Sales price for one unit of goods or service.

Vendor Business partner from whom the material and service is procured.

Warehouse Organizational division of plant for managing stored material in different bins or places.

Workflow Event-based sequence of steps processed by system and addressed to appropriate user for action.

B   About the Author

 **D. Rajen Iyer** has more than 16 years' experience in supply chain management applications and implementations. He has worked in the software consulting, apparel, aerospace, high-tech, manufacturing, and trading industries. Rajen has more than 10 years' experience with SAP, including work on Global Trade Services, Sales and Distribution, Pricing, and Materials Management.

A certified Project Management Professional, Rajen is currently leading an SAP practice with KRYAA, which focuses on GTS, Solution Extensions, and xApps. He can be reached at Rajen.Iyer@kryaa.com.

Acknowledgments

I would like to dedicate this book to all the IT professionals who sacrifice their valuable personal time in delivering system solutions. I would like to thank the two most influential persons in my life: my mother, Susila, and my wife, Padmaja, for continually believing in my ever-changing goals and in myself. My wife gave me all the support I needed to keep going in difficult times. I would like to also thank my two little angels: my three-year-old son Pranaav and one-year-old daughter Pranati, whose valuable playtimes always refreshed my mind and helped me concentrate on this book after a long day.

Last but not least; I would like to thank SAP PRESS for providing with me an opportunity to share my experience and knowledge. I hope to reach out to other dedicated professionals through this book to help them make the best of their knowledge in providing value-added solutions.

Index

Discover the power and potential of SAP for Retail

Explore SAP's various software offerings for retailers

Understand the concepts, functionality, and software architecture

approx. 300 pp., 69,95 Euro / US$ 69.95
ISBN 978-1-59229-213-4, Dec 2008

SAP for Retail

www.sap-press.com

Heike Rawe

SAP for Retail

This must-have guide presents the 20 individual products in SAP for Retail, illustrating what each do for retailers, and how they fit together. This is the first complete and comprehensive review of SAP for Retail that explains how business processes and general business concepts fit into its solution. The book is written in an easy-to-follow style, with applied real-world examples and graphics throughout. Topics covered include planning, merchandising and buying, supply chain and fulfilment, and store and multi-channel retailing.

Provides a complete guide to maximizing your SAP Plant Maintenance implementation process

Teaches how to align SAP procedures with your plant maintenance processes, teams, and best practices

Explains how to measure the

approx. 350 pp., 69,95 Euro / US$ 69.95
ISBN 978-1-59229-215-8, Oct 2008

Maximize Your Plant Maintenance with SAP

www.sap-press.com

John Hoke, Lorri Craig

Maximize Your Plant Maintenance with SAP

This book teaches plant managers and employees how to make the most out of SAP in plant maintenance. It also explains how to use SAP from a maintenance perspective, and align SAP functions with how you have to do your job. It covers important topics such as organizational preparation and refocus, common configuration and implementation issues, and the information system of plant maintenance. This is a complete reference to plant maintenance that provides real-world examples, step-by-step instructions, and practical advice.

Understand SAP Supply Network Collaboration 5.1

Learn about business processes and implementation in detail

With a comprehensive sample scenario and many tips and tricks

approx. 300 pp., 79,95 Euro / US$ 79.95
ISBN 978-1-59229-194-6, Oct 2008

Supplier Collaboration with SAP SNC

www.sap-press.com

Mohamed Hamady, Anita Leitz

Supplier Collaboration with SAP SNC

This is a comprehensive book on business processes and functionality of supplier collaboration with SAP SNC 5.1 (formerly Inventory Collaboration Hub, ICH). By using a fictitious company as an example throughout, this book introduces the business background and usage scenarios, and then moves on to cover the configuration of SNC. This important resource also shows how SNC ties in to other SAP solutions.

Teaches how to integrate MDM data into everyday business processes

Covers the benefits of integrating business partner master data processes throughout an enterprise

Provides practical, real-world case studies and solution examples

Up-to-Date for MDM 5.5 SP06

approx. 400 pp., 69,95 Euro / US$ 69.95
ISBN 978-1-59229-223-3, Sept 2008

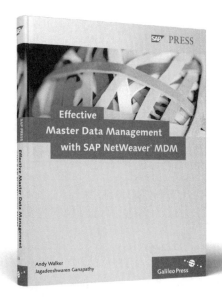

Effective Master Data Management with SAP NetWeaver MDM

www.sap-press.com

Andy Walker, Jagadeeshwaren Ganapathy

Effective Master Data Management with SAP NetWeaver MDM

This book describes the key business benefits of implementing business partner master data processes in SAP MDM. Users learn the business drivers for MDM, as well as the value of integrating with Dun & Bradstreet services. The book covers the complete process of planning for and understanding master data management and how it can specifically affect business processes. Users will understand what MDM is and what it can do for their business, and you'll develop the practical skills necessary to integrate SAP MDM effectively.

Master real-life business processes and the structuringof plant maintenance technical systems

Discover tips and tricks for implementing daily operations

Explore interfaces, reporting, and new EAM technologies – MAM, RFID, Enterprise SOA, NetWeaver Portal, and more

552 pp., 2008, with CD, 69,95 Euro / US$ 69.95
ISBN 978-1-59229-150-2

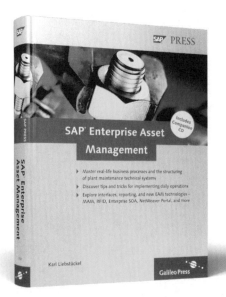

SAP Enterprise Asset Management

www.sap-press.com

Karl Liebstückel

SAP Enterprise Asset Management

This is a must-have guide for anyone interested in learning about the implementation and customization of SAP EAM. Consultants, managers, and administrators will learn about the plant maintenance process, how to evaluate which processes work best for them, and then go on to review the actual configuration steps of these processes. This book includes practical tips and best practices for implementation projects. The companion DVD contains examples, practice tests, presentations, and more. This book is up-to-date for SAP ERP 6.0.

**Master inventory optimization
using SAP ERP and SCM APO
with this updated & expanded
new edition**

**Explore inventory factors such as
inventory controlling, demand
planning, MRP, and much more**

**Learn how to improve your
forecast accuracy and planning**

705 pp., 2. edition 2008, 79,95 Euro / US$ 79.95
ISBN 978-1-59229-205-9

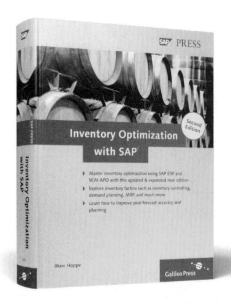

Inventory Optimization
with SAP

www.sap-press.com

Marc Hoppe

Inventory Optimization with SAP

This new edition provides a completely up-to-date reference to teach users how to manage inventory to increase profitability and operational efficiency using SAP ERP 6.0 and/or SAP SCM 5.1. New and updated topics include additional sections on Material Requirements Planning, Controlling with SAP NetWeaver BI, Vendor Managed Inventory and Supplier Managed Inventory, and much more. This is the one-stop, must-have reference for anyone who needs to improve and maximize inventory management with SAP.

Provides a comprehensive overview of the entire delivery process

Teaches functions, processes, and customization

Covers dangerous goods management, availability checks, user exits, and much more

574 pp., 2008, 79,95 Euro / US$ 79.95
ISBN 978-1-59229-169-4

Transportation Management with SAP LES

www.sap-press.com

Othmar Gau

Transportation Management with SAP LES

This in-depth reference provides readers with practical and detailed knowledge on all aspects of shipping and transportation with SAP Logistics Execution System (LES). Using this book, employees in the warehouse and shipping departments, as well as consultants, can benefit from proven best practices for working successfully with the Transportation Management module. The author describes the entire shipping and delivery process, from the creation of a delivery in the SAP system, to mapping the internal supply chain, and from transportation planning to invoicing and settlement with forwarding agencies – and everything in between. Plus, readers also learn how to master system configuration, and much more.

Find the tools and techniques you need to deliver fast and successful SAP SRM implementations

512 pp., 2008, 79,95 Euro / US$ 79.95
ISBN 978-1-59229-154-0

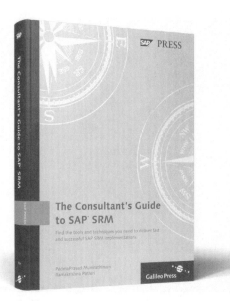

Consultant's Guide
to SAP SRM

www.sap-press.com

PadmaPrasad Munirathinam,
Ramakrishna Potluri

Consultant's Guide to SAP SRM

Find the tools and techniques you need to deliver
fast and successful SAP SRM implementations

Consultants hold many roles during an SAP implementation,
from business consultant during the blueprint phase, and
product specialist during the realization phase, to trainer
after go-live, and this book provides the information a
consultant needs to hold these roles effectively.
Based on SAP SRM 6.0, each chapter covers a specific
process of supplier relationship management, ensuring that
implementation teams can utilize their time efficiently.
Going beyond standard SRM scenarios, the book arms
consultants with practical tips for enabling complex
customer requirements, and provides insightful
troubleshooting tips and techniques.
The authors use their years of experience implementing SAP
applications to make this a must-have resource for SAP SRM
implementation teams.

2nd edition, completely revised and up-to-date for SAP ECC 6.0

Gain a comprehensive understanding of SAP MM and how it works

Learn the basics and then explore the full functionality of each part of SAP MM

588 pp., 2. edition 2008, 69,95 Euro / US$ 69.95
ISBN 978-1-59229-134-2

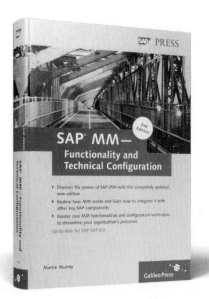

SAP MM—Functionality and Technical Configuration

www.sap-press.com

Martin Murray

SAP MM—Functionality and Technical Configuration

Fully updated for SAP ERP 6.0, this comprehensive update of the best-selling original is the ultimate MM resource. From dealing with Goods Receipt and Invoice Verification to Balance Sheet Valuation and the Material Ledger, this book is the ultimate reference for anyone looking for MM information.

Interested in reading more?

Please visit our Web site for all
new book releases from SAP PRESS.

www.sap-press.com